Beginning
Ruby on Rails™

Steven Holzner

Wiley Publishing, Inc.

Beginning Ruby on Rails™

Published by
Wiley Publishing, Inc.
10475 Crosspoint Boulevard
Indianapolis, IN 46256
www.wiley.com

Copyright © 2007 by Wiley Publishing, Inc., Indianapolis, Indiana

Published simultaneously in Canada

ISBN-13: 978-0-470-06915-8
ISBN-10: 0-470-06915-5

Manufactured in the United States of America

10 9 8 7 6 5 4 3 2 1

1B/QZ/RR/QW/IN

Library of Congress Catalog Control Number: 2006030329

To Nancy, now and always!

About the Author

Steven Holzner is the award-winning author of more than 100 programming books. He's been involved in Ruby on Rails for a long time, and does commercial Rails development. He's also been on the faculty of Cornell University and MIT, as well as having been a contributing editor for *PC Magazine*.

Credits

Acquisitions Editor
Kit Kemper

Development Editor
Maryann Steinhart

Technical Editor
David Mabelle

Production Editor
Angela Smith

Copy Editor
Kim Cofer

Editorial Manager
Mary Beth Wakefield

Production Manager
Tim Tate

Vice President and Executive Group Publisher
Richard Swadley

Vice President and Executive Publisher
Joseph B. Wikert

Project Coordinators
Heather Kolter, Ryan Steffen

Graphics and Production Specialists
Carrie A. Foster
Denny Hager
Barbara Moore
Lynsey Osborn
Laura Pence
Alicia B. South

Quality Control Technicians
John Greenough
Brian H. Walls

Proofreading and Indexing
Techbooks

Acknowledgments

The book you hold in your hands is the work of many people. I'd especially like to thank Kit Kemper, Maryann Steinhart, and all of the other Wiley editors who worked on this project for their contribution to its success.

Contents

Contents

Contents

Contents

Contents

Introduction

Congratulations, you've made the right choice—this is the book that will give you a working knowledge of Ruby and Rails. You don't have to know either Ruby or Rails—you get a guided tour of both in this book. And as you're going to see, putting Ruby on Rails is the best and easiest way to create web applications.

Who This Book Is For

This book is for anyone who wants to develop online applications using Ruby and Rails. All you have to know is HTML to read this book profitably.

On the other hand, *Beginning Ruby on Rails* is all about programming, so if you have programming experience, that will be helpful.

If you want to know how to create Ruby on Rails online applications, this book is for you. If you want to learn how to connect Ruby on Rails applications to databases, this book is for you. If you only want to learn the Ruby language, this book is for you.

How This Book Is Structured

You're going to get a working knowledge of both Ruby and Rails in this book. No experience of either is assumed, so you get the whole package here. Following is a breakdown of the book, chapter by chapter.

Chapter 1, "Welcome to Ruby," gets you started using the Ruby language. It also explains where to get and how to install both Ruby and Rails.

Chapter 2, "Conditionals, Loops, Methods, and Blocks," gives you more of the Ruby story as you delve deeper into Ruby. Understanding the material in this chapter is essential for working with Ruby on Rails.

Chapter 3, "Classes and Objects," introduces the object-oriented nature of Ruby. In fact, everything in Ruby is an object, and this chapter brings that point home.

In Chapter 4, "Welcome to Rails," you actually start putting Ruby on Rails. You'll examine the fundamentals of Rails and learn how to create a basic online application.

Chapter 5, "Building Simple Rails Applications," takes you deeper into the Rails story, including how to work with HTML controls such as text fields and checkboxes, how to use models in Rails applications, and how to work with sessions.

Chapter 6, "Connecting to Databases," explores what databases are, and how to connect to them using Ruby on Rails. It includes how to create, edit, and delete database records.

Chapter 7, "Working with Databases," provides more details on working with databases, and leads you through the creation of a shopping cart application.

Chapter 8, "Validating and Testing," is all about validating user input, using the validation support built into Rails, and testing your applications.

In Chapter 9, "Controlling the Action with the Action Controller," you work with the controller in Ruby on Rails applications, and learn to handle cookies, filters, and caching pages.

Chapter 10, "Getting the Big Picture with Views," tackles creating XML, partial views, view helpers, and more.

In Chapter 11, "Ajax and Rails," you learn all about connecting Rails with Asynchronous JavaScript and XML (Ajax), also called Web 2.0.

What You Need to Use This Book

To make the most of this book, you're going to need Ruby and Rails—both of which are available for free. You'll see how to download and install both Ruby and Rails in Chapter 1.

You also need a database server. This book uses MySQL, which is the default database server to which Rails connects. You're also going to see how to get MySQL for free and download it in this book.

That's it—the software you need is free, and it's available for free download.

Conventions

To help you get the most from the text and keep track of what's happening, a number of conventions are used throughout the book.

Try It Out

The *Try It Out* is an exercise you should work through, following the text in the book.

1. They usually consist of a set of steps.
2. Each step has a number.
3. Follow the steps through with your copy of the database.

How It Works

After each *Try It Out*, the code you've typed is explained in detail.

> **Boxes like this one hold important, not-to-be forgotten information that is directly relevant to the surrounding text.**

Tips, hints, tricks, and asides to the current discussion are offset and placed in italics like this.

As for styles in the text:

❑ New terms and important words are *highlighted* when they're introduced.

❑ Keyboard strokes appear like this: Ctrl+A.

❑ Simple filenames, URLs, and code within the text looks like so: `persistence.properties`.

❑ Code is presented in two different ways:

```
In code examples, new and important code is highlighted with a gray background.
```

```
The gray highlighting is not used for code that's less important in the present
context, or has been shown before.
```

❑ You will see some highlighted code in the middle of non-highlighted code like this:

```
<body>
  <h1>Using Ajax</h1>
  <br>
  <%= link_to_remote("Click me to use Ajax", :update => "displayDiv",
    :url => {:action => :replacer }) %>
  <br>
  <div id = "displayDiv">The new text will appear here.</div>
</body>
```

The highlighted lines represent new code or code that you will be changing.

Source Code

As you work through the examples in this book, you may choose either to type in all the code manually or to use the source code files that accompany the book. All of the source code used in this book is available for download at `http://www.wrox.com`. Once at the site, simply locate the book's title (either by using the Search box or by using one of the title lists) and click the Download Code link on the book's detail page to obtain all the source code for the book.

Because many books have similar titles, you may find it easiest to search by ISBN; this book's ISBN is 0-470-06915-5 (changing to 978-0-470-06915-8 as the new industry-wide 13-digit ISBN numbering system is phased in by January 2007).

Once you download the code, just decompress it with your favorite compression tool. Alternatively, you can go to the main Wrox code download page at `http://www.wrox.com/dynamic/books/download.aspx` to see the code available for this book and all other Wrox books.

Errata

We make every effort to ensure that there are no errors in the text or in the code. However, no one is perfect, and mistakes do occur. If you find an error in one of our books, like a spelling mistake or faulty piece of code, we would be very grateful for your feedback. By sending in errata you may save another reader hours of frustration and at the same time you will be helping us provide even higher quality information.

To find the errata page for this book, go to http://www.wrox.com and locate the title using the Search box or one of the title lists. Then, on the book details page, click the Book Errata link. On this page you can view all errata that has been submitted for this book and posted by Wrox editors. A complete book list including links to each book's errata is also available at www.wrox.com/misc-pages/booklist.shtml.

If you don't spot "your" error on the Book Errata page, go to www.wrox.com/contact/techsupport.shtml and complete the form there to send us the error you have found. We'll check the information and, if appropriate, post a message to the book's errata page and fix the problem in subsequent editions of the book.

p2p.wrox.com

For author and peer discussion, join the P2P forums at p2p.wrox.com. The forums are a Web-based system for you to post messages relating to Wrox books and related technologies and interact with other readers and technology users. The forums offer a subscription feature to e-mail you topics of interest of your choosing when new posts are made to the forums. Wrox authors, editors, other industry experts, and your fellow readers are present on these forums.

At http://p2p.wrox.com you will find a number of different forums that will help you not only as you read this book, but also as you develop your own applications. To join the forums, just follow these steps:

1. Go to p2p.wrox.com and click the Register link.
2. Read the terms of use and click Agree.
3. Complete the required information to join as well as any optional information you want to provide, and click Submit.
4. You will receive an email with information describing how to verify your account and complete the joining process.

You can read messages in the forums without joining P2P but to post your own messages, you must join.

Once you join, you can post new messages and respond to messages other users post. You can read messages at any time on the Web. If you would like to have new messages from a particular forum e-mailed to you, click the Subscribe to this Forum icon by the forum name in the forum listing.

For more information about how to use the Wrox P2P, be sure to read the P2P FAQs for answers to questions about how the forum software works as well as many common questions specific to P2P and Wrox books. To read the FAQs, click the FAQ link on any P2P page.

Welcome to Ruby

Welcome to Ruby on Rails! If you're a web developer, you're going to love Ruby on Rails — it's the easiest way to get real web applications going. If you've been a Java web programmer in the past, for example, you're going to think: this is great!

If you're used to huge, overly complex web applications, you're in for a treat — both Ruby and Rails can do a lot of the code writing for you, creating skeleton applications that you can modify easily. And if you're new to web programming, you're also in for a treat because you're getting started the right way.

Ruby is the programming language you're going to be using, and Rails is the web application framework that will put everything online. This and the next couple of chapters get you up to speed in Ruby, building the foundation you need to start putting Ruby on Rails. If you already know Ruby, you can skip this material and get directly to the online stuff.

But why just talk about it? Why not start by seeing Ruby in action? Heck, why not see Ruby on Rails in action, taking a look at just how simple it is to build a sample web application? That will give you something to keep in mind as you work through Ruby in these first few chapters. The first step, of course, is to install Ruby and Rails.

Installing Ruby and Rails

You're going to need both Ruby and Rails, so you should install both. Fortunately, that's not hard. The following sections lead you through installing on Windows, Mac OS X, and Linux/Unix.

Install Ruby and Rails on Windows

Just follow these steps to install Ruby:

1. Download the one-click installer for Ruby at `http://rubyinstaller.rubyforge.org`.

2. Click the installer to install Ruby.

Setting up Rails is just about as easy.

Select Start⇨Run. Type **cmd** in the Open field and click OK.

Then, type the following at the command prompt:

```
gem install rails --include-dependencies
```

And that's it! You've got Ruby, and you've got Rails.

Install Ruby and Rails in Mac OS X

As of Mac OS X version 10.4 (the version called Tiger), installation is more than simple—Ruby comes built in. To check that, open the Terminal application by using Finder to go to Applications⇨Utilities, double-click Terminal, and then enter **ruby -v** to check Ruby's version number.

You should see a version of Ruby that's 1.8.2 or later. If not, you're going to have to install Ruby yourself.

The locomotive project (`http://locomotive.raaum.org`) is a complete one-step install Rails environment for OS X.

Alternatively, you can download Rails yourself. To do that, you first need RubyGems, which you can pick up by going to `http://rubygems.rubyforge.org` and clicking the download link. Then go to the directory containing the download in the Terminal application and enter the following at the command prompt, updating `rubygems-0.8.10.tar.gz` to the most recent version of the download:

```
tar xzf rubygems-0.8.10.tar.gz
cd rubygems-0.8.10
sudo ruby setup.rb
```

The final step is to use RubyGems to download Rails, so enter this command:

```
sudo gem install rails --include-dependencies
```

That's it—you should be on Rails!

> **Ruby comes installed in Mac OS X, but it's not really installed all that well. For example, support for the Ruby readline library isn't working, which means that you could have problems if you want to use the interactive Ruby tool discussed later in this chapter. To fix the problem and install Ruby yourself, take a look at** `http://tech.ruby.com/entry/46`.

Install Ruby and Rails in Linux and Unix

If you're using Linux or Unix, you probably already have Ruby installed—you're going to need at least version 1.8.2 for this book. Open a shell and type **ruby -v** at the prompt—if you have version 1.8.2 or later installed, you're all set. If you don't have Ruby installed, you can find pre-built versions for your Linux/Unix installation on the Internet, or you can build it from the source, which you can find at `http:// ruby-lang.org/en`.

To build Ruby from source, download `ruby-1.8.4.tar.gz` (change that name to the most recent version), untar the file, and build it:

```
tar xzf ruby-1.8.4.tar.gz
cd ruby-1.8.4
./configure
make
make test
sudo make install
```

You're also going to need Rails, which is most easily installed with RubyGems. To get RubyGems, go to `http://rubygems.rubyforge.org` and click the download link. Then go to the directory containing the download in a shell and enter the following at the command prompt, updating `rubygems-0.8.10.tar.gz` to the most recent version of the download:

```
tar xzf rubygems-0.8.10.tar.gz
cd rubygems-0.8.10
sudo ruby setup.rb
```

All that's left is to use RubyGems to install Rails, which you can do this way:

```
sudo gem install rails --include-dependencies
```

Things very rarely go wrong with the Ruby and Rails installation process, but if there was a problem, take a look at the online help files, starting with `http://rubyinstaller.rubyforge.org/wiki/wiki.pl?RubyInstallerFAQ`.

Database System

You're also going to need to install a database system to get the most out of this book. This book uses MySQL, which you can get for free from `http://dev.mysql.com`. You will also learn how to set up Rails to work with other databases as well.

OK, now that you've got Ruby on Rails installed, how about creating a web application?

Creating a First Web Application

This and the next few chapters are on the Ruby language, which you're going to need to write Ruby on Rails web applications. But before getting into the details on Ruby, take a look at how easy it is to build a simple Ruby on Rails application. This first Rails application displays a friendly greeting message.

To organize the work you do in this book, you'll build all of your applications in a directory named rubydev. Create that directory now by typing md rubydev at the command prompt (in Windows, that might look like this):

```
C:\>md rubydev
```

Then navigate to that directory:

```
C:\rubydev>cd rubydev
C:\rubydev>
```

> If you're using Linux or Unix or Mac or some other operating system, please trans-
> late these directions as appropriate. Ruby on Rails is operating-system independent,
> so you shouldn't run into any trouble in this regard — you'll run into very few oper-
> ating system commands in this book. For example, if you're using the Bash shell,
> enter this:
>
> ```
> -bash-2.05b$ mkdir rubydev
> -bash-2.05b$ cd rubydev
> -bash-2.05b$
> ```
>
> If you're using other varieties of Linux/Unix, you see something like this:
>
> ```
> /home/steve: mkdir rubydev
> /home/steve: cd rubydev
> /home/steve/rubydev:
> ```

This first application is named hello. To tell Rails to create the hello application, type the command **rails**
and then the name of the application you want — in this case, hello. Rails creates many files for you
(most of which are omitted here for brevity):

```
C:\rubydev>rails hello
      create
      create   app/controllers
      create   app/helpers
      create   app/models
      create   app/views/layouts
      create   config/environments
      create   components
      create   db
      create   doc
      create   lib
      create   lib/tasks
      create   log
      create   public/images
      create   public/javascripts
      create   public/stylesheets
      create   script/performance
      create   script/process
      create   test/fixtures
      create   test/methodal
      create   test/integration
        .
        .
        .
      create   public/favicon.ico
      create   public/robots.txt
      create   public/images/rails.png
```

```
create    public/javascripts/prototype.js
create    public/javascripts/effects.js
create    public/javascripts/dragdrop.js
create    public/javascripts/controls.js
create    public/javascripts/application.js
create    doc/README_FOR_APP
create    log/server.log
create    log/production.log
create    log/development.log
create    log/test.log
```

Great; that sets up the framework you're going to need. The next step is to create a *controller* for the application. A controller acts as the application's overseer, as you're going to see in detail when you start working with Rails in depth later in this book. Rails has already created a new directory, hello, for the hello application, so change to that directory now:

```
C:\rubydev>cd hello
C:\rubydev\hello>
```

Then use the Ruby command `ruby script/generate controller App` to create a new controller named `App`:

```
C:\rubydev\hello>ruby script/generate controller App
      exists   app/controllers/
      exists   app/helpers/
      create   app/views/app
      exists   test/methodal/
      create   app/controllers/app_controller.rb
      create   test/methodal/app_controller_test.rb
      create   app/helpers/app_helper.rb
```

The new controller is created. In fact, here's what it looks like, in the file rubydev\hello\app\controllers\app_controller.rb (the `.rb` extension, as you've probably already guessed, stands for Ruby):

```
class AppController < ApplicationController
end
```

The controller is derived from the base class `ApplicationController` (if you don't know about inheriting, don't worry about it — that's coming up in Chapter 3). As you can see, it's a very simple file.

The controller determines the flow of navigation in an application. Each controller contains one or more actions. Each action knows how to respond when a specific input is received from the browser. Actions can call and prepare data for display in views or return other content directly to the browser. The controller will contain all the actions you want in the web application, and each action is supported with its own code.

So while the controller oversees whole web application, each action that the controller watches over contains methods as separate tasks. That makes it easy to build web applications as collections of separate tasks (actions).

The hello application uses an example action named greeting to display its message in a browser window. To create the greeting action, just add the following code to app_controller.rb, using your favorite text editor:

```
class AppController < ApplicationController
  def greeting
  end
end
```

Make sure that your text editor can save text in plain text format with the extension .rb (not the default .rtf format of Windows WordPad, for example, or the default Notepad extension .txt), and save the file after you've added the greeting action.

So you've created a web application with a controller that oversees the action and an action that acts as a task you can ask the controller to execute. You still need to display its results. In Rails, a *view* is often used to do that. A view is a web page template that the action can call and supply data to. A view can format data as a web page and display it in the browser. In other words, you can construct a full web page template with all kinds of formatting — colors, fonts, and so on — and pop the data items supplied by the action into that template in appropriate places before sending it back to the browser.

Now you've already learned three concepts vital to Ruby on Rails programming:

❑ The controller oversees the application.

❑ The action or actions in the application act as individual tasks.

❑ The view or views accept data from the actions and display that data in web pages.

In this example, no data will be passed from the action to the view template; this view will only display a friendly greeting web page, greeting.rhtml, like this:

```
<html>
  <head>
    <title>Ruby on Rails</title>
  </head>
  <body>
    <h1>Yes it's working!</h1>
  </body>
</html>
```

In Rails applications, view templates like this one have the extension .rhtml (that's so Rails knows it is an active web page that should be checked to see if you've left places where data from the action should be added). Create the greeting.rhtml file now, and store it in the rubydev\hello\app\views\app\ folder.

If you are using Windows WordPad or Notepad, you're going to notice that they have an annoying tendency to append the extension .rtf or .txt, respectively, to the end of any file whose extension they don't understand — and that includes Ruby .rb and Rails .rhtml files. So instead of greeting .rhtml, you might end up with greeting.rhtml.rtf or greeting.rhtml.txt when you try to save this file. To get around that, place the name of the file in quotation marks when you save it, such as "greeting.rhtml". That stops WordPad and Notepad from adding their default extensions.

And that's it—believe it or not, you're done. You've created your first Ruby on Rails web application. How can you see it in a web browser? Rails comes with a built-in web server that you can use for testing. To start that web server, just use `ruby script/server` at the command line, as you see here:

```
C:\rubydev\hello>ruby script/server
=> Booting WEBrick...
=> Rails application started on http://0.0.0.0:3000
=> Ctrl-C to shutdown server; call with --help for options
[2006-05-03 11:10:29] INFO  WEBrick 1.3.1
[2006-05-03 11:10:29] INFO  WEBrick::HTTPServer#start: pid=4008 port=3000
```

Now open a browser. The Ruby on Rails server operates locally, and uses port 3000, so you start the URL `http://localhost:3000`. Then you specify the web application controller's name (`app`, in this case) and the name of the web application's actions—that is, tasks—you want to execute (`greeting`). That makes the full URL `http://localhost:3000/app/greeting`.

Navigate to `http://localhost:3000/app/greeting` and you'll see the web page shown in Figure 1-1, complete with the greeting from the web application.

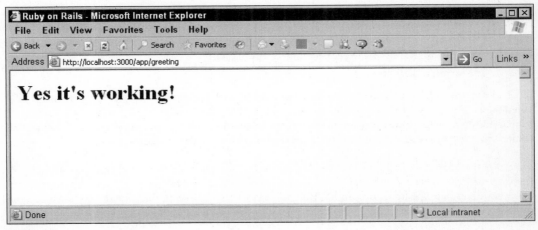

Figure 1-1

Congratulations! You've just completed and run your first Ruby on Rails application, and it took practically no time at all. To create web applications that do something more impressive, though, you need to get the Ruby language under your belt. That's what the rest of this and the next couple of chapters are all about—building the foundation you're going to need when it comes to working with Ruby on Rails.

Getting Started with Ruby

Ruby is the language that is going to make everything happen. To work with Ruby, you need a text editor of the kind you already used to get the Ruby on Rails example working, such as WordPad (Start⇨Programs⇨Accessories⇨WordPad) or Notepad (Start⇨Programs⇨Accessories⇨Notepad) in Windows.

Each Ruby program should be saved with the extension `.rb`, such as this first example, `hello.rb`, which displays a greeting from Ruby.

Try It Out   Display a Message

To get started with Ruby and make it display a welcoming message, follow these steps:

1. Start your text editor and enter the following Ruby code:

```
puts "Hello from Ruby."
```

2. Save the file as `hello.rb`. Make sure you save the file as a text file (select Text Document in the Save As Type drop-down), and if you are using Windows WordPad or Notepad, make sure you enclose the name of the file in quotes — `"hello.rb"` — before saving to prevent those editors from saving the file as `hello.rb.rtf` or `hello.rb.txt`.

3. Use Ruby to run this new program and see the results. Just enter the ruby command followed by the name of the program at the command line:

```
C:\rubydev>ruby hello.rb
Hello from Ruby.
```

How It Works

This first example is simple — it executes a line of Ruby code:

```
puts "Hello from Ruby."
```

What is `puts`? That's a *method* built into Ruby, and it stands for "put string." A method is a piece of executable code that you can pass data to — in this case, the `puts` method takes the data you pass to it (that's `"Hello from Ruby."` here) and displays it in the command window.

Note that this line of code doesn't end with a semicolon as in some other programming languages you'll see, such as Java or JavaScript. You don't need any end-of-line marker at all in Ruby. If you can't fit a Ruby statement on one line, you can tell Ruby that you are continuing that line of code on a second line by using backslashes, like this:

```
puts \
"Hello from Ruby."
```

So if you ever need to break a line of Ruby onto more than one line, just use a backslash at the end of each line — except for the last line — to indicate that more is coming.

You can also create *comments* in Ruby, using the # symbol. A comment is human-readable text that Ruby will ignore. When you use # on a line, everything you place after the # will be ignored by Ruby, although you can read it:

```
puts "Hello from Ruby."    #Display the text!
```

Working with Ruby Interactively

This first example was a success, but you should be aware that there's another way to work with Ruby interactively — you can use the interactive Ruby tool irb. You can start that tool from the command line:

```
C:\rubydev>irb
irb(main):001:0>
```

This displays the irb prompt, and you can enter your Ruby code at that prompt, such as puts "Hello from Ruby.":

```
C:\rubydev>irb
irb(main):001:0> puts "Hello from Ruby."
```

When you press the Enter key, irb evaluates your Ruby and gives you the result:

```
C:\rubydev>irb
irb(main):001:0> puts "Hello from Ruby."
Hello from Ruby.
```

Although you can create multi-line programs using irb, it's awkward, so this book sticks to entering Ruby code in files instead.

Checking the Ruby Documentation

What about documentation? Does Ruby come with any documentation that you can use to look up questions? Yes, it does, and there's more online. To handle the local version of the documentation, you use the ri tool. Just enter **ri** at the command line, followed by the item you want help with, such as the puts method:

```
C:\rubydev>ri puts
More than one method matched your request. You can refine
your search by asking for information on one of:

    IO#puts, Kernel#puts, Zlib::GzipWriter#puts
```

If more than one item matches your request, you have to choose which one to ask for more information on. In this example, the puts method of interest is part of the IO package (more on packages in Chapter 3), so request that documentation by entering **ri IO#puts** at the command line:

```
C:\rubydev>ri IO#puts
----------------------------------------------------------------- IO#puts
     ios.puts(obj, ...)    => nil
------------------------------------------------------------------
     Writes the given objects to _ios_ as with +IO#print+. Writes a
     record separator (typically a newline) after any that do not
     already end with a newline sequence. If called with an array
     argument, writes each element on a new line. If called without
```

```
        arguments, outputs a single record separator.

            $stdout.puts("this", "is", "a", "test")

    _produces:_

        this
        is
        a
        test
```

The ri tool searches the local Ruby documentation for the item you have requested and displays any help it can find. Unfortunately, that help is likely to be terse and not very helpful. Still, the local documentation can be useful, especially when it comes to examples.

Another place to turn is the online Ruby documentation site, www.ruby-doc.org. This site isn't overly easy to use, but its information is usually more complete than the local version of the documentation.

Working with Numbers in Ruby

Ruby has some great features for working with numbers. In fact, Ruby handles numbers automatically, so you need not be concerned about them. There is no limit to the size of integers you can use — a number like 12345678987654321 is perfectly fine. What's more, you make this number easier to read by using underscores every three digits from the right, like this: 12_345_678_987_654_321. You can give floating-point numbers simply by using a decimal point (you need at least one digit in front of the decimal point), like this: 3.1415. You can also give an exponent like this: 31415.0e-4. And you can give binary numbers by prefacing them with 0b (as in 0b1111), octal — base eight — numbers by prefacing them with a 0 (like this: 0355), and hexadecimal numbers — base 16 — by prefacing them with 0x (such as 0xddff).

Ruby stores numbers in a variety of types. For example, integers are stored as the Fixnum type unless they become too large, in which case they are stored as the Bignum type. And floating-point numbers are stored as the Float type. However, you don't have to worry about of this, because Ruby keeps track of a number's type internally.

Try It Out   **Working with Numbers**

To get started with numbers in Ruby, follow these steps:

1. Enter this Ruby code in a new file:

```
puts 12345
puts 3.1415
puts 31415.0e-4
puts 12_345_678_987_654_321
puts 0xddff
```

2. Save the file as numbers.rb.

3. Use Ruby to run numbers.rb:

```
C:\rubydev>ruby numbers.rb
12345
3.1415
3.1415
12345678987654321
56831
```

How It Works

This example takes several numbers and uses the `puts` method to display them in a command window. As you can see, it displays a few integers and floating-point numbers — even a hexadecimal number (which is displayed in decimal). Note the number 31415.0e-4, which is actually 31415.0×10^{-4}. Ruby handles this number as it should, and displays it in simpler format: 3.1415.

Working with Strings in Ruby

You can enclose strings in single quotes (`'Shall we watch a movie?'`) or double quotes (`"No, we certainly shall not."`). In fact, you can mix single and double quotes, as long as Ruby can keep them straight, like this: `"Did you say, 'No, we certainly shall not'?"`. However, you cannot mix double-quoted text inside a double-quoted string, or single-quoted text inside a single-quoted string, like this: `"I said, "Hello.""`, because Ruby won't know where the quotation actually ends. To fix that, you can alternate single and double quotes, like this: `"I said, 'Hello.'"` or `'I said, "Hello."'`, or you can escape quotation marks with a backslash, like this: `"I said, \"Hello.\""` or `'I said, \'Hello.\''`.

In fact, you don't even have to use single or double quotes — Ruby can add them for you if you use the `%q` (single quotes) or `%Q` (double quotes) syntax. Just use `%q` or `%Q` with a single character, and Ruby will add quotes until it sees that character again. For example, the expression `%Q/Yes, that was Cary Grant./` is the same as `"Yes, that was Cary Grant."` And it's also the same as the expression `%Q!Yes, that was Cary Grant.!`. The expression `%q/Are you sure?/` is the same as `'Are you sure?'`. You can also use pairs of delimiters, such as { and } or < and > when quoting, like this: `%Q{Yes, that was Cary Grant.}`. In fact, you can omit the Q altogether — if you do, you'll get a double-quoted string: `%/No, it wasn't Cary./` is the same as `"No, it wasn't Cary."`

You can also concatenate (join) strings together, using a +. For example, the expression `"It " + "was " + "too " + "Cary " + "Grant!"` is the same as `"It was too Cary Grant!"`.

Try It Out   Working with Strings

To get started with strings in Ruby, follow these steps:

1. Enter this Ruby code in a new file, `strings.rb`:

```
puts "Hello"
puts "Hello " + "there"
puts 'Nice to see you.'
puts %Q/How are you?/
puts %Q!Fine, and you?!
puts %q!I'm also fine, thanks.!
puts "I have to say, 'I am well.'"
puts "I'll also say, \"Things are fine.\""
```

2. Save the file as `strings.rb`.

3. Run `strings.rb` using Ruby to see the result:

```
C:\rubydev>ruby strings.rb
Hello
Hello there
Nice to see you.
How are you?
Fine, and you?
I'm also fine, thanks.
I have to say, 'I am well.'
I'll also say, "Things are fine."
```

How It Works

This example gives a good overview of the ways of working with single- and double-quoted text in Ruby. And, there's even more to come — double-quoted strings have some additional power that you'll see after the upcoming discussion on variables.

There's another way of working with text strings that you should know about in Ruby: HERE documents. HERE documents are inherited in Ruby from older languages like Perl, and they give you a shortcut for printing multiple lines to the console window. Although not in common use, you should still know what they are in case you come across them.

HERE documents let you break up strings into multiple lines; Ruby treats any text that starts with `<<TOKEN` (where TOKEN can be any uppercase word) as the beginning of a multi-line sequence, and assumes that that text ends with TOKEN. Here is an example that uses the Ruby `print` method, which prints out the text you pass it and, unlike `puts`, does not skip to the next line (that is, `print` does not add a carriage return to the text):

```
print <<HERE
Now
is
the
time
HERE
```

You don't have to use HERE as the token; you can use any word.

This displays this text:

```
Now
is
the
time
```

Although the `print` method does not skip to the next line automatically, the output here did skip to the next line. That's because a HERE document automatically inserts a newline character at the end of each line, enabling you to create multi-line text easily.

If you want to make the `print` method skip to the next line without a HERE document, use the newline character, `\n`. For example,

```
print "Now is \nthe time."
```

prints out

```
Now is
the time.
```

Storing Data in Variables

Ruby can store your data in *variables*, which are named placeholders that can store numbers, strings, and other data. You reference the data stored in a variable by using the variable's name. For example, to store a value of 34 in a variable named `temperature`, you assign that variable the value like this:

```
temperature = 34
```

Then you refer to the data in the `temperature` variable by name, as here, where you are printing out the value in the `temperature` variable (34) in a command window:

```
puts temperature
```

Here's the result:

```
34
```

Because you refer to the values in variables by using the variables' names in code, it's important to realize that there are rules for the names you can use in Ruby. A standard variable starts with a lowercase letter, *a* to *z*, or an underscore, _, followed by any number of *name characters*. A name character is a lowercase letter, an uppercase letter, a digit, or an underscore. And you have to avoid the words that Ruby reserves for itself. Here's a list of Ruby's reserved words:

__FILE__	def	in	self
__LINE__	defined?	module	super
BEGIN	do	next	then
END	else	nil	true
alias	elsif	not	undef
and	end	or	unless
begin	ensure	redo	until
break	false	rescue	when
case	for	retry	while
class	if	return	yield

It's also the Ruby convention to use underscores rather than "camel case" for multiple-word names; money_I_owe_my_cousin is good, for example, but moneyThatIOweMyCousin is not.

Some variables are named with an @ (as in @money_I_owe_my_cousin) or even @@ (as in @@money_I_owe_my_cousin). You learn about those in Chapter 3 when you write classes in Ruby.

To create a variable, you just have to use it in Ruby. You can see that for yourself in the following exercise.

Try It Out   Working with Variables

To get started with variables in Ruby, follow these steps:

1.   Enter this Ruby code in a new file, variables.rb:

```
temperature = 36
puts "The temperature is " + String(temperature) + "."
temperature = temperature + 5
puts "Now the temperature is " + String(temperature) + "."
```

2.   Save the variables.rb file.

3.   Run variables.rb to see the result:

```
C:\rubydev>ruby variables.rb
The temperature is 36.
Now the temperature is 41.
```

How It Works

This example first creates a variable named temperature and stores a value of 36 in it:

```
temperature = 36
```

Then it prints out the value in the temperature variable. Note that you convert the integer in the temperature variable to a string before trying to print it out, and you can do that with the Ruby String method — the parentheses after the String method name are to make certain that you just pass the temperature variable to the String method, not any additional text on the line:

```
puts "The temperature is " + String(temperature) + "."
```

Instead of the String method, you could use the to_s method built into all numbers — that method does the same as the String method (and in fact, the String method simply calls the number's to_s method):

```
temperature = 36
puts "The temperature is " + temperature.to_s + "."
```

Then the example uses the + operator to add 5 to the value in the temperature variable. Using operators, as you're about to see, lets you manipulate the data stored in variables:

```
temperature = temperature + 5
```

Finally, this example displays the new value stored in the temperature variable, which is 36 + 5, or 41:

```
puts "Now the temperature is " + String(temperature) + "."
```

Creating Constants

You can also create constants in Ruby. A *constant* holds a value that you do not expect to change, such as the value of pi:

```
PI = 3.1415926535
```

Note the uppercase name, PI, here. Constants in Ruby start with an uppercase letter — that's how Ruby knows they are constants. In fact, the entire name of a constant is usually in uppercase. But it's that first letter that is crucial — it must be uppercase so that Ruby knows that you intend to create a constant.

Constants are often used to collect data items that won't change at the beginning of your code so that they can be grouped together and changed easily if need be — you use the constants throughout your code, and won't have to hunt for the specific values the constants stand for and change them throughout your code if you need to change a value. For example, constants might hold Internet IP addresses:

```
IP_SERVER_SOURCE = "903.111.333.055"
IP_SERVER_TARGET = "903.111.333.056"
```

These constants, IP_SERVER_SOURCE and IP_SERVER_TARGET, can now be used throughout your code, and if you have to change them, you only need to change them in one place.

Unlike other languages, Ruby allows you to change the values in constants by assigning a new value to them:

```
CONST = 1
CONST = 2
```

However, you'll get a warning each time you do this:

```
constants.rb:2: warning: already initialized constant CONST
```

Interpolating Variables in Double-Quoted Strings

As mentioned earlier, double-quoted strings have a special property — you can display the values of variables directly in them using a process called *interpolation*. Here's how it works: you surround the expression you want placed into the double-quoted string with #{ and }, and when Ruby sees that, it'll evaluate that expression and substitute its value at that location in the string. For example, you saw this code a page or two ago:

```
temperature = 36
puts "The temperature is " + String(temperature) + "."
```

But you can get the same result using variable interpolation, like this:

```
temperature = 36
puts "The temperature is #{temperature}."
```

In this case, the term #{temperature} is evaluated to the value stored in the temperature, 36, and that result is displayed:

```
The temperature is 36.
```

Try It Out   Interpolating Variables

To get started with interpolating expressions in double-quoted strings in Ruby, follow these steps:

1. Enter this code in a new file, doublequoted.rb:

```
temperature = 36
puts "The temperature is #{temperature}."
temperature = temperature + 5
puts "Now the temperature is #{temperature}."
```

2. Save doublequoted.rb.

3. Run doublequoted.rb:

```
C:\rubydev>ruby doublequoted.rb
The temperature is 36.
Now the temperature is 41.
```

How It Works

This example interpolates the value in the temperature variable into a double-quoted string: "The temperature is #{temperature}." When Ruby sees that, it substitutes the value of the temperature variable in the double-quoted string automatically.

In fact, you can place any expression inside #{ and } in a double-quoted string and have it interpolated into the text. For example, to add 5 to the value in the temperature variable, you could simply do this:

```
temperature = 36
puts "The temperature is #{temperature}."
puts "Now the temperature is #{temperature + 5}."
```

Reading Text on the Command Line

You've seen how to print out text in a console window using puts (displays a text string) and print (displays a text string but does not skip to the next line), but what about reading text on the command line? How do you get Ruby to read text that the user has typed? The most common way is to use the built-in gets method. That method lets you read text from the command line that the user has entered, and, by default, assigns that text to the predefined variable $_, which also comes built into Ruby.

Here's one thing you should know — the `gets` method leaves the terminating newline character that the user enters when he's done entering text on the end of the string, so if the user enters `Stop` and then presses Enter, the input you'll get will be `Stop\n`, where `\n` is a newline character.

And here's another thing you should know — the built-in Ruby method `chomp` removes that newline character from the end of the text in the `$_` variable. Problem solved.

Try It Out   Reading Text

To get started reading text in Ruby, follow these steps:

1.   Enter this code in a new file, `gets.rb`:

```
print "Please enter the temperature: "
gets
chomp
puts "The temperature is #{$_}."
```

2.   Save the file and run it.

3.   Ruby displays the prompt `Please enter the temperature:` and then waits for a response from you:

```
C:\rubydev>ruby gets.rb
Please enter the temperature:
```

4.   Enter a temperature and press Enter. Ruby reads the text that you have entered, chomps the newline character off the end of it, and displays the resulting text:

```
C:\rubydev>ruby gets.rb
Please enter the temperature: 36
The temperature is 36.
```

How It Works

This code works by displaying a prompt (with `print` so Ruby doesn't skip to the next line in the command window) and using `gets` to read what the user has entered. By default, `gets` places the text it has read in the `$_` predefined variable, so you can use `chomp` to get rid of the newline character at the end of that text. Then you can display the resulting trimmed text using `puts`.

Actually, you don't need to use `$_` with `gets` — you can assign the text it reads to any variable, like this: `temperature = gets`. However, that still leaves you the problem of removing the newline character at the end of the text with `chomp`, because you do have to use `$_` with `chomp` — you can't specify a variable to `chomp`. That would make your code look like this:

```
print "Please enter the temperature: "
temperature = gets
$_ = temperature
chomp
temperature = $_
puts "The temperature is #{temperature}."
```

Creating Symbols in Ruby

You've seen how to create variables and constants, but there's more to come in Ruby, such as *symbols*. As you know, when you use a variable in Ruby code, Ruby substitutes the value of that variable for the variable itself. But what if you just wanted to use a name, without having it stand for anything? For that, you can use a Ruby symbol (called atoms in other languages), which is preceded by a colon (:). Here are a few examples:

```
:temperature
:ISP_address
:row_delimiter
```

Each of these symbols is treated simply as a name; no substitution is performed when you use them in your code.

At this point, you can think of symbols much as you would quoted strings that contain names. In fact, they are really very much like quoted strings, with a couple of technical differences — each symbol always stands for the same object (more on objects is coming up in Chapter 3), no matter where you use it in your code, which is different from strings; and comparing symbols to each other is faster than comparing strings.

Working with Operators

It's time to start working with the data stored in the variables you create. As you've already seen, you can add numbers to the values you store in variables — for example, this code added 5 to the value in the temperature variable:

```
temperature = temperature + 5
```

The code used the + addition operator to add 5 to the value in the temperature variable, and the = assignment operator to assign the result to the `temperature` variable, but many other operators are available.

Try It Out   **Using Operators**

To get started using operators in Ruby, follow these steps:

1. Enter this code in a new file, `operators.rb`:

```
value = 3
puts value
value = value + 3    #addition
puts value
value = value / 2    #division
puts value
value = value * 3    #multiplication
puts value
value = value ** 2   #exponentiation
puts value
```

2. Save `operators.rb`.

3. Run `operators.rb`:

```
C:\rubydev>ruby operators.rb
3
6
3
9
81
```

How It Works

This example shows a number of the Ruby operators (+, /, *, and **) at work. Table 1-1 describes many of the Ruby operators.

Table 1-1 Ruby Operators

Operator	Description
[ ] [ ]=	Array reference Array element set
**	Exponentiation
! ~ + −	Not Complement Unary plus Minus
* / %	Multiply Divide Modulo
+ −	Plus Minus
>> <<	Right shift Left shift
&	Bitwise And
^ |	Bitwise exclusive Or (Xor) Regular Or
 <= < > >=	Comparison operators: Less than or equal to Less than Greater than Greater than or equal to
 <=> == === != =~	Equality and pattern match operators: Less than, equal to, greater than Equal to Tests equality in a when clause of a case statement Not equal to Regular expression pattern match

Table continued on following page

Table 1-1 Continued

Operator	Description
&&	Logical And
||	Logical Or
..	Inclusive range
...	Exclusive range
?	Ternary if
:	Else
=	Assignment
	Normal assign
%=	Modulus and assign
/=	Divide and assign
-=	Subtract and assign
+=	Add and assign
*=	Multiply and assign
**=	Exponent and assign
defined?	True if symbol defined
not	Logical negation
and	Logical composition
or	
	Statement modifiers
if	
unless	
while	
until	
begin/end	Block expression

Some of the operators have assignment shortcuts; for example, this line of code

```
value = value + 3
```

can be made shorter with the += addition assignment operator, like this:

```
value += 3
```

In other words, the += shortcut operator adds its right operand to its left operand and assigns the result to the left operand. And that means that the preceding example could be rewritten using shortcut operators:

```
value = 3
puts value
value += 3    #addition
puts value
```

```
value /= 2    #division
puts value
value *= 3    #multiplication
puts value
value **= 2   #exponentiation
puts value
```

Handling Operator Precedence

Here's a question for you: what does the following Ruby statement print out?

```
puts 5 + 3 * 2
```

Does it add the 5 and 3 first, and then multiply the result (8) by 2 to get 16? Or does it multiply 3 by 2 to get 6, and then add the 5 to get 11? Let's see how Ruby answers the question:

```
C:\rubydev>ruby precedence.rb
11
```

The answer is that it multiplies the 3 by 2 first, and then adds 5, which might not be what you expected.

The reason Ruby performed the multiplication first, before the addition, is that multiplication has higher *precedence* than addition in Ruby. An operator's precedence specifies the order in which it is executed with respect to other operators in the same statement.

The operators in Table 1-1 are arranged in terms of precedence, from highest at the top to lowest at the bottom. As you can see in the table, the multiplication operator * has higher precedence than the addition operator +, which means that * will be executed first.

You can alter the execution order, if you want to, using parentheses. Just wrap the expression you want evaluated first inside parentheses, like this:

```
puts (5 + 3) * 2
```

In this case, 5 and 3 will be added first, and the result, 8, multiplied by 2, to yield 16:

```
C:\rubydev>ruby precedence.rb
16
```

Working with Arrays

There are plenty of ways to work with data in Ruby. Next up is to store it in *arrays*. Arrays act as groups of variables, and you can access each variable in an array with an index number.

For example, to create an array, you use the [] operator like this:

```
array = [1, 2, 3]
```

This creates an array with three elements, 1, 2, and 3. You access those elements using an array index like this:

```
puts array[0]        #prints 1
puts array[1]        #prints 2
puts array[2]        #prints 3
```

Note that the first element in the array corresponds to array index 0, not 1, and the second element is at index 1, the third at index 2, and so on. You can also assign values to arrays, using the array index:

```
array[0] = 4         #assigns 4 to array[0]
array[1] = 5         #assigns 5 to array[1]
array[2] = 6         #assigns 6 to array[2]
puts array[2]        #prints 6
```

As you know, Ruby variables can store text strings as well as numbers, and you can store both in arrays. Here's an example:

```
array = ["Hello", "there", "sweetie", 1, 2, 3]
```

This creates an array filled with six elements, three of which are text and three of which are numbers:

```
array = ["Hello", "there", "sweetie", 1, 2, 3]
puts array[1]        #prints "there"
puts array[4]        #prints 2
```

Arrays are handy in code because you have control over the numeric array index, which means that you can move over all the elements in an array in code, handling all the data at once. For example, you store test scores of students in a class on Ruby that you are teaching. To find the average test score, you could simply increment the array index, fetching each individual score and adding them up. Then you could divide by the total number of students.

How could you find the total number of students in the array? You could use the array's built-in `length` method, which returns the number of elements in the array:

```
array = ["Hello", "there", "sweetie", 1, 2, 3]
puts array[1]        #prints "there"
puts array[4]        #prints 2
puts array.length    #prints 6
```

Try It Out   Using Arrays

To get started using arrays in Ruby, follow these steps:

1. Enter this code in a new file, `arrays.rb`:

```
array = ["Hello", "there", "sweetie", 1, 2, 3]
puts array[0]
puts array[1]
puts array.length
array2 = Array.new
```

```
puts array2.length
array2[0] = "Banana"
array2[1] = "fish"
puts array2[0] + " " + array2[1]
puts array2.length
```

2. Save the file and run it:

```
C:\rubydev>ruby arrays.rb
Hello
there
6
0
Banana fish
2
```

How It Works

This example creates an array, fills it with data, extracts data from the array, and displays the length of the array. Then this example does something new — it creates a second array with the Array class's new method:

```
array2 = Array.new
```

That creates a new array named array2, and gives it zero length (because it doesn't have any elements in it yet):

```
puts array2.length          #prints 0
```

Now you can use this array as you did the first array in this example, assigning data to the elements in the array, and fetching data from those elements as you want:

```
array2[0] = "Banana"
array2[1] = "fish"
puts array2[0] + " " + array2[1]
puts array2.length
```

When you assign data to a new element in an array, that element is automatically created if it didn't exist before. Note that at the end of this code, puts array2.length prints out the new length of the array, which is 2.

Here's something else you should know — you don't have to place data in array elements consecutively. After creating a new array, you can fill its element 0, then skip over element 1, and fill element 2 like this, no problem:

```
array2 = Array.new
puts array2.length
array2[0] = "Banana"
array2[2] = "fish"
puts array2[0] + " " + array2[2]      #prints "Banana fish"
```

In fact, you can use *negative* array indices in Ruby as well. Negative indices count from the end of the array back to the beginning of the array. Here's an example:

```
array = ["Hello", "there", "sweetie", 1, 2, 3]
puts array[-1]            #prints 3
```

This example prints out 3, the last element in the array. It often confuses people that the first element in an array is 0, the next 1, and so on — but the last element in the array is -1 (which means negative indices start with -1, not 0), the previous one -2, the previous one -3, and so on. But that does make sense — how could negative indices start with 0? That array index is already taken. Using negative array indices, you can move backward through an entire array:

```
array = ["Hello", "there", "sweetie", 1, 2, 3]
puts array[-1]            #prints 3
puts array[-2]            #prints 2
puts array[-3]            #prints 1
```

In addition to numbers, you can use a variable (or a constant) as an array index. Here's an example:

```
array = ["Hello", "there", "sweetie", 1, 2, 3]
index_value = 0
puts array[index_value]   #prints "Hello"
index_value = 1
puts array[index_value]   #prints "there"
index_value = 2
puts array[index_value]   #prints "sweetie"
```

Want a quick way of printing out an entire array? Just use `puts` on the entire array:

```
array = ["Hello", "there", "sweetie", 1, 2, 3]
puts array
```

This code gives you:

```
Hello
there
sweetie
1
2
3
```

Using Two Array Indices

You can access the data in arrays using two indices, not just one. This works differently from other programming languages you might be used to, however. Instead of letting you work with two-dimensional arrays, in Ruby the first index is the start location and the second holds the number of elements you want to access. So you can call the first index the start point, and the second index the count of elements to access: `array[start, count]`.

For example, here's an array:

```
array = ["Hello", "there", "sweetie", 1, 2, 3]
```

Now to replace element 1, you can do this:

```
array[1] = "here"
```

That leaves you with the array

```
["Hello", "here", "sweetie", 1, 2, 3]
```

An equivalent way of doing things is to use a double index, indicating that you want to replace element 1 only, like this:

```
array = ["Hello", "there", "sweetie", 1, 2, 3]
array[1, 1] = "here"
```

You get the same result:

```
["Hello", "here", "sweetie", 1, 2, 3]
```

However, what if instead of `array[1, 1]`, you used `array[1, 2]`? Then you would be referencing two array elements, starting with the element at index 1, and this statement replaces two elements in the array, not just one:

```
array = ["Hello", "there", "sweetie", 1, 2, 3]
array[1, 2] = "here"
```

Here is the result:

```
["Hello", "here", 1, 2, 3]
```

Do you get it? The expression `array[1, 2]` referred to two elements in the array (`"there"` and `"sweetie"`), starting at index 1.

What about using a count of 0?

```
array = ["Hello", "there", "sweetie", 1, 2, 3]
array[3, 0] = "pie"
puts array
```

Here's what you get:

```
Hello
there
sweetie
pie
1
2
3
```

In other words, assigning a value to `array[3, 0]` did not replace any element in the array; it inserted a new element starting at index 3 instead.

Try It Out   **Using Two Array Indices**

To get started using two array indices in Ruby, follow these steps:

1.   Enter this code in a new file, `doubleindex.rb`:

```
array = ["Hello", "there", "sweetie", 1, 2, 3]
array[2, 1] = "pal"
puts array
array = ["Hello", "there", "sweetie", 1, 2, 3]
array[3, 0] = "pie"
puts array
array = ["Now", "is", 1, 2, 3]
array[2, 0] = ["the", "time"]
puts array
array = ["Hello", "there", "sweetie", 1, 2, 3]
array2 = array[3, 3]
puts array2
```

2.   Save the file and run it:

```
C:\rubydev>ruby doubleindex.rb
Hello
there
pal
1
2
3
Hello
there
sweetie
pie
1
2
3
Now
is
the
time
1
2
3
1
2
3
```

How It Works

This example uses double indices in arrays, and there are a few new points here. Take a look at this code:

```
array = ["Now", "is", 1, 2, 3]
array[2, 0] = ["the", "time"]
puts array
```

Here, the code inserts an entire new array, `["the", "time"]`, into the array, and you can see the results:

```
Now
is
the
time
1
2
3
```

In addition, you can extract subarrays using double indices. Take a look at this code from the example:

```
array = ["Hello", "there", "sweetie", 1, 2, 3]
array2 = array[3, 3]
puts array2
```

This extracts a second array, `array2`, from the first array. This second array is made up of the elements in the first array starting at element three, and continuing for three elements, as you can see when the code displays the array:

```
1
2
3
```

Working with Hashes

Arrays are powerful, but isn't there some way to work with a collection of data using words instead of numbers as indices? You might have a set of relatives who owe you money, for example, and it's hard to remember the numbers you gave to them — is `money_I_am_owed[1]` the money your brother Dan or your sister Claire owes you?

There is a solution; you can use *hashes*. A hash, sometimes called an associative array or a dictionary, is much like an array in that it holds a collection of data, but you can index it using text strings as well as numbers.

To create a hash, you use curly braces, `{` and `}`, not square braces (`[]`) as with arrays. Here's an example:

```
money_I_am_owed = {"Dan" => "$1,000,000", "Claire" => "$500,000"}
```

Here, `"Dan"` is a hash *key* (in hashes, the index is usually called the key), and `"$1,000,000"` is the *value* associated with that key in the hash. The => operator separates the keys from the values.

You can extract data from the hash by using its keys. For example, to find out the amount your brother Dan owes you, you can use this code:

```
money_I_am_owed = {"Dan" => "$1,000,000", "Claire" => "$500,000"}
puts money_I_am_owed["Dan"]
```

Note that to access data in a hash, you use [ ], as with an array, not { } as you might expect (and as you use in other languages).

This code will display:

```
C:\rubydev>ruby hashes.rb
$1,000,000
```

Not bad — certainly a lot easier to remember that your brother corresponds to index 1 and money_I_am_ owed[1] the amount of money he owes you. In fact, you can use numbers as keys as well if you want to:

```
money_I_am_owed = {1 => "$1,000,000", 2 => "$500,000"}
puts money_I_am_owed[1]
```

This code will display:

```
C:\rubydev>ruby hashes.rb
$1,000,000
```

Try It Out   **Using Hashes**

To get started using hashes in Ruby, follow these steps:

1. Enter this code in a new file, hashes.rb:

```
pizza = {"first_topping" => "pepperoni", "second_topping" => "sausage"}
puts pizza["first_topping"]
puts pizza
puts pizza.length
receipts = {"day_one" => 5.03, "day_two" => 15_003.00}
puts receipts["day_one"]
puts receipts["day_two"]
```

2. Save the file and run it:

```
C:\rubydev>ruby hashes.rb
pepperoni
first_toppingpepperonisecond_toppingsausage
2
5.03
15003.0
```

How It Works

This example puts hashes to work, and there are a few things to note here. First, using puts on a hash in Ruby doesn't result in as nice a display as it does for arrays. For example:

```
pizza = {"first_topping" => "pepperoni", "second_topping" => "sausage"}
puts pizza
```

gives you:

```
first_toppingpepperonisecond_toppingsausage
```

Second, you can use the `length` method on hashes just as you can on arrays. For example:

```
pizza = {"first_topping" => "pepperoni", "second_topping" => "sausage"}
puts pizza.length
```

gives you:

```
2
```

Finally, you can store numbers — and for that matter, all kinds of data — in hashes, not just text. This code:

```
receipts = {"day_one" => 5.03, "day_two" => 15_003.00}
puts receipts["day_one"]
puts receipts["day_two"]
```

gives you:

```
5.03
15003.0
```

Working with Ranges

There's another data construct that you should know about — Ruby *ranges*. In the real world, you encounter all kinds of ranges all the time — Monday through Friday, May through July, 1 to 10, a to z, and so on. Ruby gives you an easy way to specify ranges.

To create a range, use the `..` operator. For example, here's how you might create the range 1 to 4:

```
my_range = 1..4
```

That creates the range 1, 2, 3, 4. A handy way of seeing that is to convert the range into an array using the range's `to_a` method, and then simply print out the result array:

```
my_range = 1..4
puts my_range
```

This gives you:

```
1
2
3
4
```

You can also use the `...` operator, which is the same thing except that the final item in the range is omitted. So this range:

```
my_new_range = 1...4
```

actually gives you 1, 2, 3 — not 1, 2, 3, 4, as you can see by printing it out:

```
my_new_range = 1...4
puts my_new_range
```

Here's what you get:

```
1
2
3
```

Ranges are going to be useful in the next chapter, when you want Ruby to do something over and over again. Using a range, you can specify the data items that you want Ruby to work with in such cases.

Try It Out   Using Ranges

To get started using ranges in Ruby, follow these steps:

1. Enter this code in a new file, ranges.rb:

```
range = 1..5              #creates 1, 2, 3, 4, 5
puts range.to_a
range = 1...5             #excludes the 5
puts range.to_a
range = "a".."e"          #creates "a", "b", "c", "d", "e"
puts range.to_a
puts range.min            #prints "a"
puts range.max            #prints "e"
range = "alpha".."alphe"
puts range.to_a
```

2. Save the file and run it.

```
C:\rubydev>ruby ranges.rb
1
2
3
4
5
1
2
3
4
a
b
c
d
e
a
e
alpha
alphb
alphc
alphd
alphe
```

The `range min` and `max` methods return the first and last elements in an array:

```
range = "a".."e"        #creates "a", "b", "c", "d", "e"
puts range.min          #prints "a"
puts range.max          #prints "e"
```

This code displays:

```
a
e
```

And note this code:

```
range = "alpha".."alphe"
puts range.to_a
```

which results in:

```
alpha
alphb
alphc
alphd
alphe
```

As you can see, Ruby attempts to be smart about how it constructs ranges for you.

Here's a final note: You have to create ranges in ascending sequence. For example, whereas this will work:

```
(1..10).to_a
```

this will give you an empty array:

```
(10..1).to_a
```

Summary

In this chapter, you got the basics of Ruby down, including how to:

❑ Install Ruby and Rails, simply by downloading and uncompressing binary files.

❑ Use the `puts` method to display messages.

❑ Read the Ruby documentation using the `ri` command.

❑ Create variables in Ruby just by using them. You name Ruby variables by starting with a lower-case letter, a to z, or an underscore (_) followed by any number of lowercase letters, uppercase letters, digits, or underscores.

❑ Name and use constants in Ruby (the names of constants — whose values are not supposed to be changed — start with a capital letter).

❑   Use Ruby operators.

❑   Use arrays and hashes to group data together into handy data constructs.

❑   Construct Ruby ranges using the .. and ... operators.

In the next chapter, you learn to work with conditionals, loops, methods, and much more. Before you move on, though, work through the following exercises to test your understanding of the material covered in this chapter. The solutions to these exercises are in Appendix A.

Exercises

1. Use a negative index to access the third element in this array: `array = [1, 2, 3, 4, 5, 6, 7, 8]`.

2. Construct a hash that will act the same as the array introduced in the previous exercise, as far as the `[]` operator is concerned.

3. Use a range to create the array introduced in exercise 1.

Conditionals, Loops, Methods, and Blocks

The previous chapter got you started with Ruby, and now it's time to really dig in. This chapter covers conditionals like the `if` statement; loops that let you iterate over sections of code; creating your own methods; and blocks, a special Ruby construct that can be called like pseudo-methods. All of these are essential to working with Ruby, and you're going to need all this stuff in the upcoming chapters.

It's All about Making Choices: the if Statement

Although the syntax is a little different, the Ruby `if` statement works just like the `if` statement does in other languages. In the previous chapter, you saw examples of storing and displaying the current temperature—how about making decisions based on that temperature?

Try It Out   Use the if Statement

In this exercise you use the Ruby `if` statement to make a choice. Here are the steps:

1. Start your editor and enter this Ruby code:

```
temperature = 76

if temperature > 65 && temperature < 85
  puts "Picnic time!"
end
```

2. Save the file as `if.rb`.

3. Use Ruby to run this new program and see the results:

```
C:\rubydev\ch02>ruby if.rb
Picnic time!
```

How It Works

This example is easy enough — it simply uses an `if` statement to check whether the temperature is right for a picnic. The simple form of an `if` statement looks like this:

```
if Boolean [then | :]
    code
end
```

The Boolean is a true-false condition such as `temperature > 65 && temperature < 85`. This is a compound condition that uses > (the greater-than operator) to check whether the value in the temperature variable is greater than 65, and < (the less-than operator) to check whether it's less than 85. Here are the standard conditional operators in Ruby:

Operator	Meaning
==	equal to
>	greater-than
<	less-than
>=	greater-than or equal to
<=	less-than or equal to

The example connects the two conditions it tests together with && (the and operator), which means that both conditions — temperature must be greater than 65 and less than 85 — must be true for the overall expression to be true.

The or operator (| |) specifies that either the first operand or the second one needs to be true for the overall expression to be true; otherwise, the overall expression is false.

Note the `[then | :]` term in the preceding general expression for an `if` statement:

```
if Boolean [then | :]
```

This indicates that you can use the keyword `then` or a colon or neither after the Boolean condition to check. The square braces mean that both the `then` keyword and the colon are optional. You won't use either of them here.

One final item: Ruby `if` statements end with the `end` keyword. You may be used to other languages where curly braces (`{}`) are used, but in Ruby, you use `end`.

OK, good so far. But what if it isn't picnic time?

Using else Clauses in if Statements

If the Boolean true-false condition in an `if` statement isn't true, the code inside the `if` statement isn't executed, but any code in an `else` clause of that same `if` statement is executed. Try it out.

Try It Out   Use an else Clause

Follow this example to see how the Ruby `else` clause works:

1. Start your editor and enter the following code:

```
temperature = 43
if temperature > 65 && temperature < 85
  puts "Picnic time!"
else
  puts "Sorry, no picnic today."
end
```

2. Save the file as `else.rb`.

3. Use Ruby to run this new program and see the results:

```
C:\rubydev\ch02>ruby else.rb
Sorry, no picnic today.
```

How It Works

This example shows how the code in an `else` clause in an `if` statement executes when the Boolean condition for the `if` statement is false—in this case, there was no picnic today:

```
temperature = 43
if temperature > 65 && temperature < 85
  puts "Picnic time!"
else
  puts "Sorry, no picnic today."
end
```

Here's what an `if` statement with an `else` clause looks like in general—note that the `else` clause is optional:

```
if Boolean [then | :]
  code
[else
  code ]
end
```

There's more to `if` statements—you can add `elsif` clauses to perform more tests, and evaluate code if those tests turn out to be true.

Using elsif Clauses in if Statements

You can choose to run one of several code blocks, depending on the conditionals. That's where Ruby's `elsif` clause comes in. Here's the syntax:

```
if (condition1)
  code to be executed if condition1 is true
elsif (condition2)
```

```
      code to be executed if condition2 is true
   else
      code to be executed if condition1 and condition2 are not true
```

It basically says if condition1 is true, its code runs; if it isn't, then condition2 is checked. If condition2 is true, its code runs; if it isn't, then the else code runs.

> **This is the** `elsif` **clause. Ruby does not have an** `elseif` **clause, and plenty of Ruby programmers still get caught typing** `elseif`. **Be careful.**

Try It Out   Use an elsif Clause

Here's an example of how to use the Ruby `elsif` clause:

1. Start your editor and enter the following code:

```
temperature = 76

if temperature > 85
  puts "Too hot!"
elsif temperature < 65
  puts "Too cold!"
else
  puts "Picnic time!"
end
```

2. Save the file as `elsif.rb`.

3. Use Ruby to run this new program and see the results:

```
C:\rubydev\ch02>ruby elsif.rb
Picnic time!
```

How It Works

This example uses an `elsif` clause to check a second Boolean condition when the main Boolean condition in the `if` statement turns out to be false. The value in the temperature variable was set to 76, so the main Boolean condition in the `if` statement (`temperature > 85`) is false.

Ruby went on to check the condition specified in the `elsif` clause (`temperature < 65`) and, if that were true, would have executed the code in that clause (`puts "Too cold!"`). However, the Boolean condition for the `elsif` statement turned out to be false, so Ruby executed the code in the `else` clause (`puts "Picnic time!"`).

Here's the general syntax of the full `if` statement, including as many optional `elsif` clauses as you want to put in:

```
if Boolean [then | :]
  code
[elsif
  code
```

```
[elsif
   code
]...
]
[else
   code ]
end
```

And that's it for the Ruby `if` statement. But there are some other choice statements you'll want to use: `unless` and `case`. The following sections explore them.

Using the unless Statement

If you like the `if` statement, you'll like the `unless` statement. As you can gather from its name, the `unless` statement simply operates in the logically reverse sense from the `if` statement — it executes its code if its condition turns out to be `false`. The following exercise demonstrates how the Ruby `unless` statement works.

Try It Out   Use an unless Statement

1. Start your editor and enter this code:

```
temperature = 76

unless temperature < 65 || temperature > 85
  puts "Picnic time!"
else
  puts "Sorry, no picnic today."
end
```

2. Save the file as `unless.rb`.

3. Use Ruby to run this new program and see the results:

```
C:\rubydev\ch02>ruby unless.rb
Picnic time!
```

How It Works

This code uses the `unless` statement to check the temperature. The code displays the message "Picnic time!" unless the temperature is less than 65 or greater than 85.

Here's the syntax of the full `unless` statement:

```
unless Boolean [then | :]
  code
]
[else
  code ]
end
```

You can't use `elsif` in `unless` statements, and there is no such thing as an `unlessif` clause.

Note that you can simply negate the condition tested in an `unless` statement and use the `!` logical negation operator — which switches false to true and true to false — to change from `unless` to `if`. For example, this code does the same as the preceding example:

```
temperature = 76
if !(temperature < 65 || temperature > 85)
  puts "Picnic time!"
else
  puts "Sorry, no picnic today."
end
```

Using if and unless as Modifiers

Here's something cool that Ruby borrows from other languages like Perl: you can use `if` and `unless` to modify general Ruby statements. That means you can add `if` and `unless` clauses to general Ruby statements. For example, this code:

```
if funds < 0
  puts "Uh oh."
end
```

can be written more simply this way:

```
puts "Uh oh." if funds < 0
```

Here's an example:

```
temperature = 76

puts "Picnic time!" unless temperature < 65 || temperature > 85
```

Use Ruby to run this program and the result is:

```
Picnic time!
```

The example uses an `unless` clause as a modifier to check the value in the temperature variable:

```
temperature = 76
puts "Picnic time!" unless temperature < 65 || temperature > 85
```

The code could also be written using `if` as a modifier instead:

```
temperature = 76
puts "Picnic time!" if temperature > 65 && temperature < 85
```

So which should you use, `if` and `unless` statements, or `if` and `unless` as statement modifiers?

Generally, you should stick with `if` and `unless` statements for clarity. However, if you've got a single statement whose operation isn't central to the rest of the code, you can use `if` and `unless` modifiers. The rationale here is that because `if` and `unless` modifiers come after the rest of the statement, they can easily be missed by someone scanning your code. Of course, the way you actually write your code, including using `if` and `unless` modifiers, is up to you.

Using the case Statement

Ruby also supports a `case` statement, much like the `switch` statement in other languages. This one is much like a multi-path `if` statement, and it's a powerful one.

For example, what if you had a variable named `command` containing one of several possible instructions and you want to pick the correct behavior based on the instruction, such as `"Stop"`, it contains? You could use a ladder of `if` and `elsif` clauses — or you could use the `case` statement.

Check it out for yourself in the following exercise.

Try It Out   **Use a case Statement**

1.   Start your editor and enter the following code:

```
command = "Stop"

case command
when "Go"
  puts "Going"
when "Wait"
  puts "Waiting"
when "Turn"
  puts "Turning"
when "Stop"
  puts "Stopping"
else
  puts "I can't understand that."
end
```

2.   Save the file as `case.rb`.

3.   Use Ruby to run the new program and see the results:

```
C:\rubydev\ch02>ruby case.rb
Stopping
```

How It Works

That's the way the `case` statement works — as a collection of `when` clauses, followed by an optional `else` clause. The code for the first match found is executed, and if no match is found, the code in the `else` statement is executed. In this case, the command matched `"Stop"`:

```
command = "Stop"

case command
when "Go"
  puts "Going"
when "Wait"
```

```
    puts "Waiting"
when "Turn"
    puts "Turning"
when "Stop"
    puts "Stopping"
else
    puts "I can't understand that."
end
```

This example also could be written as an `if` statement with a collection of `elsif` and `else` clauses:

```
command = "Stop"
if command == "Go"
    puts "Going"
elsif command == "Wait"
    puts "Waiting"
elsif command == "Turn"
    puts "Turning"
elsif command == "Stop"
    puts "Stopping"
else
    puts "I can't understand that."
end
```

But using a `case` statement is simpler. Here's the general format of the Ruby `case` statement:

```
case value
    when expression [, comparison]...[then | :]
        code
    when expression [, comparison]...[then | :]
        code
    .
    .
    .
    [else
        code]
end
```

Using the Ternary Operator

It's worth pointing out that in addition to `if`, `unless`, and `case`, Ruby supports another operator that lets you make choices: the ternary operator, `?:`. You may have seen this operator in other languages; here's how you use it:

```
result = condition ? true_value : false_value
```

Here, `result` is assigned `true_value` if `condition` is `true`, and `false_value` if condition is `false`. For example, say you're trying to get the price of a pizza. With up to three toppings, the price should be $4.99, but with more than three toppings, the price jumps to $5.99. Here's how you could set a variable named `price` with the correct price, based on the value in a variable named `toppings`:

```
price = toppings > 3 ? 5.99 : 4.99
```

You can use ranges in `case` statements, like this:

```
temperature = 76
case temperature
when 0...65
  puts "Too cold!"
when 85...120
  puts "Too hot!"
when 65...85
  puts "Picnic time!"
else
  puts "Temperature out of reasonable range!"
end
```

You can also use a `case` statement to make an assignment in this second form of the `case` statement, which omits the value to test, as you see in the following code (`case2.rb`):

```
temperature = 76

message = case
when (0...65) === temperature
  "Too cold!"
when (85...120) === temperature
  "Too hot!"
when (65...85) === temperature
  "Picnic time!"
else
  "Temperature out of reasonable range!"
end

puts message
```

The example shows how you can check whether a value is in a certain range by using ===, the case equality operator. If temperature is inside the range `0...65`, for example, then `(0...65) === temperature` will be true. This `case` statement checks the various conditions in the when clauses, and assigns the value associated with the first one whose condition is `true` to the message variable. After the `case` statement has been executed, the message variable is displayed.

> *Here's another way to check whether a value is in a certain range. Use the* `include?` *method like this:* `(0...65).include?(temperature)`. *This expression returns true if the value in the temperature variable is in the range* `0...65`.

Using Loops

One of the most important aspects of programming languages is the capability to execute code repeatedly over a whole set of data, as when you're adding up the contents of a huge array. What are computers good for if not handling repetitive tasks like that? That's where loops come in, and Ruby supports a number of them.

Using the while Loop

The `while` loop may be familiar to you from other programming languages. It executes its contained code while a condition that you specify remains true.

Here's an example:

```
while($_ != "q")
   puts "Running..."
   print "Enter q to quit: "
   gets
   chomp
end
```

Run this program and enter various letters, followed by a q to make the program quit:

```
Running...
Enter q to quit: r
Running...
Enter q to quit: u
Running...
Enter q to quit: b
Running...
Enter q to quit: y
Running...
Enter q to quit: q
```

This example uses a `while` loop and the `gets` method to read input from the user, and keeps printing out `Running...` until the user types q. That's easy enough to do — all you have to do is to check the input in the `$_` variable from the `gets` method, and if it's q, quit. Otherwise, you keep looping.

Here's the formal specification for the `while` loop:

```
while condition [ do | : ]
   code
end
```

You recall that Ruby's `if` statement has a logically opposite counterpart — the `unless` statement. In much the same way, the `while` loop also has a counterpart — the `until` loop.

Using the until Loop

If you understand the `while` loop, the `until` loop is simple — the only difference is that `until` keeps looping while its condition remains *false*, or not true.

For example:

```
until($_ == "q")
puts "Running..."
print "Enter q to quit: "
gets
chomp
end
```

Use Ruby to run this program and then enter various letters, followed by a q to make the program quit:

```
Running...
Enter q to quit: r
Running...
Enter q to quit: a
Running...
Enter q to quit: i
Running...
Enter q to quit: l
Running...
Enter q to quit: s
Running...
Enter q to quit: q
```

This example simply switches the logical sense of the test from the previous topic to make the code work:

```
until($_ == "q")end
```

In the previous example, the code ran while $_ variable did not equal q; here, it runs until $_ equals q.

Here's the formal specification for the until loop:

```
until condition [ do | : ]
   code
end
```

As you can see, there's not much difference between while and until loops — the logical sense of the condition is opposite, but that's all. Which one you use is a matter of taste, although there are cases where one or the other can make the code slightly easier to read. For example, here's a loop that keeps going until there is a panic:

```
until(panic)
   #do something
end
```

And here's one that keeps going while there is no panic:

```
while(!panic)
   #do something
end
```

The first loop is slightly easier to understand at first glance.

Using while and until as Modifiers

As with the if and unless statements, you can use while and until as statement modifiers. That actually has limited utility because it's pretty hard to make an interesting loop out of a single statement, but it's still available in Ruby.

The following Try It Out shows you how to use while as a modifier.

Try It Out   **Use while as a Loop Modifier**

1.   Start your editor and enter the following code:

```
value = 0

value += 1 while value < 100

puts value
```

2.   Save the file as `modifiers2.rb`.

3.   Use Ruby to run this new program:

```
C:\rubydev\ch02>ruby modifiers2.rb
100
```

How It Works

This example uses the `while` keyword as a modifier, incrementing the value in a variable to 100 before displaying the resulting value:

```
value = 0
value += 1 while value < 100
puts value
```

That's it for the `while` and `until` loops. But there's one more to look at: the `for` loop.

Using the for Loop

Ruby has a `for` loop (but it is not your standard `for` loop of other languages), which has a loop index. This one's more like the `for...in` or `foreach` loop that you see in some languages, because it's designed to be used with collections. You use Ruby's `for` loop with items like arrays and ranges.

Here is an example:

```
for value in 1..10
  puts "This is iteration " + value.to_s
end

print "Your pizza comes with "

for item in ["pepperoni", "sausage", "olives"]
  print item + " "
end
```

And here's its example output:

```
This is iteration 1
This is iteration 2
This is iteration 3
This is iteration 4
This is iteration 5
```

```
This is iteration 6
This is iteration 7
This is iteration 8
This is iteration 9
This is iteration 10
Your pizza comes with pepperoni sausage olives
```

This example uses a `for` loop and prints out a range and an array. You specify in the `for` loop the name of the variable you want filled with the current item from the collection, and then you refer to that variable in the body of the loop (and notice that this code uses the `to_s` method of integers to convert that integer into a string):

```
for value in 1..10
  puts "This is iteration " + value.to_s
end

print "Your pizza comes with "
for item in ["pepperoni", "sausage", "olives"]
  print item + " "
end
```

Here's the general form of the `for` loop:

```
for variable [, variable...] in collection [do | :]
  code
end
```

Using the Ruby Iterators

In addition to the defined loops, Ruby supports *iterators*, which are actually methods built into the items you're working with. They let you create loops — and they can often take the place of more sophisticated loops in other languages.

For example, say you want to work with a `for` loop of the kind you see in traditional programming languages — one that uses a loop index, something like the following, written in Java:

```
double grades[] = {88, 99, 73, 56, 87, 64};
double sum, average;

sum = 0;

for (int loop_index = 0; loop_index < grades.length; loop_index++) {
  sum += grades[loop_index];
}

average = sum / grades.length;

System.out.println(average);
```

How could you translate this code into Ruby? You could use the `upto` iterator, which is what traditional `for` loops translate into in Ruby. The following code (`scores.rb`) converts the preceding code into Ruby:

```
grades = [88, 99, 73, 56, 87, 64]

sum = 0

0.upto(grades.length - 1) do |loop_index|
  sum += grades[loop_index]
end

average = sum / grades.length

puts average
```

Note these lines:

```
0.upto(grades.length - 1) do |loop_index|
  sum += grades[loop_index]
end
```

The `upto` method creates a loop up to and including `grades.length - 1`. Each time through the loop, the variable `loop_index` is filled with the current value of the loop index. (You enclose the variable you want to use as the loop index in upright bars — | | — and then include the code to execute.)

There's also a `downto` iterator, which starts at a higher number and loops to a lower number.

What if you don't want to increment the loop index by one every time? For that, you can use the `step` iterator. For example, say that you want to add the even numbers from 4 to 12—here's how you could do that using `step`:

```
puts "What's the answer?"

sum = 0

4.step(12, 2) do |even_value|
  sum += even_value
end

puts "The answer is " + sum.to_s
```

This code displays the answer, 40. The first number inside the parentheses is the upper bound you want to loop to, and the second number is the value you want to add to the current loop index value each time through the loop.

To iterate a set number of times, use the `times` iterator:

```
5.times do
  puts "You're going to see this five times, whether you want to or not!"
end
```

Here's the result:

```
You're going to see this five times, whether you want to or not!
You're going to see this five times, whether you want to or not!
You're going to see this five times, whether you want to or not!
You're going to see this five times, whether you want to or not!
You're going to see this five times, whether you want to or not!
```

You don't have to use a fixed value such as 5 to make this kind of a loop work, of course; you could use a value in a variable like this:

```
five = 5

five.times do
  puts "You're going to see this five times, whether you want to or not!"
end
```

If you have a collection, such as an array or a range, you can also use the Ruby each iterator to create a loop. Here's an example:

```
grades = [88, 99, 73, 56, 87, 64]

sum = 0

grades.each do |grade|
  sum += grade
end

average = sum / grades.length

puts average
```

This is a cool iterator. Note this code:

```
grades.each do |grade|
  sum += grade
end
```

It uses the each iterator to loop over all items in the grades array. Each time through the loop, the current grade is placed in a variable named grade, and added to the total running sum. Very handy.

The loop iterator, on the other hand, isn't as useful because it just keeps going forever. For example, if you did this:

```
loop do
  puts "Hello again."
end
```

the hapless user would see endless lines of "Hello again." scrolling up the screen. However, you can configure a loop iterator and make it more useful if you use the break statement, coming up in the next section. First, put an iterator to work in the following Try It Out.

Try It Out Use an Iterator

1. Start your editor and enter the following code:

```
fruits = ["peaches", "pumpkins", "apples", "oranges"]

print "We offer "

0.upto(fruits.length - 1) do |loop_index|
  print fruits[loop_index] + " "
end
```

2. Save the file as iterators.rb.

3. Use Ruby to run this new program:

```
C:\rubydev\ch02>ruby iterators.rb
We offer peaches pumpkins apples oranges
```

How It Works

This example uses the upto iterator to create a loop similar to a for loop from other languages, looping over the fruits array:

```
fruits = ["peaches", "pumpkins", "apples", "oranges"]

0.upto(fruits.length - 1) do |loop_index|
  print fruits[loop_index] + " "
end
```

The part of this code that starts with the do and ends with the end is actually a Ruby block, and blocks are coming up soon in this chapter. You don't have to use do...end to delimit a block—you can use curly braces ({}):

```
0.upto(fruits.length - 1) { |loop_index|
  print fruits[loop_index] + " "
}
```

Although this might feel more natural to Java and C++ programmers, the Ruby convention is coming to be that you use {} to surround a block that is a single line of code, and you use do...end when your block contains multiple lines. So the preceding code might be better written as:

```
0.upto(fruits.length - 1) { |loop_index| print fruits[loop_index] + " " }
```

Working with break, redo, and next in Loops

There are three keywords that you can use with loops and iterators: break, redo, and next. Here's what they do:

❑ break—Ends the immediately enclosing loop (that is, if you have nested loops, break ends only the loop it's in, not any loop that encloses that loop).

❑ redo—Repeats the current loop iteration (without reevaluating the loop's condition or getting the next item from an iterator).

❑ next — Skips to the end of the current iteration (which makes the loop or iterator skip on to the next iteration or item).

For example, to display the reciprocals (that is, one over the number) of various integers — but not 1/0 (because attempting to calculate that would make the program fail); you could avoid calculating 1/0 this way with next:

```
-10.upto(10) do |number|
  next if number == 0
  puts "1/" + number.to_s + " = " + (1 / Float(number)).to_s
end
```

The keyword next is followed by a condition. If that condition is true, the next statement skips on to the next iteration.

In this case, next if number == 0 makes the code skip the attempt to divide 1 by 0. Note the use of the Float method here, which converts integers to floats, so that the reciprocals can be calculated properly. Here's what you get when you execute this code — note that 1/0 is missing:

```
C:\rubydev\ch02>ruby break.rb
1/-10 = -0.1
1/-9 = -0.111111111111111
1/-8 = -0.125
1/-7 = -0.142857142857143
1/-6 = -0.166666666666667
1/-5 = -0.2
1/-4 = -0.25
1/-3 = -0.333333333333333
1/-2 = -0.5
1/-1 = -1.0
1/1 = 1.0
1/2 = 0.5
1/3 = 0.333333333333333
1/4 = 0.25
1/5 = 0.2
1/6 = 0.166666666666667
1/7 = 0.142857142857143
1/8 = 0.125
1/9 = 0.111111111111111
1/10 = 0.1
```

Take the break statement for a test drive in the following Try It Out.

Try It Out   Use a break Statement

1.   Start your editor and enter the following code:

```
loop do
  puts "Running..."
  print "Enter q to quit: "
  gets
  chomp
  break if $_ == "q"
end
```

2. Save the file as `break.rb`.

3. Use Ruby to run the new program:

```
C:\rubydev\ch02>ruby break.rb
Running...
Enter q to quit: r
Running...
Enter q to quit: u
Running...
Enter q to quit: b
Running...
Enter q to quit: y
Running...
Enter q to quit: q
```

How It Works

This code uses the `loop` iterator, which is a dangerous thing, because, unless you make other provisions, it loops on forever. However, you are making other provisions here by using the `break` statement, which breaks the loop if the user enters q:

```
loop do
  puts "Running..."
  print "Enter q to quit: "
  gets
  chomp
  break if $_ == "q"
end
```

When the user does enter q, the `break` statement comes alive and breaks the loop, ending the application.

Using the retry Statement

The `retry` statement will start a loop or iterator over entirely. That can be useful if you need to re-run a particular loop iteration.

Here's an example:

```
1.upto(10) do |number|
  puts "1/" + number.to_s + " = " + (1 / Float(number)).to_s
  print "Enter r to retry: "
  gets
  chomp
  retry if $_ == "r"
end
```

When you run this program, it continues looping until it completes or until you enter an r, as this example output shows:

```
1/1 = 1.0
Enter r to retry: n
1/2 = 0.5
Enter r to retry: n
```

```
1/3 = 0.333333333333333
Enter r to retry: n
1/4 = 0.25
Enter r to retry: n
1/5 = 0.2
Enter r to retry: n
1/6 = 0.166666666666667
Enter r to retry: n
1/7 = 0.142857142857143
Enter r to retry: r
1/1 = 1.0
Enter r to retry: n
1/2 = 0.5
Enter r to retry: n
1/3 = 0.333333333333333
Enter r to retry:
```

Entering an r restarts the loop, as you can see.

Creating and Calling a Method

You've been using all kinds of Ruby methods already, from `puts` to the array length method. And of course, you can create your own methods in Ruby; here's an example:

```
def greeting
  puts "Hello, pilgrim."
end
```

This defines a method named `greeting` that, when called, displays the message `"Hello, pilgrim."`. You use the `def` and `end` keywords to define a method in Ruby.

As you already know, you call a method simply by giving its name:

```
greeting
```

And the code gives you what you expect:

```
"Hello, pilgrim."
```

Here's another example:

```
def welcome
  puts "Welcome to Ruby methods."
end

welcome
```

Run the program with Ruby and you get:

```
Welcome to Ruby methods.
```

`def` and `end` define the `welcome` method:

```
def welcome
   puts "Welcome to Ruby methods."
end
```

In a change from the code you've written so far, which executes as soon as the program runs, the code in methods does not run until the method is called. This example calls the `welcome` method this way:

```
def welcome
   puts "Welcome to Ruby methods."
end

welcome
```

Calling the `welcome` method executes the code that prints out the message.

That's all fine as far as it goes, but most of the time, you've passed data to the method you've called. Let's tackle that now.

Passing Arguments to a Method

It's easy enough to pass arguments to the methods you define in Ruby; you just give the names of the arguments you want to pass to a method when you define that method, and then you can refer to those arguments by name inside the body of the method.

For example, here's how you could define a method named `greeting` to take an argument, `message`:

```
def greeting(message)

end
```

Then, inside the body of the method, you refer to the argument by name:

```
def greeting(message)
   puts message
end
```

Now all you've got to do is to pass an argument to the method:

```
def greeting(message)
   puts message
end

greeting("Hello from Ruby.")
```

The parentheses in the call are optional, so the following works as well:

```
greeting "Hello from Ruby."
```

Either way, you get the result you wanted—the method read your argument and printed it out:

```
Hello from Ruby.
```

Here's another example:

```
def putter(first_word, second_word, third_word)
  puts first_word + " " + second_word + " " + third_word
end

putter "Hello", "from", "Ruby."
```

The program's output is:

```
Hello from Ruby.
```

Note that if you have multiple arguments, you can separate them with commas in the arguments list:

```
def putter(first_word, second_word, third_word)
```

And again, you don't have to use parentheses when calling a method and passing arguments to that method:

```
putter "Hello", "from", "Ruby."
```

That's all fine if you have a set number of arguments, but what if you have a variable number of arguments to pass to a method?

Passing a Variable Number of Arguments

You can create methods that take a variable number of arguments by prefixing the last argument in a method's argument list with an asterisk (*). That makes the final argument into an array, containing a variable number of elements, each of which corresponds to an argument passed to the method.

Here's an example:

```
def putter(first_word, *others)
  puts first_word + " " + others.join(" ")
end

putter "Hello", "from", "Ruby."
```

Run this program in Ruby and the output is:

```
Hello from Ruby.
```

This code is much like your typical, everyday method, except that the last argument is preceded by an asterisk, which means that it's an array. To handle that array, you can use the `join` method to connect the words in the array, separating them with a space:

```
puts first_word + " " + others.join(" ")
```

The `join` method is a cool one; if you want to separate the items in an array with a comma and a space, you could do this: `others.join(", ")`.

You can do the reverse as well—expand arrays in method calls and in the definitions of methods. For example, say you had this code:

```
def putter(first_word, second_word, third_word)
  puts first_word + " " + second_word + " " + third_word
end
```

And you store text in an array:

```
array = ["there ", "sweetie."]

def putter(first_word, second_word, third_word)
  puts first_word + " " + second_word + " " + third_word
end
```

Then you could call the method like this, prefixing the array with an asterisk:

```
array = ["there ", "sweetie."]

def putter(first_word, second_word, third_word)
  puts first_word + " " + second_word + " " + third_word
end
```

```
putter "Hello ", *array
```

That expands the array into method arguments automatically. The output would be:

```
Hello there sweetie.
```

Returning a Value from a Method

All Ruby methods return a value (although nothing says you have to make use of that value if you don't want to). You can use the `return` statement, as in this example, which simply adds two values and returns the result:

```
def adder(operand_one, operand_two)
  return operand_one + operand_two
end
```

Because the Ruby way of doing things is for a method to return the last value calculated, though, you can omit the `return` keyword if you want. That would make the `adder` method look like this:

```
def adder(operand_one, operand_two)
  operand_one + operand_two
end
```

```
def adder(operand_one, operand_two)
  operand_one + operand_two
end
```

Omitting the `return` keyword is the Ruby convention, although you are free to keep it in your code — in fact, leaving it out sometimes results in some pretty unclear code. You work with the `return` statement in the following exercise.

Try It Out   Return a Value from a Method

1. Start your editor and enter this code:

```
number = 3

def incrementer(value)
   return value + 1
end

puts number.to_s + " + 1 = " + incrementer(number).to_s
```

2. Save the file as `incrementer.rb`.

3. Use Ruby to run this new program:

```
C:\rubydev\ch02>ruby incrementer.rb
3 + 1 = 4
```

How It Works

This example creates a method named `incrementer` to which you pass a number. `incrementer` takes that number, adds one to it, and passes the result back:

```
def incrementer(value)
   return value + 1
end
```

To use the method, you have only to pass a number to it:

```
def incrementer(value)
   return value + 1
end
```

```
puts number.to_s + " + 1 = " + incrementer(number).to_s
```

In this case, you're passing the value of the variable number (3) to the method, and you get 4 back. Very nice. Of course, you can also omit the `return` keyword in the `incrementer` method, making it look like this:

```
number = 3

def incrementer(value)
   value + 1
end
```

```
puts number.to_s + " + 1 = " + incrementer(number).to_s
```

Returning Multiples Values from a Method

You can return multiple values from methods as well, much like you can in languages like Perl. Unlike Perl's special list construct, however, Ruby uses arrays to return multiple values.

To return multiple values, all you have to do is to separate them with a comma:

```
return a, b, c
```

Here's an example:

```
def greeting()
    return "No", "worries"
end

array = greeting

puts array.join(" ")
```

The result of this code is:

```
No worries
```

Because it's returning multiple values from a method, Ruby returns an array:

```
def greeting()
    return "No", "worries"
end
```

```
array = greeting
```

In fact, Ruby makes it easy to handle multiple return values—no need to work with arrays explicitly at all. All you have to do is to assign the return value of the called method to a comma-separated list of variables, like this:

```
def greeting()
    return "No", "worries"
end
```

```
word_one, word_two = greeting
```

Then you're free to print out the results:

```
No worries
```

For that matter, you can pass full arrays to methods in Ruby, and return arrays as well. For example, this code:

```
array = [1, 2, 3, 4]

def returner(array)
```

```
      return array
   end

   array2 = returner(array)

   puts array2
```

returns:

```
   1
   2
   3
   4
```

Making Use of Scope

Declaring variables inside a method gives them local *scope*. Scope is an item's visibility in your code, and the variables you declare inside a method are only visible to your code inside that method — that is, they have *local* scope.

Scope is an important concept to master. Dividing your code into methods effectively breaks it into self-contained sections — the items declared in those methods are restricted to those methods. Because each method is independent, you can divide and conquer larger programming tasks, and the variables declared locally can't be confused with the variables declared outside a method.

See how it works by working through the following exercise.

Try It Out   Use Local Scope

1.   Start your editor and enter the following code:

```
text = "No worries."

def greeting()
  text = "No problems."
  puts text
end

greeting

puts text
```

2.   Save the file as scope.rb.

3.   Use Ruby to run this new program:

```
C:\rubydev\ch02>ruby scope.rb
No problems.
No worries.
```

How It Works

This code declares a variable named `text` (`text = "No worries."`), and then declares and uses a variable, also named `text`, in a method named `greeting`:

```
text = "No worries."

def greeting()
  text = "No problems."
  puts text
end
```

Then it calls the `greeting` method, which displays the version of the `text` variable inside it (`"No problems."`):

```
text = "No worries."

def greeting()
  text = "No problems."
  puts text
end
```

```
greeting
```

Finally, the code prints out the original `text` variable, which displays `"No worries."`:

```
text = "No worries."

def greeting()
  text = "No problems."
  puts text
end
```

```
greeting
```

```
puts text
```

Working with Blocks

A block is a section of code that can be passed to a method much like passing an argument. A block is delimited with `{}`:

```
{ puts "Hello there!" }
```

or do and end:

```
do
  puts "Hello there!"
end
```

Generally, you use { } for a one-line block, and do..end for a multi-line block. You can use a block after the name of the method you're calling, like this:

```
greeting {puts "Hello there!"}
```

How do you reach the code in the block from inside the method? You use the yield statement, which is designed for exactly that purpose. Here's an example:

```
def greeting()
   yield
end

greeting {puts "Hello there!"}
```

The result of this code is:

```
Hello there!
```

The code declares a method named greeting:

```
def greeting()
   yield
end
```

Then it calls that method:

```
greeting {puts "Hello there!"}
```

The yield statement in the greeting method calls the code in the block, which executes the code in the block — and that gives you the results you see when you run this code: Hello there!

You can execute the yield statement any number of times:

```
def greeting()
   yield
   yield
   yield
end

greeting {puts "Hello there!"}
```

When you call the new greeting method, the code block is called three times — once for each yield statement. In this case, you get:

```
Hello there!
Hello there!
Hello there!
```

The method you're calling can take standard arguments in addition to a block. Just place those arguments in parentheses before the code block, like this:

```
greeting("yes", "no", "yes") {"Hello there!"}
```

Passing Data to Blocks

You can pass data to code clocks used with methods simply by passing that data to the `yield` statement. Here's an example:

```
def greeting()
  yield "Hello", "there"
end
```

Then you can read the passed data in the code block much as you can with passed arguments to a method. Take a look at another example:

```
def greeting()
  yield "Hello", "there!"
end

greeting {|word_one, word_two | puts word_one + " " + word_two}
```

The result of this program is:

```
Hello there!
```

This code declares a method named `greeting`, designed to pass data to code blocks, and then it calls that method.

Note the syntax: the arguments passed to the code block will be named using the names inside the vertical bars, | and |. After you've named those arguments, you can use them in the code block, much as you would use passed arguments to a method.

So not only can you pass arguments to a method, you can also pass code blocks — and the method can even pass arguments to that code block. And if you pass a new set of arguments to the code block, like this:

```
def greeting()
  yield "Hello", "there!"
  yield "Bye", "now."
end

greeting {|word_one, word_two | puts word_one + " " + word_two}
```

that data is also passed to the code block, and you get this result:

```
C:\rubydev\ch02>ruby blockarguments.rb
Hello there!
Bye now.
```

You can use code blocks with Ruby iterators like `each`, `upto`, `downto`, and `times`. Here's an example:

```
["Hello", "there", "sweetie."].each {|word| puts word}
4.upto(8) {|loop_index_value| puts loop_index_value}
4.times {print "X"}
```

And here are the results of this code:

```
Hello
there
sweetie.
4
5
6
7
8
XXXX
```

Using BEGIN and END Blocks

There are two special blocks you should know about: BEGIN and END. The code in a block labeled with the keyword BEGIN is run automatically when a Ruby program is loaded, and the code in a block labeled END is automatically run when the program finishes.

Here's an example:

```
BEGIN {puts "Hi "}

puts "there "

END {puts "sweetie."}
```

And its results:

```
Hi
there
sweetie.
```

This code uses a BEGIN block, normal code, and an END block. As you can see from the results, the code in the BEGIN block is run first, followed by the normal code. The last thing that runs is the code in the END block.

Summary

In this chapter, you got a number of essential Ruby skills under your belt. You learned how to:

- ❏ Use the if statement to make choices, so you can create branching code in your programs.
- ❏ Add else clauses to if statements, providing for alternate code execution.
- ❏ Use elsif clauses in if statements, to provide alternate execution with additional condition tests.
- ❏ Use the unless statement, which is the same as an if statement, but with the logical testing of its condition reversed.
- ❏ Use if and unless as statement modifiers.

- ❏ Put the `case` statement to work, enabling you to handle multiple conditionals as if you were creating a ladder of `if` statements — but easier.

- ❏ Iterate over code multiple times with the `while` loop.

- ❏ Use the `until` loop, which is the same as the `while` loop, except that the logical testing of its condition is reversed.

- ❏ Use `while` and `until` as statement modifiers.

- ❏ Work with Ruby iterators.

- ❏ Create and call a method, using the `def` and `end` delimiters around the code for the method.

- ❏ Pass arguments to methods, and return values, including multiple values, from a method.

- ❏ Work with code blocks and methods.

In the next chapter, you learn to work with classes, objects, inheritance, and much more. Before proceeding, however, try the exercises that follow to test your understanding of the material covered in this chapter. The solutions to these exercises are in Appendix A.

Exercises

1. Create a method that calls itself — a technique called *recursion* — to calculate *factorials*. A factorial is the product of the number times all the other whole numbers down to one — for example, the factorial of 6, written as 6!, is $6 \times 5 \times 4 \times 3 \times 2 \times 1 = 720$.

2. Construct a method named `printer` that you can call with some text, which then calls a code block to print out that text.

3. Create a method named `array_converter` that takes four arguments and returns them in an array.

Classes and Objects

Everything is an object or object-oriented in Ruby. Don't believe it? Try entering this code in a Ruby program:

```
puts 1.+(2)
```

What the heck does that do? It adds 1 and 2 and displays a value of 3, the same as if you had entered puts 1 + 2. The reason this is the same as 1 + 2 is that numbers are considered objects in Ruby, so 1 is an object, not just a numeric literal as in many other languages. As an object, it can have both data and methods built into it — that's the whole idea behind objects, encapsulating functionality. Among other things, the object 1 has a method named + built in that supports the + operator, so the expression 1.+ is simply calling the + method of the 1 object. And you can pass 2 to the + method, as you see: 1.+(2).

Yes, it looks funny. And it's not something you'd normally write in a program. But it does illustrate that everything in a Ruby program is either an object (such as 1) or object-oriented (such as the + method).

It also means that numbers have built-in methods you haven't seen yet, such as the abs absolute value method. This line of code prints the absolute value of −1, which is 1:

```
puts -1.abs
```

Before you tackle classes and objects, it's best to have some understanding of encapsulation.

All about Encapsulation

You may well know about classes and objects and be eager to work with them in Ruby. But if you're not, it's worth taking a moment to understand the concept of classes and objects. Originally, programmers wrote simple programs, just line after line of code. Then programs started getting longer, and programmers needed a way to break things up, so they invented methods, in which code was divided into callable chunks.

But not even methods proved to be enough, and the idea of an object—a piece of code that can contain not only methods, but also data—was born. And you wrap everything up—a process called *encapsulation*—in a handy item called an object. Being able to wrap both data and methods into an object makes that object far more self-contained. The idea is to divide and conquer your program, and being able to create objects makes your program much more divisible.

For example, think of a refrigerator. What it does is actually quite remarkable—it checks the temperature, turns on the compressor, circulates air and coolant, and so on. If you had to do that yourself, all spread through the rest of your code, it'd be easy to get lost and start making mistakes. But wrap everything into an easily conceptualized object, a "refrigerator," and all that it does is internal to the refrigerator—checking the temperature, circulating what it needs to circulate, even turning on the light when the door opens. That means that instead of having to take care of turning on pumps and the like throughout your code while you are attending to other tasks, you can simply use an object, a refrigerator, with a readily understandable function: it keeps food cold.

So now in your code, when you need to keep food cold, you can store it in the refrigerator. The internal details of how the refrigerator works is up to the refrigerator, and you don't have to bother with it. You've been able to divide and conquer.

An important part of working with objects is that they should be easily conceptualized. For example, a refrigerator is readily understood. An object that is part refrigerator, part stove, and part hairdryer is not so easily thought of—it's not a handy object. So when separating your code into objects, take the time to divide things up into a set of objects that makes sense—in other words, sets of objects that help rather than hinder the programming process.

You use classes to create objects. That is, a class is an object's *type*. For example, the number 1 may be an object in Ruby, but the class you use to create that number object is named `Fixnum`. So classes come first, objects second. You can think of classes as cookie cutters, and objects as the cookies you create from the classes.

Enough talk. Let's get to some code.

Creating a Class

To create a class in Ruby, you simply use the `class` statement. For example, here's how you'd create a new class named `Animal`:

```
class Animal
end
```

That's your first class in Ruby—easy. Of course, there's nothing going on here—you have to add some data and/or methods, and you'll see that in a little while. One thing to note: names of classes in Ruby start with a capital letter (and, as an interesting side note, that makes class names constants).

Here's another example:

```
class Animal
  def initialize
    @color = "red"
```

```
      end

    def get_color
      return @color
    end
  end
```

This code starts by creating the `Animal` class, and then adds a method named `initialize`:

```
class Animal
  def initialize

  end
end
```

In Ruby, the `initialize` method is called automatically when you use a class to create an object. In this example, the code adds an *instance variable* named `@color` that stores the color of the animal to the `initialize` method:

```
class Animal
  def initialize
    @color = "red"
  end
end
```

An instance variable is one in which you can store the data in an object—an *instance* of a class is an object. You've already seen local variables in methods, like the following, where the local variable is named sum:

```
def adder(operand_one, operand_two)
  sum = operand_one + operand_two
  return sum
end
```

Local variables do not retain their values between method calls. On the other hand, instance variables hold their values for as long as the object is in existence. That's what helps make objects self-contained: the capability to store data.

In Ruby, you prefix instance variables—those variables designed to store the data in an object (you can consider them object variables)—with an at sign (@), which is what tells Ruby that you're creating an instance variable that should hold on to its data, not a local variable that should be re-initialized each time a method is called.

The new `Animal` class also adds a method named `get_color`, which returns the color of animal objects created from this class:

```
class Animal
  def initialize
    @color = "red"
  end

  def get_color
    return @color
  end
end
```

Now when you create objects of the `Animal` class, you can call those objects' `get_color` method, and the return value will be `"red"`. In the next section, you create objects using this class.

Creating an Object

You use the `new` method to create an object in Ruby. For example, to create an object of the `Animal` class you created in the previous section, you could do this:

```
class Animal
  def initialize
    @color = "red"
  end
  def get_color
    return @color
  end
end
```

```
animal = Animal.new
```

`animal` is a new instance of the `Animal` class. The new object's name starts with a lowercase letter, just as any variable name would. There's a reason for that: objects are stored in variables (remember, everything is an object, so you've already been doing this), therefore object names obey the Ruby naming conventions for variables.

Here's another example:

```
class Animal
  def initialize
    @color = "red"
  end

  def get_color
    return @color
  end
end

animal = Animal.new
puts "The new animal is " + animal.get_color
```

The result of executing this code is:

```
The new animal is red
```

The code first creates the `Animal` class and then creates a new object named `animal`. The `animal` object has the `get_color` method built into it, so you can call that method like this:

```
puts "The new animal is " + animal.get_color
```

Very cool — you've created your first Ruby class and created an object from that class.

However, the class is not all that dynamic; the animal's color is always red. Nothing much changes. But you can change that by using a constructor.

Using a Constructor to Configure Objects

Using new actually calls the initialize method of a class to create a new object:

```
class Animal
  def initialize
    @color = "red"
  end

  def get_color
    return @color
  end
end
```

The initialize method has a special name — it's the class's *constructor*, which you use to construct new objects. And you can also use the constructor to configure the objects you create. Take a look at the following example:

```
class Animal
  def initialize(color)
    @color = color
  end

  def get_color
    return @color
  end
end

animal = Animal.new("brown")
puts "The new animal is " + animal.get_color
```

The result of executing this code is:

```
The new animal is brown
```

The code starts by creating the Animal class, and giving the initialize method an argument, color:

```
def initialize(color)
  @color = color
end
```

Because color is stored in an instance variable, the object stores that color, making it ready for use. A get_color method is created to return the color:

```
def get_color
  return @color
end
```

And when it comes time to create an `animal` object, you can pass the color of the animal to the constructor, which stores it so that the `get_color` method will return that color:

```
animal = Animal.new("brown")
puts "The new animal is " + animal.get_color
```

As you can see, you've configured your new object by passing data to the constructor, which was stored inside the object. That's what constructors are for — configuring the new objects you create. For example, you could create a new object by calling the `Animal` class's constructor again this way:

```
animal = Animal.new("brown")
puts "The new animal is " + animal.get_color

animal_two = Animal.new("orange")
```

And the newly created object would have its own color. The last line of code prints out "The new animal is orange":

```
animal = Animal.new("brown")
puts "The new animal is " + animal.get_color

animal_two = Animal.new("orange")
puts "The new animal is " + animal_two.get_color
```

Understanding Ruby Attributes

Externally visible aspects of an object are called *attributes* in Ruby. Attributes are data items that are accessible outside the object. There are three basic attributes: readable, writable, and readable/writable.

Creating Readable Attributes

The `Animal` class contains an instance variable (`@color`) and a method for accessing that color (`get_color`). `get_color` is called an *accessor* method in object-oriented programming; you use accessor methods to access values inside an object. Using an accessor method gives the object control over access to the variables that make up its internal state, such that you could make sure, for example, that only legal values were assigned to the `@color` instance variable.

Here's how to create an accessor method named `color` that will return the value in the `@color` variable:

```
class Animal
  def color()
    @color
  end

  def initialize(color)
    @color = color
  end
end

animal = Animal.new("brown")
puts "The new animal is " + animal.color
```

This code creates an accessor method named `color`, and then uses that method to extract the value of the `@color` variable from the `animal` object. `color` here (as in `animal.color`) is called an *attribute*.

The `color` attribute is a *readable attribute* of the `animal` object because you can read the value of the internal `@color` instance variable using it. It's easy to create readable attributes for objects, and Ruby makes it even easier, as you can see in this example:

```
class Animal
  attr_reader :color

  def initialize(color)
    @color = color
  end
end

animal = Animal.new("brown")
puts "The new animal is " + animal.color
```

The output of this code is:

```
The new dog is brown
```

Once again, the example begins by creating the `Animal` class. Then it adds the statement `attr_reader :color`:

```
class Animal
  attr_reader :color

  def initialize(color)
    @color = color
  end
end
```

This statement creates the `@color` instance variable—and also creates an accessor method with the same name (`color`). So using `attr_reader :color` is an easy way to create a readable attribute. This example's result is identical to the longer code you saw earlier.

Creating Writable Attributes

What if you want to change the color of the animal at runtime? For that, you can use writable attributes, which you support using an accessor method followed with an equals sign (=). Here's how you assign data to such accessor methods:

```
class Animal
  attr_reader :color

  def color=(color)
    @color = color
  end

  def initialize(color)
    @color = color
  end
end
```

This new version of the `Animal` class now has a readable and writable attribute: `color` — and you can both read and write that attribute, as follows:

```
animal = Animal.new("brown")
puts "The new animal is " + animal.color
animal.color = "red"
puts "Now the new animal is " + animal.color
```

This code gives you:

```
C:\rubydev\ch03>ruby writable.rb
The new animal is brown
Now the new animal is red
```

That's one way to create a writable attribute — a method with an equals sign at the end of its name. But as with readable attributes, Ruby also gives you a quick way to create writable attributes, as you'll see in this Try It Out.

Try It Out   Use a Writable Attribute

1. Start your editor and enter this Ruby code:

```
class Animal
  attr_reader :color
  attr_writer :color

  def initialize(color)
    @color = color
  end
end

animal = Animal.new("brown")
puts "The new animal is " + animal.color
animal.color = "red"
puts "Now the new animal is " + animal.color
```

2. Save the file as `writable.rb`.

3. Execute the new code:

```
C:\rubydev\ch03>ruby writable.rb
The new dog is brown
Now the new animal is red
```

How It Works

You first create the `Animal` class, giving a readable attribute, `color`:

```
class Animal
  attr_reader :color

  def initialize(color)
    @color = color
  end
end
```

Then you use the statement `attr_writer :color` to create the writable `color` attribute:

```
class Animal
  attr_reader :color
  attr_writer :color

  def initialize(color)
    @color = color
  end
end
```

Using `attr_writer :color` is the same as if you had done this:

```
class Animal
  attr_reader :color

  def color=(color)
    @color = color
  end

  def initialize(color)
    @color = color
  end
end
```

Now you not only can read the `color` attribute, but also write to it.

Creating Readable and Writable Attributes

Using `attr_reader` lets you create readable attributes in objects, and using `attr_writer` lets you create writable attributes. What if you want to create an attribute that is both readable and writable? You could use both `attr_reader` and `attr_writer`, of course, but there's a simpler way in Ruby — you can use `attr_accessor`:

```
class Animal
  attr_accessor :color

  def initialize(color)
    @color = color
  end
end

animal = Animal.new("brown")
puts "The new animal is " + animal.color
animal.color = "red"
puts "Now the new animal is " + animal.color
```

This code creates a readable and writable attribute named `color`, with the following result:

```
The new dog is brown
Now the new animal is red
```

Chapter 3

Basing One Class on Another

The `Animal` class is a good one, but all it does is record an animal's color. There's more to an animal than that, such as how many feet it has, what sound it makes, how long its fur is, and so on. In other words, the `Animal` class is a good starting point, but you may want to create a more specific class, such as a `Dog` class, based on the `Animal` class.

The `Dog` class will inherit all that the `Animal` class has, and you can add more on top of the `Animal` class to the `Dog` class. So, for example, if the `Animal` class has a `get_color` method, and the `Dog` class is based on the `Animal` class, `Dog` objects will also have a `get_color` method built in. And you can also add other methods, such as `get_sound`, which returns the sound the dog makes, to the `Dog` class.

Basing one class on another is called *inheritance*. Here's an example of creating a class named `A` and then using the `A` class as a base class for another class, `B`:

```
class A
 .
 .
 .
end

class B < A
 .
 .
 .
end
```

Note that the syntax `class B < A` indicates that the `B` class inherits all that `A` class has. Now you can use all the members — the data and methods — of the `A` class when you create `B` objects.

Try It Out   Use Inheritance

You work with inheritance in Ruby in this exercise:

1.   Start your editor and enter the following Ruby code:

```
class Animal
  def initialize(color)
    @color = color
  end

  def get_color
    return @color
  end
end

class Dog < Animal
  def initialize(color, sound)
    super(color)
    @sound = sound
  end

  def get_sound
```

```
      return @sound
    end
  end

  dog = Dog.new("brown", "Bark")
  puts "The new dog is " + dog.get_color
  puts "The new dog says: " + dog.get_sound + " " + dog.get_sound
```

2. Save the file as `constructor.rb`.

3. Execute the new code:

```
C:\rubydev\ch03>ruby inheritance.rb
The new dog is brown
The new dog says: Bark Bark
```

How It Works

This example starts by creating the `Animal` class and giving the `initialize` method an argument, `color`, which is stored as an instance variable:

```
class Animal
  def initialize(color)
    @color = color
  end

  def get_color
    return @color
  end
end
```

Then it creates the `Dog` class, which is based on the `Animal` class:

```
class Dog < Animal
    .
    .
    .
end
```

The `Dog` class keeps track of not just the dog's color, but also the dog's sound, so you pass the constructor both those items:

```
class Dog < Animal
  def initialize(color, sound)
      .
      .
      .
  end
end
```

The constructor of the `Animal` class, on the other hand, takes only one argument, `color`:

```
class Animal
  def initialize(color)
```

```
      @color = color
   end
      .
      .
      .

   end
```

To pass the color to the constructor of the base class, that is, the Animal class, you use the special super method, built into Ruby for just that purpose — the base class, Animal, is called the super class, and the derived class, Dog, is called the subclass:

```
class Dog < Animal
   def initialize(color, sound)
     super(color)
   end
      .
      .
      .

   end
```

That passes the color back to the Animal class's constructor and stores the color in the instance variable @color. The sound the animal makes is stored in an instance variable in the Dog class:

```
class Dog < Animal
   def initialize(color, sound)
     super(color)
     @sound = sound
   end
      .
      .
      .

   end
```

The Dog class inherits the get_color method from the Animal class, so you don't need to add that method to this class. However, to return the sound the dog makes, you're going to need a get_sound method in the Dog class, like this:

```
class Dog < Animal
   def initialize(color, sound)
     super(color)
     @sound = sound
   end

   def get_sound
     return @sound
   end
 end
```

That completes the Dog class, which is based on the Animal class. Now you can create a new Dog animal:

```
dog = Dog.new("brown", "Bark")
```

Because the constructor now takes two arguments, you pass two arguments to `new`—the color of the new dog and the sound it makes. Now you can call the new `dog` object's `get_color` method to get the dog's color:

```
dog = Dog.new("brown", "Bark")
puts "The new dog is " + dog.get_color
```

You can also use the `Dog` class's `get_sound` method to get the sound the dog makes:

```
dog = Dog.new("brown", "Bark")
puts "The new dog is " + dog.get_color
puts "The new dog says: " + dog.get_sound + " " + dog.get_sound
```

After creating the new dog object and calling `get_color` and `get_sound`, here are the results you see:

```
The new dog is brown
The new dog says: Bark Bark
```

Understanding Ruby's Object Access

Objects are all about wrapping up functionality, and that often means making things private inside the object—not accessible outside the object. Ruby gives you three levels of access:

❑ **Public methods**—Can be called from anywhere in your code. There's no restriction on these.

❑ **Protected methods**—Can be called only inside objects of the class that defines those methods, or objects of classes derived from that class. In other words, access is kept "in the family."

❑ **Private methods**—Can only be called inside the current object. These are the most restricted of all.

Ruby defines keywords to match—`public`, `protected`, and `private`—which are called *access modifiers*. In the `Animal` class, you could have used the keyword `public` for the `get_color` method:

```
class Animal
  def initialize(color)
    @color = color
  end

  public
  def get_color
    return @color
  end
end

animal = Animal.new("brown")
puts "The new animal is " + animal.get_color
```

But the default is `public`, so you don't really need to use that keyword. When you use an access modifier, all the methods that follow are defined with that access, until you use a different access modifier. The following example makes `get_color` public, but `get_feet` and `get_sound` private:

```
class Animal
  def initialize(color)
    @color = color
  end

  public
  def get_color
    return @color
  end

  private
  def get_feet
    return "four"
  end

  def get_sound
    return "Bark"
  end
end
```

Using Protected Access

The default access modifier `public` makes all methods in an object accessible to the environment outside that object. But that's not always desirable — you may have some methods you want to keep internal to the object. In the earlier analogy of an object as a refrigerator, for example, there might be plenty of methods you want to keep inside the refrigerator: `start_pump`, `start_circulating_fan`, `check_temperature`, and so on. You could make those `protected` in the `Refrigerator` class.

Ruby handles protected methods differently from the usual object-oriented programming language. You use the `protected` keyword primarily when you want to give an object access to the internal data of another object. A protected method can be called by any object of the same class, or by any object of a class derived from that class (that is, by any subclass). Take a look at the following Try It Out to see this in action.

Try It Out   Use Protected Access

In this exercise, you use access in Ruby:

1. Start your editor and enter this Ruby code:

```
class Animal
  def initialize(color)
    @color = color
  end

  protected
  def get_color
    return @color
  end
end

class Dog < Animal
  def initialize(color)
```

```
    @animal = Animal.new(color)
  end

  def get_info
    return @animal.get_color
  end
end

dog = Dog.new("brown")
puts "The new animal is " + dog.get_info

animal2 = Animal.new("red")
puts "The new animal is " + animal2.get_color
```

2. Save the file as `protected.rb`.

3. Execute this new code:

```
C:\rubydev\ch03>ruby protected.rb
The new animal is brown
protected.rb:26: protected method `get_color' called for #<Animal:0x27b7790 @col
or="red"> (NoMethodError)
```

How It Works

This example first creates the `Animal` class and makes the `get_color` method protected:

```
class Animal
  def initialize(color)
    @color = color
  end

  protected
  def get_color
    return @color
  end
end
```

Then the code creates a new class, `Dog`, which in turn creates an `animal` object and accesses the protected `Animal` class's `get_color` method. This is fine, because you're accessing the protected `get_color` method from an object that is derived from the `Animal` class:

```
class Dog < Animal
  def initialize(color)
    @animal = Animal.new(color)
  end

  def get_info
    return @animal.get_color
  end
end
```

Finally, the code tries to create a new `animal` object outside any object, and access the protected `get_golor` method:

```
animal2 = Animal.new("red")
puts "The new animal is " + animal2.get_color
```

You saw the results — the call to the protected `Animal` `get_color` method worked when it was inside an object derived from the `Animal` class, but not when it was outside such a class. That's how the `protected` keyword works in Ruby.

Using Private Access

When you make a method private, it's not accessible outside the object it's defined in — not even inside other objects of the same or a derived class, as it is when the method is protected.

Here's an example:

```
class Animal
  def initialize(color)
    @color = color
  end

  private
  def get_color
    return @color
  end
end

class Dog < Animal
  def initialize(color)
    @animal = Animal.new(color)
  end

  def get_info
    return @animal.get_color
  end
end

dog = Dog.new("brown")
puts "The new animal is " + dog.get_info

animal2 = Animal.new("red")
puts "The new animal is " + animal2.get_color
```

Here's the code's output:

```
private.rb:23: undefined method `get_info' for #<Animal:0x27b7b38 @color="brown"
> (NoMethodError)
```

This example creates the `Animal` class and makes the `get_color` method `private`:

```
class Animal
  def initialize(color)
    @color = color
  end

  private
```

```
    def get_color
      return @color
    end
  end
```

Then it creates a new class, `Dog`, that tries to create an `Animal` object and call its private `get_color` method:

```
class Dog < Animal
  def initialize(color)
    @animal = Animal.new(color)
  end

  def get_info
    return @animal.get_color
  end
end
```

Finally, it also tries to access the private `get_color` method outside any object:

```
animal2 = Animal.new("red")
puts "The new animal is " + animal2.get_color
```

The result? Total failure — you can't even access a private method of a class from a subclassed object:

```
C:\rubydev\ch03>ruby private.rb
private.rb:23: undefined method `get_info' for #<Animal:0x27b7b38 @color="brown"
> (NoMethodError)
```

That's how the private access modifier works — you can only call private methods inside the object where they're declared.

Overriding Methods

You can override methods in Ruby as you can in other object-oriented languages. When you define a method in a class, you can redefine that method in a derived class, and that's what overriding is all about — redefining a method in a derived class.

Take a look at this example:

```
class Animal
  def initialize(color)
    @color = color
  end

  def get_color
    return @color
  end
end

class Dog < Animal
  def initialize(color)
```

```
      super(color)
    end

    def get_color
      return "blue"
    end
  end

  dog = Dog.new("brown")
  puts "The new dog is " + dog.get_color
```

The output is:

```
  The new dog is blue
```

This example creates the `Animal` class and defines the `get_color` method as usual. However, this time, the code defines a new class, `Dog`, that overrides the `get_color` method, and simply returns a value of `blue`, producing blue dogs:

```
class Dog < Animal
  def initialize(color)
    super(color)
  end

  def get_color
    return "blue"
  end
end
```

Now create a new dog and color it brown:

```
dog = Dog.new("brown")
puts "The new dog is " + dog.get_color
```

But the result is always going to be the same — you're going to get a blue dog because the `get_color` method has been overridden:

```
  The new dog is blue
```

That's how method overriding goes — all you have to do is to redefine the method.

Creating Class Variables

You create instance variables by prefixing a variable name with @. You can also create *class variables* by prefixing a variable's name with @@. A class variable is shared by all instances of a class, so, for example, if you change the value in that variable in one object, it's changed for all objects (unlike instance variables, which are internal to the object).

Here's an example of using class variables in Ruby:

```ruby
class Animal
  @@number_animals = 0

  def initialize(color)
    @color = color
    @@number_animals += 1
  end

  def get_color
    return @color
  end  .

  def get_number_animals
    return @@number_animals
  end
end

dog = Animal.new("brown")
cat = Animal.new("striped")
squirrel = Animal.new("gray")

puts "Number of animals is " + squirrel.get_number_animals.to_s
```

The result of this code is:

```
Number of animals is 3
```

The example creates a class variable, `@@number_animals`, to hold the number of created animals:

```ruby
class Animal
  @@number_animals = 0
        .
        .
        .
```

Every time a new animal is created, `@@number_animals` is incremented:

```ruby
class Animal
  @@number_animals = 0

  def initialize(color)
    @color = color
    @@number_animals += 1
  end
        .
        .
        .
```

You determine the number of animals by using the `get_number_animals` method, which returns the value in `@@number_animals`:

```ruby
class Animal
  @@number_animals = 0

  def initialize(color)
    @color = color
    @@number_animals += 1
  end

  def get_color
    return @color
  end

  def get_number_animals
    return @@number_animals
  end
end
```

Next, the code makes a few animal objects, and displays the total number of such objects:

```ruby
dog = Animal.new("brown")
cat = Animal.new("striped")
squirrel = Animal.new("gray")

puts "Number of animals is " + squirrel.get_number_animals.to_s
```

This produces, as it should, a value of 3:

```
Number of animals is 3
```

Creating Class Methods

Besides class variables, you can create *class methods* in Ruby. You can call a class method using just the name of the class — you don't have to create an object before you can use the method. This has some advantages, such as saving you the step of having to create an object before calling a method, but you can't use instance data with a class method because you don't actually have an object to store data in. So class methods are useful, but only as long as you don't want to store the data you're working on.

Try It Out   Use a Class Method

You work with class methods in this exercise:

1.   Start your editor and enter this Ruby code:

```ruby
class Mathematics
  def Mathematics.add(operand_one, operand_two)
    return operand_one + operand_two
  end
```

```
end

puts "1 + 2 = " + Mathematics.add(1, 2).to_s
```

2. Save the file as `classmethods.rb`.

3. Execute this new code:

```
C:\rubydev\ch03>ruby classmethods.rb
1 + 2 = 3
```

How It Works

This example creates a class method, `add`, whose purpose is to add together two numbers. You create a class method in Ruby by prefixing its name with the name of the class, followed by a dot (`.`). That looks like this for the `add` method in the `Mathematics` class:

```
class Mathematics
  def Mathematics.add(operand_one, operand_two)
    return operand_one + operand_two
  end
end
```

Every time you want to add two numbers together now, you can use the `Mathematics.add` method — without first needing to create an object:

```
puts "1 + 2 = " + Mathematics.add(1, 2).to_s
```

On occasion, you might want to make a class's constructor private, and you can do that with the line `private_class_method :new` *in the definition of a class. When a constructor is private, it can't be called by outside code, so you should then add a public method, such as a method named* `create`, *that calls the private constructor to create new objects. Doing this gives you more control over the creation process. For example, you could store the new object in a class variable and not create another if that variable already holds an object — which makes sure that no more than one object of your class will be created.*

Creating Modules

When you start working with a large number of classes, you may want to group those classes together into *modules*. That makes it easier to work with larger collections of classes. To create a module, you use the `module` keyword. You can place modules and the code that uses them in the same file, or break them out among separate files.

Try It Out   Create a Module

To create a module in Ruby, follow these steps:

1. Start your editor and enter the following Ruby code:

```
module Mathematics
  def Mathematics.add(operand_one, operand_two)
```

```
      return operand_one + operand_two
   end
end
```

2. Save the file as `mathematics.rb`.

3. Enter the following code in a new file:

```
module Sentence
   def Sentence.add(word_one, word_two)
      return word_one + " " + word_two
   end
end
```

4. Save the file as `sentence.rb`.

5. Enter the following code in another new file:

```
require 'mathematics'
require 'sentence'

puts "2 + 3 = " + Mathematics.add(2, 3).to_s
```

6. Save the file as `usemodules.rb`, and execute the new code:

```
C:\rubydev\ch03>ruby usemodules.rb
2 + 3 = 5
```

How It Works

This example creates two modules, Mathematics and Sentence, both of which have an `add` method:

```
module Mathematics
   def Mathematics.add(operand_one, operand_two)
      return operand_one + operand_two
   end
end

module Sentence
   def Sentence.add(word_one, word_two)
      return word_one + " " + word_two
   end
end
```

The Mathematics `add` method adds two numbers, and the Sentence `add` method adds two words together with a space to create a sentence. The `add` method looks much like a class method — unlike classes, you cannot create instances (that is, objects) of modules in Ruby.

Giving both these modules an `add` method points out another use of modules — because you have to prefix the module method to use with the module's name, you can keep the two methods separate: there's no chance that Ruby will confuse one `add` method with the other.

The Mathematics module goes in a file named `mathematics.rb`, and the Sentence module goes into a file named `sentence.rb`. You can include their code in other files with the Ruby `include` statement:

```
include 'mathematics.rb'
include 'sentence.rb'
```

However, there's a shortcut that assumes you're using `.rb` files — you can use the `require` statement instead:

```
require 'mathematics'
require 'sentence'
```

Now you're free to use the `add` methods, as in this code, which uses `Mathematics.add` to add two numbers:

```
require 'mathematics'
require 'sentence'

puts "2 + 3 = " + Mathematics.add(2, 3).to_s
```

You can also store classes inside modules. Here's an example — the `Adder` class, which you can place the `add` method inside of:

```
module Mathematics
  class Adder
    def Adder.add(operand_one, operand_two)
      return operand_one + operand_two
    end
  end
end
```

And you can access methods inside classes inside modules if you use the Ruby scope resolution operator (`::`) like this:

```
module Mathematics
  class Adder
    def Adder.add(operand_one, operand_two)
      return operand_one + operand_two
    end
  end
end
```

```
puts "2 + 3 = " + Mathematics::Adder.add(2, 3).to_s
```

That's the way you have to reach classes inside modules, using the `::` scope resolution operator (and you can reach classes nested inside of classes the same way).

Creating Mixins

Although it's true that you can't create an instance of a module, you can create a *mixin* using a module. Doing so includes the code in a module inside a class and gives you a way of inheriting from multiple modules at the same time.

Take a look at this example:

```ruby
module Adder
  def add(operand_one, operand_two)
    return operand_one + operand_two
  end
end

module Subtracter
  def subtract(operand_one, operand_two)
    return operand_one - operand_two
  end
end

class Calculator
  include Adder
  include Subtracter
end

calculator = Calculator.new()

puts "2 + 3 = " + calculator.add(2, 3).to_s
```

Executed, the output of the code is:

```
2 + 3 = 5
```

This example creates two modules, Adder and Subtracter, one of which has an add method, and the other of which has a subtract method. add and subtract are declared like normal instance methods, not class methods, so you can inherit them and use them as instance methods:

```ruby
module Adder
  def add(operand_one, operand_two)
    return operand_one + operand_two
  end
end

module Subtracter
  def subtract(operand_one, operand_two)
    return operand_one - operand_two
  end
end
```

Then the code mixes these two modules into a class, Calculator:

```ruby
class Calculator
  include Adder
  include Subtracter
end
```

Now objects of the `Calculator` class have access to both the `add` and `subtract` methods. Here's how you might use the `add` method, for example:

```
calculator = Calculator.new()

puts "2 + 3 = " + calculator.add(2, 3).to_s
```

Summary

In this chapter, you learned the details of working with classes and objects in Ruby, including how to:

- ❏ Create classes and objects.
- ❏ Use a constructor to configure objects by storing data in them.
- ❏ Create readable, writable, and readable/writable attributes using, respectively, `attr_reader`, `attr_writer`, and `attr_accessor`.
- ❏ Base one class on another, a process called inheritance.
- ❏ Denote the access of methods in classes by using the `public`, `protected`, and `private` specifiers.
- ❏ Override methods by redefining them in an inherited class.
- ❏ Create instance variables, which store instance data, and to store class variables, which are shared over all instances of the class.
- ❏ Create class methods, which you don't need an object to use, and create modules.
- ❏ Create mixins, which let you support de facto multiple inheritance.

In the next chapter, you start creating web applications with Rails. Before proceeding, however, try the exercises that follow to test your understanding of the material covered in this chapter. The solutions to these exercises are in Appendix A.

Exercises

1. Create a class named `Vehicle`, and pass the color of the vehicle to the constructor. Include a method named `get_color` to return the vehicle's color. Print out the color of the vehicle.

2. Construct a new class named `Car` based on the `Vehicle` class, and override the `get_color` method so it always returns blue. Print out the color of the car.

3. Create a `Car` class based on two modules, one that contains a `get_color` method, and one that contains a `get_number_of_wheels` method. Print out the color of the car, and the number of wheels.

Welcome to Rails

Now that you've gotten the Ruby you need under your belt, it's time to turn to Rails. Rails is the vehicle that brings Ruby to the Web in this book, and here's where it all starts.

Among other things in this chapter, you learn how to:

- ❑ Use Rails to create an application framework.
- ❑ Use the WEBrick web server.
- ❑ Generate a controller.
- ❑ Create an action by adding a method to a controller.
- ❑ Create a view template.
- ❑ Add a second action to a web application.
- ❑ Render any template.
- ❑ Link to actions from views.

Putting Ruby on Rails

Rails is a web application framework that uses Ruby as its programming language, and as you're going to see, the scripts that come with Rails will do a lot of the work for you. In fact, that's one of the key concepts of Rails: favor convention over configuration. That means that Rails will not only build skeleton applications for you, but will also stock those applications with defaults so that you don't have to configure everything from scratch. If you're used to a web framework like Java Servlets, this will come as a big relief — and no XML configuration files are involved in building Rails applications.

As discussed in Chapter 1, this book creates examples in a directory named rubydev, so if you haven't created that directory, do so now at the command prompt. That looks something like this in Windows:

```
C:\>md rubydev
```

Next, change directories to the rubydev directory. Again in Windows, that would look something like this:

```
C:\>md rubydev
C:\>cd rubydev
C:\rubydev>
```

Because this is Chapter 4, the examples from this chapter will go in a directory named ch04, so create that directory now:

```
C:\>md rubydev
C:\rubydev>cd rubydev
C:\rubydev>md ch04
```

Finally, change to the ch04 directory:

```
C:\>md rubydev
C:\rubydev>cd rubydev
C:\rubydev>md ch04
C:\rubydev>cd ch04
C:\rubydev\ch04>
```

The best way to get started is with an example, so in this chapter you'll build an application named "first" that displays a welcoming message from Rails.

Creating the Application Framework

Rails can do most of the work in creating your application. In fact, all you need to do is use the command `rails applicationName` — in this case, `rails first` — at the command line in the rubydev directory. Rails creates the files you're going to need:

```
C:\rubydev\ch04>rails first
      create
      create  app/controllers
      create  app/helpers
      create  app/models
      create  app/views/layouts
      create  config/environments
      create  components
      create  db
      create  doc
      create  lib
      create  lib/tasks
      create  log
      create  public/images
      create  public/javascripts
      create  public/stylesheets
      create  script/performance
      create  script/process
      create  test/fixtures
```

```
create   test/functional
create   test/integration
create   test/mocks/development
create   test/mocks/test
create   test/unit
create   vendor
create   vendor/plugins
create   tmp/sessions
create   tmp/sockets
create   tmp/cache
create   Rakefile
create   README
create   app/controllers/application.rb
create   app/helpers/application_helper.rb
create   test/test_helper.rb
create   config/database.yml
create   config/routes.rb
create   public/.htaccess
create   config/boot.rb
create   config/environment.rb
create   config/environments/production.rb
create   config/environments/development.rb
create   config/environments/test.rb
create   script/about
       .
       .
       .
```

Wow, that's a lot of files, and a lot of new directories (and only about half of them are shown here). Here is the new directory structure of the rubydev\ch04\first directory:

```
rubydev
|__ch04
   |__first
      |__README
      |__app
      |  |__controllers
      |  |__models
      |  |__views
      |  |__helpers
      |
      |__config
      |__components
      |__db
      |__doc
      |__lib
      |__public
      |__script
      |__test
      |__tmp
      |__vendor
```

The README document that is automatically generated and placed in the rubydev\ch04\first directory contains an explanation of these directories, and here's what it looks like (you're going to become familiar with all this information before you finish this book):

app
  Holds all the code that's specific to this particular application.

app/controllers
  Holds controllers that should be named like weblog_controller.rb for
  automated URL mapping. All controllers should descend from
  ActionController::Base.

app/models
  Holds models that should be named like post.rb.
  Most models will descend from ActiveRecord::Base.

app/views
  Holds the template files for the view that should be named like
  weblog/index.rhtml for the WeblogController#index action. All views use eRuby
  syntax. This directory can also be used to keep stylesheets, images, and so on
  that can be symlinked to public.

app/helpers
  Holds view helpers that should be named like weblog_helper.rb.

app/apis
  Holds API classes for web services.

config
  Configuration files for the Rails environment, the routing map, the database, and
  other dependencies.

components
  Self-contained mini-applications that can bundle together controllers, models,
  and views.

db
  Contains the database schema in schema.rb. db/migrate contains all
  the sequence of Migrations for your schema.

lib
  Application specific libraries. Basically, any kind of custom code that doesn't
  belong under controllers, models, or helpers. This directory is in the load path.

public
  The directory available for the web server. Contains subdirectories for images,
  stylesheets,
  and javascripts. Also contains the dispatchers and the default HTML files.

script
  Helper scripts for automation and generation.

test
  Unit and functional tests along with fixtures.

vendor
  External libraries that the application depends on. Also includes the plugins
  subdirectory.
  . This directory is in the load path.

Running the Application

To launch your new application, start by changing directories to the new first directory:

```
C:\rubydev\ch04>cd first
```

There are a number of short Ruby programs in the rubydev\ch04\first\script directory for use with your new application. The server script launches the web server WEBrick, which comes with Rails, so enter **ruby script/server** at the command line:

```
C:\rubydev\ch04\first>ruby script/server
=> Booting WEBrick...
=> Rails application started on http://0.0.0.0:3000
=> Ctrl-C to shutdown server; call with —help for options
[2006-05-16 12:26:22] INFO  WEBrick 1.3.1
[2006-05-16 12:26:22] INFO  ruby 1.8.2 (2004-12-25) [i386-mswin32]
[2006-05-16 12:26:22] INFO  WEBrick::HTTPServer#start: pid=1684 port=3000
```

This starts the WEBrick server on port 3000 of your local host, which means you can access your application at the URL `http://localhost:3000/`. To see that, open a browser on your machine and navigate to that URL, as shown in Figure 4-1.

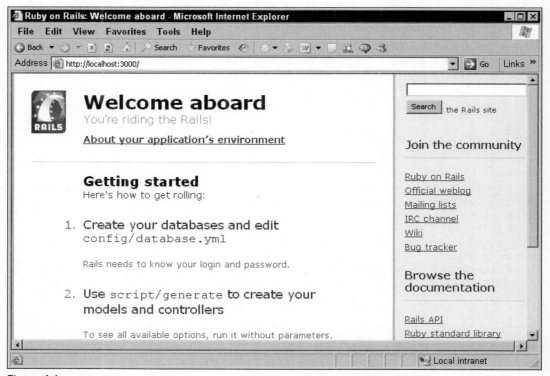

Figure 4-1

The web page displays a cheery message, indicating that you're now riding the Rails. Not bad. To end the WEBrick session now, follow the directions displayed when WEBrick started, such as pressing Ctrl+C in Windows.

Creating the Controller

The process of making the application do something for you begins when you create a *controller* for the application. The controller is like the boss of the application: it's the overseer that makes things happen. As mentioned in Chapter 1, and as discussed more thoroughly in this chapter, Rails uses a model-view-controller (MVC) architecture in its web applications. The controller part is essential to any application, so you're going to need to create one.

After stopping WEBrick, in the rubydev\ch04\first directory, use the Ruby command `ruby script/generate controller Hello` to create a new controller named `Hello`:

```
C:\rubydev\ch04\first>ruby script/generate controller Hello
      exists   app/controllers/
      exists   app/helpers/
      create   app/views/hello
      exists   test/functional/
      create   app/controllers/hello_controller.rb
      create   test/functional/hello_controller_test.rb
      create   app/helpers/hello_helper.rb
```

That creates a new controller for your application. The code for the controllers in your application appears in the rubydev\ch04\first\controllers directory, and now you'll find a file named `hello_controller.rb` in that directory — that's the support file for your new controller.

This file is long and complex. Just kidding — here's what's in it:

```
class HelloController < ApplicationController
end
```

Here's one of the places where Rails favors convention over configuration — your entire `HelloController` class inherits just about all it needs from the `ApplicationController` class. That class is supported in `application.rb`, also in the rubydev\ch04\first\controllers directory — here are its contents:

```
# Filters added to this controller will be run for all controllers in the
application.
# Likewise, all the methods added will be available for all controllers.
class ApplicationController < ActionController::Base
end
```

In other words, `ApplicationController` inherits from `ActionController::Base` — that is, the `Base` class in the `ActionController` module. You'll see more on `ActionController::Base` throughout this book.

Using the Rails Documentation

If you want, you can take a look at the Rails documentation for classes like `ActionController::Base`. To do so, just enter the command **gem_server** on the command line:

```
C:\rubydev\ch04\first>gem_server
```

Then navigate your browser to `http://localhost:8808` to see the Rails documentation.

Testing the Controller

All right, how far can you get with a web application that has a controller? You can test that out immediately in your browser.

Try It Out   Display a Message

To test a web application that has only a controller, follow these steps:

1.   Start the WEBrick server:

```
C:\rubydev\ch04\first>ruby script/server
```

2.   Navigate to `http://localhost:3000/hello`.

3.   You should see the results in Figure 4-2, where a message lets you know that "No action responded to index".

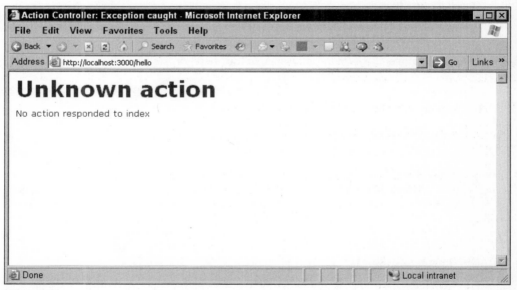

Figure 4-2

How It Works

The way you construct URLs to reach Ruby on Rails applications is simple — you append the name of the controller to the end of the URL, as you did here: `http://localhost:3000/hello`. However, as you've just seen, having only a controller isn't enough. What's missing?

As indicated in the message in Figure 4-2, you need a Rails action in addition to the controller. Controllers are the boss of the application, but you don't usually do a lot of reprogramming of the controller to make your application work. Instead, you give it a number of tasks to execute, and those tasks are called *actions*.

Creating an Action

Controllers can execute actions to make a web application do something, and you can easily add actions to the web application in Rails. The idea is that a controller is the boss of the application, and it calls various actions, each of which performs a separate task. So you can think of web applications as collections of tasks, implemented by the actions, which are driven by the controller.

This example is going to have an action named `there` that will make the application display some text in your web browser. You can specify the action you want the controller to take in the URL you navigate to. To ask the `hello` controller to execute the `there` action, navigate to `http://localhost:3000/hello/there` — you just specify the controller's name first in the URL, followed by the action you want the controller to execute. Rails decodes the URL and sends your request to the appropriate controller, which in turn calls the appropriate action.

Creating the `there` action is easy in Rails — actions are supported by methods in the controller's `.rb` file. That's all there is to it.

Try It Out   Create an Action

To add the action named `there` to the controller, follow these steps:

1. Edit your `hello_controller.rb` file in rubydev\ch04\first\app\controllers from this:

```
class HelloController < ApplicationController
end
```

to this, adding a new method named `there`:

```
class HelloController < ApplicationController
  def there
  end
end
```

2. Save `hello_controller.rb`.

3. Start the WEBrick server:

```
C:\rubydev\ch04\first>ruby script/server
```

4. Navigate to `http://localhost:3000/hello/there`. You should see the results shown in Figure 4-3, where a message tells you: "Missing template ./script/../config/../app/views/hello/there.rhtml".

Figure 4-3

How It Works

In Rails, you create an action by adding a method to a controller, and that's what you did here — you added the `there` action. You can reach this new action by navigating to `http://localhost:3000/hello/there`. However, when you do, you get the "Missing template..." Something is missing.

You need a view.

Creating a View

You've created a web application, added a controller to handle requests from the user, and added an action to let the controller respond to those requests. But you still need some way of returning a result to the user.

Associating a response with your action is done by creating a *view* in Rails applications. A view is just what it sounds like — a way of seeing some result. After your application is all done, it displays its results in a view.

Already you're picking up vital pieces of Ruby on Rails terminology — the controller is the boss of a web application, actions are tasks that controllers can perform, and views give the controller a way to display the results of the application.

You use a *template* to create a view. A template is a skeleton web page that will display your results in a browser; at runtime, an action can store data throughout that template so that your web page shows the data formatted as you want it.

Creating a template is easy — templates are just web pages with the extension `.rhtml`. That extension makes Rails read the file and pops into it any data from the action you want displayed before sending the template back to the browser.

In this example, the action is just a rudimentary, empty method named `there` in the controller:

```
class HelloController < ApplicationController
  def there
  end
end
```

The file, `hello_controller.rb`, is in rubydev\ch04\first\app\controllers because it's the support code for the `hello` controller's `there` action. Rails will automatically connect a view template to this action if you give the template the action's name — `there.rhtml`, in this case — and place it in rubydev\ch04\first\app\views\hello. In other words, to establish a view template for the `hello` controller's `there` action, you can create a file named `there.rhtml` and store it in the rubydev\ch04\first\app\views\hello directory.

Try It Out   Create a View

To add a view to the application, follow these steps:

1. Start your text editor and place this text in it:

```
<html>
  <head>
    <title>Using Ruby on Rails</title>
  </head>
  <body>
    <h1>Welcome to Ruby on Rails</h1>
    This is your first Ruby on Rails application.
    <br>
    <br>
    Using this application, you've been introduced to
    controllers, actions, and views.
    <br>
    <br>
    Not bad for a first example!
  </body>
</html>
```

2. Save this file as `rubydev\ch04\first\app\views\hello\there.rhtml`.

3. Start the WEBrick server:

```
C:\rubydev\ch04\first>ruby script/server
```

4. Navigate to `http://localhost:3000/hello/there`. Figure 4-4 shows the new web page — mission accomplished.

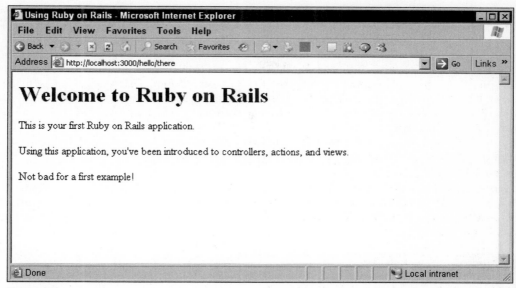

Figure 4-4

How It Works

This example shows how to connect a sample view template to an action, displaying a sample, static web page — there.rhtml — in the browser. All you had to do was to place there.rhtml into rubydev\ch04\first\app\views\hello to connect the template to the hello controller's there action.

You've completed your first Ruby on Rails web application. Note that only two files were involved — hello_controller.rb and there.rhtml:

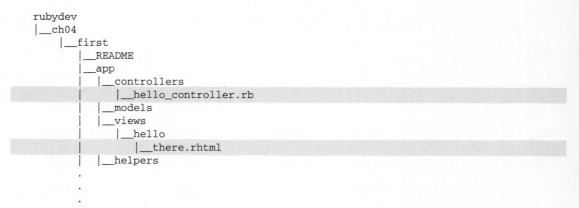

Introducing Model-View-Controller Architecture

Now let's take the application apart so you can get a good idea how such applications work. Control starts in the browser, when the user enters the URL for the application. That sends a request to the web server, which decodes the URL and sends the request from the browser on to the controller. The controller can have a number of actions to select from — there's just one in this case, but you can add as many methods as you want to `hello_controller.rb`. The controller passes the request on to the appropriate action, as specified in the URL in this case. The action in this example didn't really do anything, just used a view template to return data to the browser. Figure 4-5 shows what the process looks like schematically.

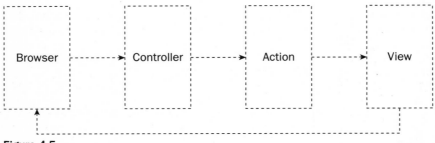

Figure 4-5

In fact, this is a specific case of a more general picture — the model-view-controller picture. Figure 4-6 shows what that picture looks like in overview.

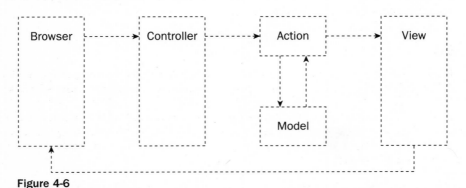

Figure 4-6

It's going to be helpful to take this picture apart, piece by piece, to get the full model-view-controller story. In the early days of web applications, all the code was heaped together into a single document, which ran when you accessed it from a browser. However, as online applications got longer and longer, it became a good idea to split out the presentation code from the rest of the code to make maintenance and debugging easier. That led to a whole new breed of applications. But even that architecture in turn has been superceded by the addition of the model for data handling. Enter the MVC architecture, which all starts with the controller.

The Controller

When the user enters a URL into his browser, a request is sent from the browser to the web server. If your web server supports Rails, it's going to hand the request from the browser off to a Rails controller of the kind you've already seen.

The controller supervises the entire application, handling requests as needed. For example, the controller can decode the URL you've already seen — http://localhost:3000/hello/there — to know that you're requesting the action named there.

Controllers can also route requests between the web pages of an application — so far, the application you've seen only has one web page, but it's a rare application that stops at one web page. Most have multiple pages, and the controller can route the user from page to page.

At its most basic, a controller just inherits from the ApplicationController class, which in turn inherits from the ActionController::Base class — the ActionController module is the one that contains the support for controllers in Rails:

```
class HelloController < ApplicationController
end
```

And as you've also already seen, you create actions simply by adding methods to the controller:

```
class HelloController < ApplicationController
  def there
  end
end
```

The controller calls the various actions, and when the actions have done their thing, the controller passes the results of the application on to a view.

The View

A view is responsible for displaying the results of an action. There can be many different views in a web application, because web applications can display many different pages in the user's browser.

The view you've seen so far has been static, but of course you usually want to display data in the view. That means that an action will typically pass data on to the view, and you're going to see how to do that in this chapter. Rails view templates often allow you to insert data into them before they are sent back to the user's browser by the controller.

In other words, you use views to interact with the user. When you want to read data from the user, you send a view with various HTML controls such as text fields, listboxes, text areas, and so on. When the user clicks the Submit button, that data is passed to your application's controller, which hands it off to an action, which in turn passes it to a view that is sent back to the browser.

Views are supported with the ActionView modules in Rails, and you're going to see a great deal about that support in this book. In fact, in Rails, controllers and views are so tightly integrated that together, the ActionView and ActionController modules are referred to as the ActionPack.

So the controller routes requests to actions, and the actions send views to the user's browser. What more do you need?

101

The Model

You also need the *model* in a Rails application. The model handles the data processing that takes place in a web application. Actions can interact with the model to handle the data churning that needs to be done.

For example, the model is where you can place the business rules of an application that figure the tax and/or shipping on an order from the user. Or you can check a database to see whether an item is in stock. Or you can look up a user's information from another database.

That is, the model is the number cruncher in the application. It has no clue about its environment, and knows nothing about being on a web server as part of an online application. You just hand it data and tell it what to do. It does the data-handling work, and returns the result. Typically, actions pass data into the model and then retrieve the results.

Rails is written especially to handle databases, and the model is where that support is. You can base models on the Rails `ActiveRecord` module — note, not `ActionRecord`, but `ActiveRecord`.

That's the overview of the model-view-controller architecture that Rails uses. Because Rails applications are broken up into these components, it's important to know what they do. You've already seen the controller and view at work in your first Rails web application, and you're going to see how to work with models soon.

So far, the view has been pretty static, just displaying a welcome message. It's time to add some more functionality there.

Giving the View Something to Do

The view for the `there` action, `there.rhtml`, has the extension `.rhtml`, because that extension tells Rails to open the file and execute any parts that can be executed before sending the results back to the browser. What's to execute? You can embed Ruby code in `.rhtml` files, and that code is run before the file is sent to the browser.

In Rails, embedded Ruby in `.rhtml` pages is run using a processor called ERb, for Embedded Ruby. As with various online scripting languages, such as PHP or JavaServer Pages (JSP), you surround the Ruby code you want to have executed with the markup `<%` and `%>`. For example, to add 2 + 3, you could do that this way in `there.rhtml`:

```
<html>
  <head>
    <title>Using Ruby on Rails</title>
  </head>
  <body>
    <h1>Welcome to Ruby on Rails</h1>
    This is your first Ruby on Rails application.
    <br>
    <br>
    Using this application, you've been introduced to
    controllers, actions, and views.
    <br>
```

```
    <% 2 + 3 %>
    <br>
    Not bad for a first example!
  </body>
</html>
```

This executes the expression 2 + 3, but doesn't display anything in the web page. To insert text into a page you use different markup (<%= and %>), like this:

```
Using this application, you've been introduced to
controllers, actions, and views.
<br>
<%= 2 + 3 %>
<br>
```

You can mix HTML and ERb as well; for example, this:

```
Using this application, you've been introduced to
controllers, actions, and views.
<br>
2 + 3 = <%= 2 + 3 %>
<br>
```

displays:

```
Using this application, you've been introduced to
controllers, actions, and views.
<br>
2+ 3 = 5
<br>
```

You create an active view, which will execute code and show you the results, in the following Try It Out.

Try It Out   Create an Active View

1. Change directories to rubydev\ch04:

```
C:\rubydev\ch04\first>cd \rubydev\ch04
```

2. Create a new application named `viewer`:

```
C:\rubydev\ch04>rails viewer
```

(Remember, Rails creates a big batch of files for your new application.)

3. Change directories to rubydev\ch04\viewer:

```
C:\rubydev\ch04>cd viewer
```

4. Create a new controller named `Look`:

```
C:\rubydev\ch04\viewer>ruby script/generate controller Look
```

Again, Rails provides code for the controller in your application in the rubydev\ch04\viewer\controllers directory, including a file named `look_controller.rb`, which is the support file for your new controller.

5. Add an action named `at` to the new controller, rubydev\ch04\viewer\app\controllers\look_controller.rb:

```
class LookController < ApplicationController
  def at
  end
end
```

6. Add a view template to the application as rubydev\ch04\viewer\app\views\look\at.rhtml:

```
<html>
  <head>
    <title>Using Views</title>
  </head>
  <body>
    <h1>Working With Views</h1>
    This is an active view in a Ruby on Rails application.
    <br>
    <br>
    2 + 3 = <%= 2 + 3 %>
    <br>
    <br>
    This page executes Ruby code on-the-fly.
  </body>
</html>
```

7. Save this file as rubydev\ch04\viewer\app\views\look\at.rhtml.

8. Start the WEBrick server:

```
C:\rubydev\ch04\viewer>ruby script/server
```

9. Navigate to `http://localhost:3000/look/at`. Figure 4-7 shows the results, the new web page in which Rails adds 2 + 3 together, giving you 5.

How It Works

This example displays a view where Rails passes an expression to the Ruby ERb processor for evaluation:

```
<br>
2 + 3 = <%= 2 + 3 %>
<br>
<br>
```

Here, 2 + 3 evaluates to 5, and because that expression is evaluated inside the <%= and %> markup, 5 is placed in the web page. The result is:

```
<br>
2 + 3 = 5
<br>
<br>
```

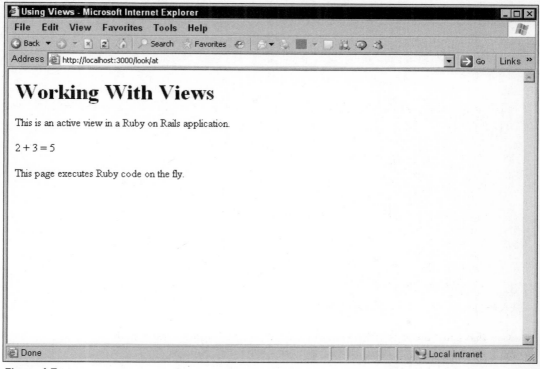

Figure 4-7

Mixing Ruby Code and HTML Inside the View

You can mix HTML and Ruby code together in an .rhtml page. For example, to display some text three times, you could use a 3.times do loop. All you have to do is to make sure the Ruby code is inside <% and %>, and that no HTML is inside that <% and %> markup.

Give it a try in the following exercise.

Try It Out   Mix Ruby Code and HTML

To mix Ruby and HTML, follow these steps:

1. Modify the view template of the application, rubydev\ch04\viewer\app\views\look\at.rhtml, adding this Ruby/HTML code:

```
<html>
  <head>
```

```
      <title>Using Views</title>
   </head>
   <body>
      <h1>Working With Views</h1>
      This is an active view in a Ruby on Rails application.
      <br>
      <br>
      2 + 3 = <%= 2 + 3 %>
      <br>
      <br>
      Do loops work?
      <br>
      <% 3.times do %>
      Yes! <br>
      <% end %>
      <br>
      This page executes Ruby code on-the-fly.
   </body>
</html>
```

2. Save the file.

3. Start the WEBrick server:

```
C:\rubydev\ch04\viewer>ruby script/server
```

4. Navigate to `http://localhost:3000/look/at`. Figure 4-8 shows the results: Rails executed the `3.times do loop`, displaying Yes! three times. Not bad.

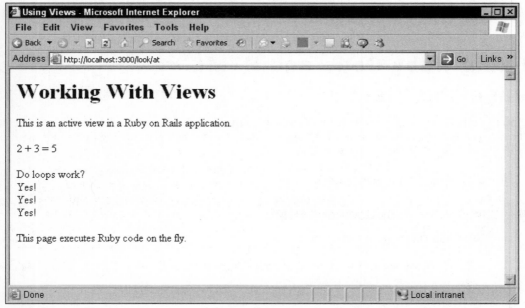

Figure 4-8

What About puts?

What about using `puts`? Can you use `puts` to display text in a web page? For example, what if you executed this code:

```html
<html>
  <head>
    <title>Using Views</title>
  </head>
  <body>
    <h1>Working With Views</h1>
    This is an active view in a Ruby on Rails application.
    <br>
    <br>
    2 + 3 = <%= 2 + 3 %>
    <br>
    <% puts "Hi" %>
    <br>
    This page executes Ruby code on the fly.
  </body>
</html>
```

When you look at this new version of the view in your browser, however, nothing's changed—where did the "Hi" you printed out go? It was printed out in the console. Take a look at the console where WEBrick is running; you'll see the "Hi":

```
C:\rubydev\ch04\viewer>ruby script/server
=> Booting WEBrick...
=> Rails application started on http://0.0.0.0:3000
=> Ctrl-C to shutdown server; call with —help for options
[2006-05-17 12:55:08] INFO  WEBrick 1.3.1
[2006-05-17 12:55:08] INFO  ruby 1.8.2 (2004-12-25) [i386-
mswin32]
[2006-05-17 12:55:08] INFO  WEBrick::HTTPServer#start: pid=1416
port=3000
127.0.0.1 - - [17/May/2006:13:07:47 Eastern Standard Time] "GET
/look/at HTTP/1.
1" 200 270
- -> /look/at
Hi
```

This points out that, true to its nature, `puts` is a console-oriented method. You can't use it to display text in web pages. However, `puts` still has uses in web applications—you can use it to print text to the console, such as error or diagnostic messages. That's useful when you're developing or debugging Rails applications and you want to know what's going on behind the scenes.

How It Works

This example mixes Ruby and HTML together by setting up a loop and executing the body of the loop (the HTML Yes!) three times:

```
Do loops work?
<br>
<% 3.times do %>
Yes! <br>
<% end %>
```

The result is that the HTML is displayed three times in the web page:

```
<br>
Yes! <br>
Yes! <br>
Yes! <br>
<br>
```

That's how you can mix Ruby code with HTML. In fact, .rhtml pages are usually made up of mixes of Ruby and HTML.

However, you shouldn't place too much Ruby code in a view, because the view's job is primarily to display results, not create those results. Instead, you normally perform calculations in the action, and pass the results of those calculations on to the view.

Passing Data from an Action to a View

Take a look at this new version of the view at.rhtml, which uses the Ruby Time.now method to display the current time:

```
<html>
  <head>
    <title>Using Views</title>
  </head>
  <body>
    <h1>Working With Views</h1>
    This is an active view in a Ruby on Rails application.
    <br>
    <br>
    2 + 3 = <%= 2 + 3 %>
    <br>
    <br>
    Do loops work?
    <br>
    <% 3.times do %>
    Yes! <br>
    <% end %>
    <br>
    The time is now <%= Time.now %>
    <br>
    <br>
```

```
      This page executes Ruby code on the fly.
   </body>
</html>
```

That works fine, and you'll see the time displayed in your web browser in this page. However, because the code in the view is there primarily to display results, you could argue that the current time is better calculated in an action and the results passed to the view. Tackle that in the following Try It Out.

Try It Out   Pass Data from an Action to a View

To pass data from an action to a view, follow these steps:

1. Modify the at action in the controller of the application, rubydev\ch04\viewer\app\ controllers\look_controller.rb, adding this Ruby code:

```
class LookController < ApplicationController
   def at
      @time_now = Time.now
   end
end
```

2. Save the file as rubydev\ch04\viewer\app\controllers\look_controller.rb.

3. Modify the view template of the application, rubydev\ch04\viewer\app\views\look\at.rhtml, adding this Ruby/HTML code:

```
<html>
   <head>
      <title>Using Views</title>
   </head>
   <body>
      <h1>Working With Views</h1>
      This is an active view in a Ruby on Rails application.
      <br>
      <br>
      2 + 3 = <%= 2 + 3 %>
      <br>
      <br>
      Do loops work?
      <br>
      <% 3.times do %>
      Yes! <br>
      <% end %>
      <br>
      The time is now <%= @time_now %>
      <br>
      <br>
      This page executes Ruby code on the fly.
   </body>
</html>
```

4. Save this file as rubydev\ch04\viewer\app\views\look\at.rhtml.

5. Start the WEBrick server:

```
C:\rubydev\ch04\viewer>ruby script/server
```

6. Navigate to `http://localhost:3000/look/at`. Figure 4-9 shows an example result (yours will have your current time and date).

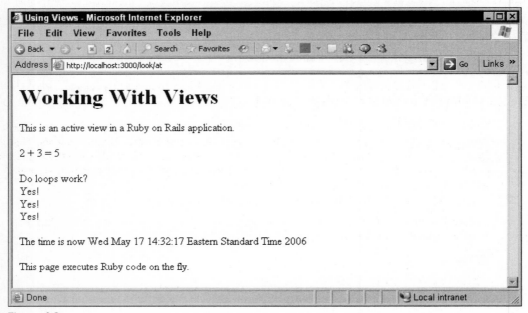

Figure 4-9

How It Works

This example creates an instance variable, `@time_now`, in the `at` action and then, in the view template connected to that action, you can refer to the same instance variable. This code inserts the value of `@time_now` into the final web page:

```
The time is now <%= @time_now %>
```

That's all there is to it — the instance variable in the action is available to your code in the action template as well.

Making instance variables available to views is a nice feature in Rails. It saves you some time compared to other MVC frameworks, where you have to do special work to export data from an action into a view. In Rails, all you have to do is to refer to the action's instance variables by name in the view, and you have instant access to them.

This means that you can perform your calculations in the action and automatically have them sent over to the views, no pesky method calls or exports needed. In fact, Rails even breaks the rules a little on your behalf here — technically speaking, the instance variables in the action should be private to the action object, but in Rails, they're shared with the view connected to that action. A technical breach of the rules, but so handy that no one minds. How does Rails know which view belongs to which action? It checks the app/views directory for a subdirectory with the name of the controller, and if it finds it, Rails checks inside it for an .rhtml file with the same name as the action.

In MVC applications, you're supposed to break the code up into model-view-controller parts, and the fact that instance variables are automatically exported into the view makes it easier for you to do so.

Escaping Sensitive Text

Here's something you should know now that you're displaying text in web pages using Ruby on Rails. On occasion, web pages can contain sensitive text that can be misinterpreted by the browser. That happens when those pages contain characters such as <, &, and @ that are not intended as HTML markup. For example, to display the text "I say that here<there alphabetically." (in other words, that "here" comes before "there" alphabetically) in a web page:

```
<html>
  <head>
    <title>Using Views</title>
  </head>
  <body>
    <h1>Working With Views</h1>
    This is an active view in a Ruby on Rails application.
    <br>
    <br>
    2 + 3 = <%= 2 + 3 %>
    <br>
    <br>
    Do loops work?
    <br>
    <% 3.times do %>
    Yes! <br>
    <% end %>
    <br>
    The time is now <%= @time_now %>
    <br>
    <br>
    I say that here<there alphabetically.
    <br>
    <br>
    This page executes Ruby code on the fly.
  </body>
</html>
```

This text contains a < character that is not intended to be interpreted as markup, but is, as you can see in Figure 4-10, near the bottom. The browser interpreted <there as the beginning of an HTML element, with the result that the line is truncated.

111

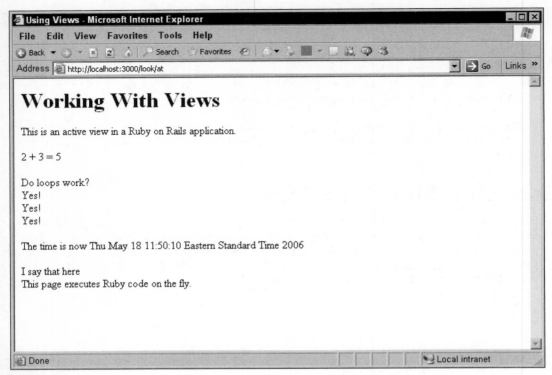

Figure 4-10

To fix that, you can use the h method in .rhtml pages. That method converts sensitive characters into their HTML entity equivalents — for example, the sensitive < character becomes <, which makes the browser display a < character, instead of interpreting < as the beginning of HTML markup. The process of converting sensitive characters into entities is called *escaping*.

You have to quote the text you want to pass to the h method, and of course, because you're executing Ruby code, you have to surround it with <%= and %>:

```
<br>
<br>
<%= h("I say that here<there alphabetically.") %>
<br>
<br>
```

This creates and inserts the text into the web page — note the escaped less-than character:

```
I say that here&lt;there alphabetically.
```

And you can see the results in Figure 4-11, where things look as they should. So anytime you have characters in your output that could be misinterpreted by the browser, think of the h method.

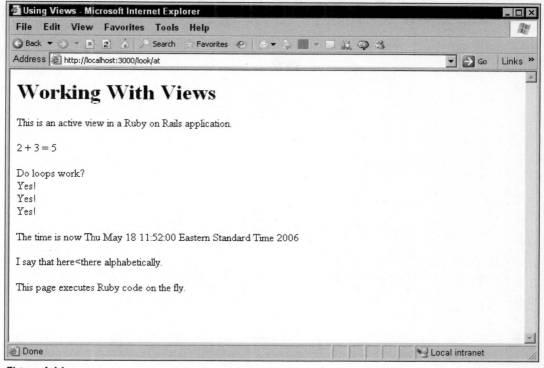

Figure 4-11

Adding a Second Action

Up to this point, your Rails applications have only supported a single action, but as you know, actions are like tasks in web applications, and applications can perform many tasks. How about adding a second action and seeing what can be done with it?

Try It Out   **Create an Application with Two Actions**

To create an application with two views, follow these steps:

1. Create a new application named `double` in rubydev\ch04:

```
C:\rubydev\ch04>rails double
      create
      create  app/controllers
      create  app/helpers
      create  app/models
      create  app/views/layouts
      create  config/environments
      create  components
```

```
      create   db
      create   doc
      create   lib
      create   lib/tasks
      create   log
      create   public/images
          .
          .
          .
```

2. Change directories to the double directory:

```
C:\rubydev\ch04>cd double
C:\rubydev\ch04\double>
```

3. Create a controller named Goto:

```
C:\rubydev\ch04\double>ruby script/generate controller Goto
      exists   app/controllers/
      exists   app/helpers/
      create   app/views/goto
      exists   test/functional/
      create   app/controllers/goto_controller.rb
      create   test/functional/goto_controller_test.rb
      create   app/helpers/goto_helper.rb
```

4. Edit rubydev\ch04\double\app\controllers\goto_controller.rb, which now looks like this:

```
class GotoController < ApplicationController
end
```

to support two actions, work and lunch:

```
class GotoController < ApplicationController
  def work
  end

  def lunch
  end
end
```

5. Place the following HTML in the work view template, rubydev\ch04\double\app\views\
goto\work.rhtml:

```
<html>
  <head>
    <title>Using Two Views</title>
  </head>
  <body>
    <h1>Working With Two Views</h1>
    <br>
    <br>
    <h1>Get back to work!</h1>
    <br>
    <br>
    This is an active view in a Ruby on Rails application.
  </body>
</html>
```

6. Place this HTML in the lunch view template,
rubydev\ch04\double\app\views\goto\lunch.rhtml:

```html
<html>
  <head>
    <title>Using Two Views</title>
  </head>
  <body>
    <h1>Working With Two Views</h1>
    <br>
    <br>
    <h1>Lunch time!</h1>
    <br>
    <br>
    This is an active view in a Ruby on Rails application.
  </body>
</html>
```

7. Start the WEBrick server:

```
C:\rubydev\ch04\double>ruby script/server
```

8. Navigate to `http://localhost:3000/goto/work`; you should see the results shown in Figure
4-12, where you see the new web page — time to get back to work!

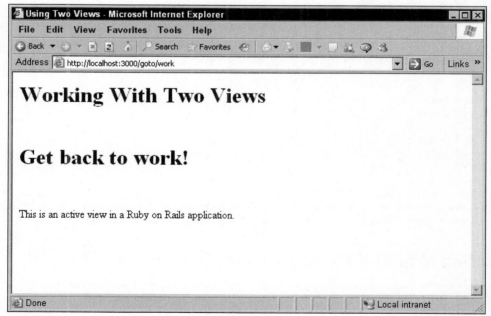

Figure 4-12

9. Now navigate to `http://localhost:3000/goto/lunch`; you should see the results shown in
Figure 4-13, where you see it's time for lunch.

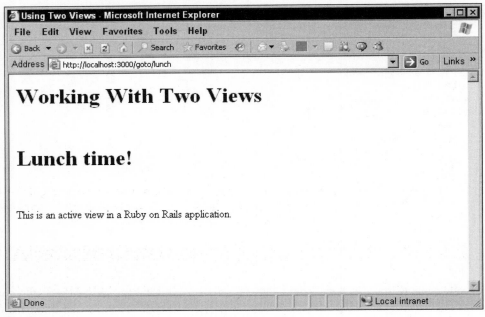

Figure 4-13

How It Works

This example creates two actions in the controller:

```
class GotoController < ApplicationController
  def work
  end

  def lunch
  end
end
```

And you can access the `work` action as `http://localhost:3000/goto/work` and the `lunch` action as `http://localhost:3000/goto/lunch`. So it's relatively easy to use multiple actions in a Rails application—in fact, you can have an unlimited number of actions in a Rails application.

Selecting Which View to Render

Now that you're dealing with multiple actions, can you select which view to call at runtime? You certainly can.

Try It Out   **Select Which View to Display**

To select which view to display, follow these steps:

1.   Edit rubydev\ch04\double\app\controllers\goto_controller.rb, adding this code:

```
class GotoController < ApplicationController
  def work
    if Time.now.hour == 12
      render(:action => :lunch)
    end
  end
  def lunch
  end
end
```

2.   Start the WEBrick server:

```
C:\rubydev\ch04\double>ruby script/server
```

3.   Navigate to `http://localhost:3000/goto/work`. The results, shown in Figure 4-14, tell you that it's time for lunch — even though the URL is `http://localhost:3000/goto/work`, not `http://localhost:3000/goto/lunch`.

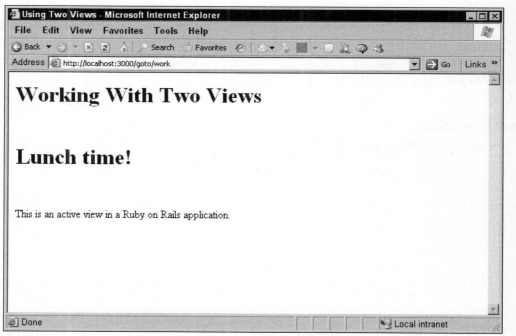

Figure 4-14

How It Works

This example adds code to the `work` action that checks to see if the hour of the day is 12, in which case, it's lunch time. You use the `render` method to draw a view, and `render(:action => :lunch)` draws the view associated with the `lunch` action.

This is particularly useful if you want the flexibility of selecting among multiple views from a single action. For example, you may want to display an error page this way (more on handling errors coming up later), or just select from multiple web pages, as in this example, where the action displays a lunch time page if it's lunch time.

You can use the `render` method alone if you're through processing and just want to jump to the view connected to your action:

```
def work
  if Time.now.hour == 12
   render(:action => :lunch)
  else
   render
  end
```

Rendering Any Template

You don't need to call another action's view; you can render any template — not just those connected to actions — simply by giving the template's path (including the file extension). That means you can associate multiple views with one action easily — just create multiple `.rhtml` templates and you're in business.

Try It Out   Call a Template File Directly

To call a template file directly, follow these steps:

1. Edit rubydev\ch04\double\app\controllers\goto_controller.rb, adding this code (change this code to match the path to your `lunch.rhtml` file as needed — if you're not using Windows, use the path `"./goto/lunch.rhtml"`):

```
class GotoController < ApplicationController
  def work
   if Time.now.hour == 12
    render(:file => 'C:\rubydev\ch04\double\app\views\goto\lunch.rhtml')
   end
  end
end
```

2. Start the WEBrick server:

```
C:\rubydev\ch04\double>ruby script/server
```

3. Navigate to `http://localhost:3000/goto/work`; you should see the lunch page even though you navigated to the work page.

How It Works

This example adds code to the `work` action, illustrating how you can render a view template using the `render(:file => path)` form of the `render` method. Powerful.

Linking to Another Action

You can also *link* from a view to another action, using the `link_to` method, which creates hyperlinks. Now you can support multiple-action applications by linking from page to page. The following Try It Out shows you how to use `link_to`.

Link to an Action

To link to another action, follow these steps:

1. Edit rubydev\ch04\double\app\views\goto\work.rhtml, adding this code:

```
<html>
  <head>
    <title>Using Two Views</title>
  </head>
  <body>
    <h1>Working With Two Views</h1>
    <br>
    <br>
    <h1>Get back to work!</h1>
    <br>
    <br>
    <%= link_to "Go to lunch.", :action => "lunch" %>
    <br>
    <br>
    This is an active view in a Ruby on Rails application.
  </body>
</html>
```

2. Start the WEBrick server:

```
C:\rubydev\ch04\double>ruby script/server
```

3. Navigate to `http://localhost:3000/goto/work`; you should see the `Go to lunch` link, as shown in Figure 4-15.

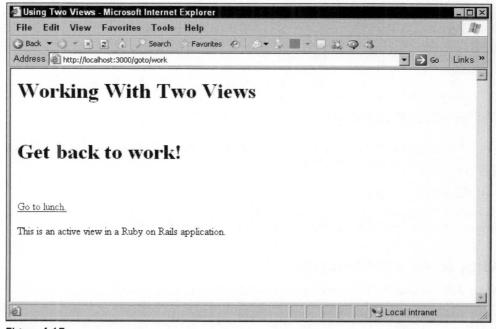

Figure 4-15

4. Click the link. That should take you back to the lunch page, as you see in Figure 4-16.

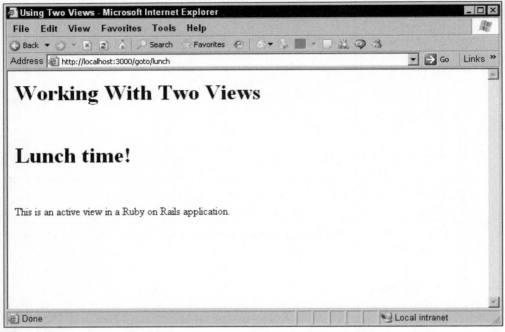

Figure 4-16

How It Works

This example adds code to the work view to link to another action from a view template — in this case, the code links to the lunch action, and that action is called when you click the link. Here's the HTML `<a>` link that's actually created by this code:

```
<a href="/goto/lunch">Go to lunch.</a>
```

Congratulations — now you're able to link from a view to an action using Ruby on Rails.

Summary

In this chapter, you got the basics of Rails applications down, including how to:

❑ Use Rails to create an application framework (`rails applicationName`).

❑ Use the WEBrick web server.

❑ Generate a controller (`ruby script/generate controller Name`).

❑ Add methods to controllers to create **actions**.

❑ Create view templates.

❑ Add a second action to a web application.

❑ Render any template as well as another action's view.

❑ Link views and actions.

In the next chapter, you learn to work with models, handle HTML controls like text fields, and more. Before proceeding, however, try the exercises that follow to test your understanding of the material covered in this chapter. You can find the solutions to these exercises in Appendix A.

Exercises

1. Create a web application named `test` with a controller named `do` and an action named `greeting` that displays the text "Hello".

2. Modify the test application to store its "Hello" message in the `greeting` action.

3. Add a second action named `greeting2` that displays "Hello again" and link to it from the `greeting` action's view template.

Building Simple Rails Applications

Nothing is more fundamental in web applications than communicating with the user through HTML controls. In this chapter, you learn how to read the data the user places in controls such as text fields and checkboxes, enabling you to communicate with the user. You'll also build and use models, and handle sessions. In later chapters, you'll see that Rails provides some tools that make the process of communicating to databases almost automatic.

Accessing Data the User Provides

You need to be able to read the data the user places in controls so that your application can take appropriate action. The following sections show you how to read data from several controls: text fields, checkboxes, radio buttons, and select controls.

Reading Data from Text Fields

Probably the most basic HTML control is the text field, which lets the user enter text. At its most fundamental, you can create a text field using the HTML <input> element:

```
<input type="text" name="text1">
```

Note the name of the text field, "text1" — you can access the data in the text field in your Rails code using that name and a hash named *params*.

Try It Out   Read Data from a Text Field

To read data from a text field, follow these steps:

1. Create a new application named `textfields`:

```
C:\rubydev\ch05>Rails textfields
        .
        .
        .
```

2. Change directories to the textfields directory:

```
C:\rubydev\ch05>cd textfields
C:\rubydev\ch05\textfields>
```

3. Add a controller named `look`:

```
C:\rubydev\ch05\textfields>ruby script/generate controller Look
```

4. Create a new file, rubydev\ch05\textfields\public\input.html, adding this code:

```
<html>
  <head>
    <title>Using Text Fields</title>
  </head>
  <body>
    <h1>Working With Text Fields</h1>
    This Ruby on Rails application lets you read data from text fields.
    <br>
    <form action = "\look\at" >
      Please enter your name.
      <br>
      <input type="text" name="text1">
      <br>
      <br>
      <input type="submit"/>
    </form>
  </body>
</html>
```

5. Edit rubydev\ch05\textfields\app\controllers\look_controller.rb, adding this code:

```
class LookController < ApplicationController
  def at
    @data = params[:text1]
  end
end
```

6. Create a new view template for the application, rubydev\ch05\textfields\app\views\look\at.rhtml:

```html
<html>
  <head>
    <title>Reading data from text fields</title>
  </head>
  <body>
    <h1>Reading data from text fields</h1>
    This Ruby on Rails application reads data from text fields.
    <br>
    <br>
    Your name is <%= @data %>.
    <br>
    <br>
  </body>
</html>
```

7.   Start the WEBrick server:

```
C:\rubydev\ch05\textfields>ruby script/server
```

8.   Navigate to `http://localhost:3000/input.html`. Figure 5-1 shows the resulting web page, where a text field appears with a prompt. Enter your name in the text field.

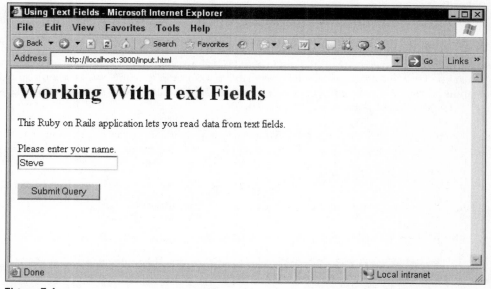

Figure 5-1

9.   Click Submit Query.

10.   Your name should be displayed, similar to the results in Figure 5-2. Success!

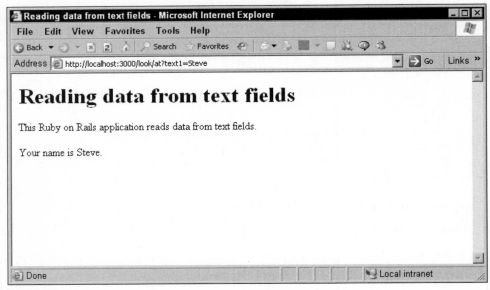

Figure 5-2

How It Works

This example places a web page in rubydev\ch05\textfields\public. That's the directory that's accessed if you just open the web application without specifying a controller/action pair — when you navigate to a web application without a controller, as `http://localhost:3000` if you're using WEBrick, you'll see public\index.html in your browser.

The web page, `input.html`, creates an HTML form that assigned its `action` attribute the text `"\look\at"`, which means the data in the form will be sent to the \look\at controller\action:

```
<form action = "\look\at" >
```

You also need a Submit button, and to end the HTML `<form>` element:

```
<form ...
...
  <input type="submit"/>
</form>
```

The data from this form is accessible in the `at` action, using the `params` hash. This is a special Rails hash that holds data entered by the user into HTML controls. To retrieve the data from the text field named `text1`, pass the symbol `:text1` to the `params` hash, and store the retrieved text in an instance variable named `@data`:

```
def at
  @data = params[:text1]
end
```

All that's left is to display the data stored in the @data instance variable in the view:

```
<br>
Your name is <%= @data %>.
<br>
```

And that's it — you've been able to read the text that the user entered into a text field in a Rails application. Congratulations.

This example uses GET, the default method for sending results to a web server. Using GET is less secure than the other method, POST, because GET uses URL-encoding — your data is pasted on the end of the URL sent to the server, and it's visible. If you prefer to use the more secure POST method, you just have to set the method attribute to "post":

```
<form action = "\look\at" method = "post">
```

And the example will work as before.

Reading Data from Checkboxes

After text fields, the most basic HTML control is the checkbox, which lets the user select or deselect it, displaying or hiding a check mark. You can create checkboxes using the HTML <input> element:

```
<input type="checkbox" name="check1">
```

In the following exercise, you create a checkbox element and read its data.

Try It Out   **Read Data from a Checkbox**

To read data from a checkbox, follow these steps:

1.   Create a new application named checkboxes:

```
C:\rubydev\ch05>Rails checkboxes
     .
     .
     .
```

2.   Change directories to the checkboxes directory:

```
C:\rubydev\ch05>cd checkboxes
C:\rubydev\ch05\checkboxes>
```

3.   Add a controller named look:

```
C:\rubydev\ch05\checkboxes>ruby script/generate controller Look
     .
     .
     .
```

4. Create a new file, rubydev\ch05\checkboxes\public\input.html, adding this code:

```html
<html>
  <head>
    <title>Using Checkboxes</title>
  </head>
  <body>
    <h1>Working With Checkboxes</h1>
    This Ruby on Rails application lets you read data from checkboxes.
    <br>
    <form action = "\look\at">
      Would you like a raise?
      <br>
      <input type="checkbox" name="check1">Yes
      <br>
      <br>
      <input type="submit"/>
    </form>
  </body>
</html>
```

5. Edit rubydev\ch05\checkboxes\app\controllers\look_controller.rb, adding this code:

```ruby
class LookController < ApplicationController
  def at
    @data = params[:check1]
  end
end
```

6. Create a new view template for the application, rubydev\ch05\checkboxes\app\views\look\at.rhtml:

```html
<html>
  <head>
    <title>Reading data from text fields</title>
  </head>
  <body>
    <h1>Reading data from text fields</h1>
    This Ruby on Rails application reads data from text fields.
    <br>
    <br>
    <% if @data %>
    You clicked yes.
    <% else %>
    You did not click yes.
    <% end %>
    <br>
    <br>
  </body>
</html>
```

7. Start the WEBrick server:

```
C:\rubydev\ch05\checkboxes>ruby script/server
```

8. Navigate to `http://localhost:3000/input.html`. Figure 5-3 shows the result—a web page with a checkbox and a prompt—do you want a raise?

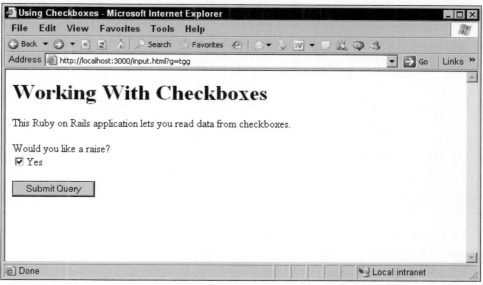

Figure 5-3

9. Select—or don't select (if you don't want a raise)—the checkbox, and click Submit Query. The resulting web page (see Figure 5-4) displays your selection.

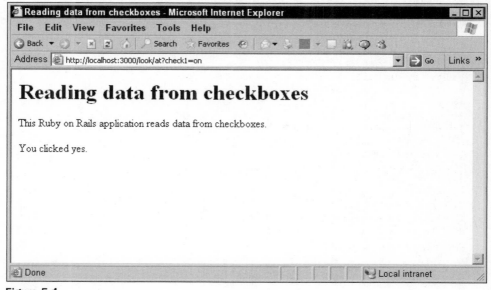

Figure 5-4

How It Works

Like the previous example, this one places a web page in its public directory, which is rubydev\ch05\ checkfields\public. The web page includes an HTML form that will send its data to the look\at controller\action, and a checkbox:

```
<form action = "\look\at">
  ...
  ...
    <input type="checkbox" name="check1">Yes
```

The data from checkboxes is passed to your code using true/false values, so in the action, @data will be left holding true if the user selected the check1 checkbox, and false otherwise:

```
def at
  @data = params[:check1]
end
```

The following code lines check which value @data holds — true or false — in the view template:

```
<br>
<% if @data %>
You clicked yes.
<% else %>
You did not click yes.
<% end %>
<br>
```

And that's all you need — you can work with checkboxes in Rails applications.

Reading Data from Radio Buttons

Radio buttons are similar to checkboxes except you group radio buttons together by giving them the same name, while also giving them different values. Here's how that looks in an application named radios:

```
<html>
  <head>
    <title>Using Radio Buttons</title>
  </head>
  <body>
    <h1>Working With Radio Buttons</h1>
    This Ruby on Rails application lets you read data from radio buttons.
    <br>
    <form action = "\look\at">
      Select your new car's color.
      <br>
      <input type="radio" name="radios1" value="red">red
      <input type="radio" name="radios1" value="green">green
      <input type="radio" name="radios1" value="blue">blue
      <br>
      <br>
      <input type="submit"/>
    </form>
  </body>
</html>
```

The `params` hash for `radios1` will contain the value of the radio button selected by the user, and you can extract that data in the action:

```
class LookController < ApplicationController
  def at
    @data = params[:radios1]
  end
end
```

Then in the view, all that remains is to display the user's selection:

```
<html>
  <head>
    <title>Reading data from radio buttons</title>
  </head>
  <body>
    <h1>Reading data from radio buttons</h1>
    This Ruby on Rails application reads data from radio buttons.
    <br>
    <br>
    You selected <%= @data %>.
    <br>
    <br>
  </body>
</html>
```

You can see the opening page of this application, `http://localhost:3000/input.html`, in Figure 5-5.

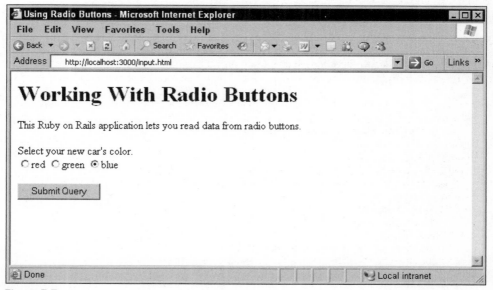

Figure 5-5

When you select a radio button and click the Submit Query button, the application tells you which radio button you selected, as you see in Figure 5-6.

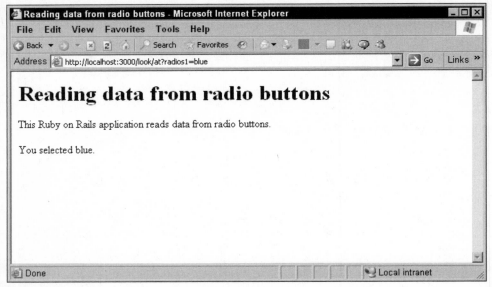

Figure 5-6

And that's all there is to it — now you're able to handle radio buttons as well as text fields and check-boxes. Ready for select controls, which display those drop-down list boxes?

Reading Data from Select Controls

As you might expect, working with select controls isn't hard. You create a select control with the `<select>` element in HTML, and fill it with `<option>` elements. Here's what the `input.html` page might look like in a new application, `selects`, which asks you to choose your new car's color:

```html
<html>
  <head>
    <title>Using Select Controls</title>
  </head>
  <body>
    <h1>Working With Select Controls</h1>
    This Ruby on Rails application lets you read data from select controls.
    <br>
    <form action = "\look\at">
      Select your new car's color.
      <br>
      <select name="select1" >
        <option value="red">red
        <option value="green">green
        <option value="blue">blue
      </select>
      <br>
      <br>
      <input type="submit"/>
```

```
      </form>
    </body>
  </html>
```

And you can read that data in the action like this:

```
class LookController < ApplicationController
  def at
    @data = params[:select1]
  end
end
```

Finally, you display the user's selection in the view:

```
<html>
  <head>
    <title>Reading data from select controls</title>
  </head>
  <body>
    <h1>Reading data from select controls</h1>
    This Ruby on Rails application reads data from select controls.
    <br>
    <br>
    You selected <%= @data %>
    <br>
    <br>
  </body>
</html>
```

Not so bad — in fact, much as if you were just working with a text field, as far as the Ruby code goes. You can see the opening web page in Figure 5-7.

Figure 5-7

When you select a car color and click Submit Query, you'll see the color you chose displayed in the view, as shown in Figure 5-8.

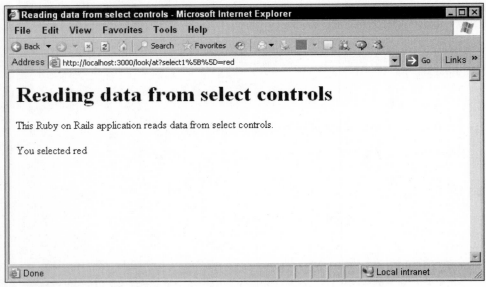

Figure 5-8

The real trick is to let the user make multiple selections, and that's just what you'll do in the following Try It Out.

Try It Out   **Read Multiple Selections from a Select Control**

To read multiple selections from a select control, follow these steps:

1. Create a new application named `selects`:

```
C:\rubydev\ch05>Rails selects
    .
    .
    .
```

2. Change directories to the selects directory:

```
C:\rubydev\ch05>cd selects
C:\rubydev\ch05\selects>
```

3. Add a controller named `look`:

```
C:\rubydev\ch05\selects>ruby script/generate controller Look
    .
    .
    .
```

4. Create a new file, rubydev\ch05\selects\public\input.html, adding this code:

```html
<html>
  <head>
    <title>Using Select Controls</title>
  </head>
  <body>
    <h1>Working With Select Controls</h1>
    This Ruby on Rails application lets you read data from select controls.
    <br>
    <form action = "\look\at">
      Select your new car's color.
      <br>
      <select name="select1[]" multiple size="3">
        <option value="red">red
        <option value="green">green
        <option value="blue">blue
      </select>
      <br>
      <br>
      <input type="submit"/>
    </form>
  </body>
</html>
```

5. Edit rubydev\ch05\selects\app\controllers\look_controller.rb, adding this code:

```ruby
class LookController < ApplicationController
  def at
    @data = params[:select1]
  end
end
```

6. Create a new view template for the application, rubydev\ch05\selects\app\views\look\at.rhtml:

```html
<html>
  <head>
    <title>Reading data from select controls</title>
  </head>
  <body>
    <h1>Reading data from select controls</h1>
    This Ruby on Rails application reads data from select controls.
    <br>
    <br>
    You selected <% for data in @data %>
    <%= data %>
    <% end %>
    <br>
    <br>
  </body>
</html>
```

7. Start the WEBrick server:

```
C:\rubydev\ch05\selects>ruby script/server
```

8. Navigate to `http://localhost:3000/input.html`. Figure 5-9 shows the web page, where you can make multiple selections for a multi-color car.

Figure 5-9

9. Select your colors, and click Submit Query. Figure 5-10 shows the result: your selection is displayed.

Figure 5-10

How It Works

To create a multiple-select list box, you use a multiple attribute in the `<select>` element, and set its size attribute (causing it to stay open, rather than act as a drop-down list — you can't make multiple selections in a drop-down list control). The trick as far as Rails goes is to append `[]` to the name of the control so that Rails knows you're dealing with a multiple-select control:

```
<select name="select1[]" multiple size="3">
```

Now the item you recover from the `params` hash will be an array, holding the multiple selections the user made:

```
@data = params[:select1]
```

And you can loop over that array in the view template, showing the selected colors:

```
You selected <% for data in @data %>
<%= data %>
<% end %>
```

Very nice.

Using Rails Shortcuts for HTML Controls

Rails supports shortcuts for HTML controls such as text fields and list controls, enabling you to set up those controls easily. For example, you can create text fields with the `text_field_tag` method, as you'll do in this Try It Out.

Try It Out   Create a Text Field with text_field_tag

To create a text field using the Rails `text_field_tag`, follow these steps:

1.   Create a new application named `textfields2`:

```
C:\rubydev\ch05>Rails textfields2
    .
    .
    .
```

2.   Change directories to the textfields2 directory:

```
C:\rubydev\ch05>cd textfields2
C:\rubydev\ch05\textfields2>
```

3.   Add a controller named `look`:

```
C:\rubydev\ch05\textfields2>ruby script/generate controller Look
    .
    .
    .
```

4. Edit rubydev\ch05\textfields2\app\controllers\look_controller.rb, adding this code:

```ruby
class LookController < ApplicationController
  def at
    @data = params[:text1]
  end

  def input
  end
end
```

5. Create a new view template for the application, rubydev\ch05\textfields2\app\views\look\ input.rhtml:

```html
<html>
  <head>
    <title>Using Text Fields</title>
  </head>
  <body>
    <h1>Working With Text Fields</h1>
    This Ruby on Rails application lets you read data from text fields.
    <br>
    <%= start_form_tag ({:action => "at"}, {:method => "post"}) %>
      Please enter your name.
      <br>
      <%= text_field_tag ("text1", "", {"size" => 30}) %>
      <br>
      <br>
      <input type="submit"/>
    <%= end_form_tag %>
  </body>
</html>
```

6. Create another new view template for the application, rubydev\ch05\textfields2\app\views\ look\at.rhtml:

```html
<html>
  <head>
    <title>Using HTML Control Shortcuts</title>
  </head>

  <body>
    <h1>Using HTML Control Shortcuts</h1>
    This application uses Rails HTML control shortcuts.
    <br>
    <br>
    Your name is <%= @data %>.
    <br>
    <br>
  </body>
</html>
```

7. Start the WEBrick server:

```
C:\rubydev\ch05\modeler>ruby script/server
```

8. Navigate to `http://localhost:3000/look/input`. Figure 5-11 shows the web page in which the application displays a text field.

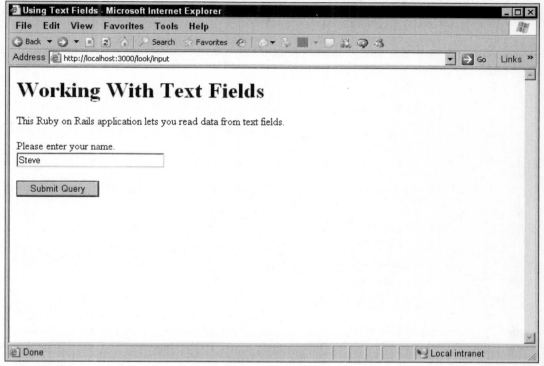

Figure 5-11

9. Enter your name and click the Submit Query button. The application displays your name on the web page (see Figure 5-12).

How It Works

This example uses the Rails `start_form_tag` method and the `text_field_tag` method to create a text field in a form. Here's how you can create the `<form>` element using `start_form_tag` and `end_form_tag`:

```
<%= start_form_tag ({:action => "at"}, {:method => "post"}) %>
  Please enter your name.
  <br>
  <br>
  <br>
  <input type="submit"/>
<%= end_form_tag %>
```

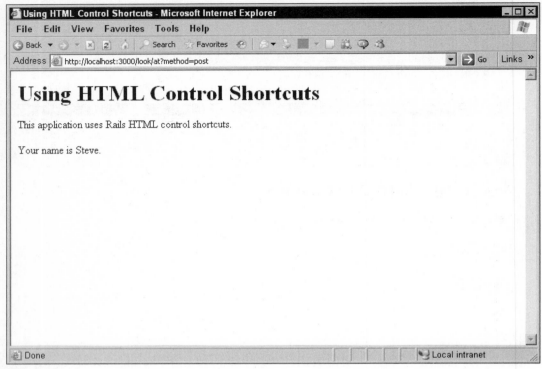

Figure 5-12

You pass the `start_form_tag` method a hash specifying the action, and an optional hash specifying options — the two possible options are `:method`, which can be `"get"` or `"post"` and `:multipart`, which can be `"true"` or `"false"`.

You create the text field using `text_field_tag` and pass the method the name of the text field (`"text1"` here), the original text you want to have appear in the text field when it first appears (just `""` here — an empty string, signifying no text), and an optional hash that can take settings for the standard HTML options `:disabled`, `:maxsize`, and `:size`:

```
<%= text_field_tag ("text1", "", {"size" => 30}) %>
```

There's also a `check_box_tag` method to create checkboxes, a `radio_button_tag` method to create radio buttons, and so on. For example, you use `check_box_tag`, where the checked argument can be true or false, and you can use the hash to pass HTML options for the checkbox: `check_box_tag(name, value, checked, {...})`. Here's how to set up a page with a checkbox using `check_box_tag`, in the `checkboxes2` application, as rubydev\ch05\checkboxes2\app\views\look\input.rhtml:

```
<html>
  <head>
    <title>Using Checkboxes</title>
  </head>
```

```
   <body>
     <h1>Working With Checkboxes</h1>
     This Ruby on Rails application lets you read data from checkboxes.
     <br>
     <%= start_form_tag ({:action => "at"}, {:method => "post"}) %>
       Would you like a raise?
       <br>
       <br>
       <%= check_box_tag ("check1", "Yes", false) %>Yes
       <br>
       <br>
       <input type="submit"/>
     <%= end_form_tag %>
   </body>
 </html>
```

And you set up the controller named `look` with two actions, `input` and `at`:

```
class LookController < ApplicationController
  def at
    @data = params[:check1]
  end

  def input
  end
end
```

Finally, here's what the `at` action's view, rubydev\ch05\checkboxes2\app\views\look\at.rhtml, looks like:

```
<html>
  <head>
    <title>Reading data from checkboxes</title>
  </head>
  <body>
    <h1>Reading data from checkboxes</h1>
    This Ruby on Rails application reads data from checkboxes.
    <br>
    <br>
    <% if @data %>
    You clicked yes.
    <% else %>
    You did not click yes.
    <% end %>
    <br>
    <br>
  </body>
</html>
```

This code works just as the checkboxes example you saw earlier did, except that it uses `check_box_tag` to create a checkbox. Working with select controls is similar. Here's how to create a multiple-select control in the input view of a new version of the selects application you saw earlier, `selects2`:

```
<html>
  <head>
    <title>Using Select Controls</title>
  </head>
  <body>
    <h1>Working With Select Controls</h1>
    This Ruby on Rails application lets you read data from select controls.
    <br>
    <%= start_form_tag ({:action => "at"}, {:method => "post"}) %>
    Select your new car's color.
    <br>
    <br>
    <%= select_tag ("select1[]", "<option value='red'>red<option
value='green'>green<option value='blue'>blue", {:multiple => true}) %>
    <br>
    <br>
    <input type="submit"/>
    <%= end_form_tag %>
  </body>
</html>
```

You pass `select_tag` the name of the select control, the option tags for use inside the select control, and a hash for HTML options, such as `:multiple`. Here's what the controller looks like:

```
class LookController < ApplicationController
  def at
    @data = params[:select1]
  end

  def input
  end
end
```

Here's the `at` view:

```
<html>
  <head>
    <title>Reading data from select controls</title>
  </head>
  <body>
    <h1>Reading data from select controls</h1>
    This Ruby on Rails application reads data from select controls.
    <br>
    <br>
    You selected <% for data in @data %>
    <%= data %>
    <% end %>
    <br>
    <br>
  </body>
</html>
```

Now all you have to do is to navigate to `http://localhost:3000/look/input`, and you'll see the same results as in the selects application earlier.

Working with Models

So far, you've seen controllers and you've seen views. That's two-thirds of the MVC equation. Now let's delve into working with *models*, the real data-crunchers in your application. That's what this next application is all about — seeing where models fit into Ruby on Rails web applications.

Try It Out **Use a Model**

To use a model, follow these steps:

1. Create a new application named `modeler`:

```
C:\rubydev\ch05>Rails modeler
```

2. Change directories to the modeler directory:

```
C:\rubydev\ch05>cd modeler
C:\rubydev\ch05\modeler>
```

3. Add a controller named `look`:

```
C:\rubydev\ch05\modeler>ruby script/generate controller Look
```

4. Create a new file, rubydev\ch05\modeler\app\models\cruncher.rb, placing this code in that file:

```
class Cruncher
  def crunch
    return 5
  end
end
```

5. Edit rubydev\ch05\modeler\app\controllers\look_controller.rb, adding this code:

```
class LookController < ApplicationController
  def at
    @cruncher = Cruncher.new
    @data = @cruncher.crunch
  end
end
```

6. Create a new view template for the application, rubydev\ch05\modeler\app\views\look\
at.rhtml:

```
<html>
  <head>
    <title>Using Models</title>
  </head>
  <body>
    <h1>Working With Models</h1>
    This application fetches data from a model.
    <br>
    <br>
    The fetched data is: <%= @data %>.
    <br>
```

```
      <br>
    </body>
  </html>
```

7. Start the WEBrick server:

```
C:\rubydev\ch05\modeler>ruby script/server
```

8. Navigate to `http://localhost:3000/input.html`.

9. You should see the web page in Figure 5-13, where the application has fetched the data, the number 5, from the model.

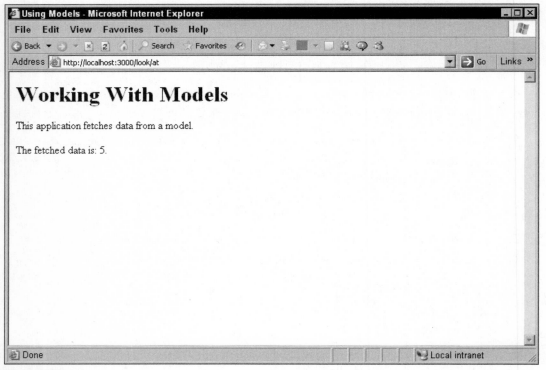

Figure 5-13

How It Works

To create a model, all you have to do is to place an `.rb` file in the application's models directory, such as `cruncher.rb` in this example. This first model simply is made up of a class named `Cruncher` and a method named `crunch`, which returns a value of 5:

```
class Cruncher
  def crunch
    return 5
  end
end
```

How do you use a model? You create an object of the model in an action and use that object's methods. In this example, that means creating an object of the `Cruncher` class and calling the `crunch` method to recover the data from the model:

```
class LookController < ApplicationController
  def at
    @cruncher = Cruncher.new
    @data = @cruncher.crunch
  end
end
```

Remember, the model contains the number-crunching business rules in the application — it doesn't know it's involved in a web application at all. It's the data handler in the application. Now you know how to add a model to a Rails application — just place the `.rb` file for the model in the models directory and create an object of the model class in an action. Then you're free to interact with the model as you want. Figure 5-14 illustrates how the model fits into a Ruby on Rails application.

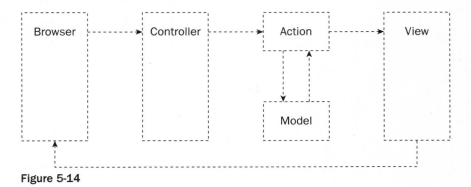

Figure 5-14

And now that you're working with models, you can use the Rails HTML control shortcuts to integrate the data the user enters into HTML controls.

Tying Controls to Models

Rails supports a number of methods — `text_field`, `select`, `check_box`, and so on — you can use to connect HTML controls directly to models. (These are not the same as the `text_field_tag`, `select_tag`, and so on methods that you saw earlier). For example, here's how you use `text_field` to create a text field and connect it to a model:

```
text_field(object_name, method, {...})
```

Here, `object_name` is the name of your model object, `method` is the accessor name of the data you want to tie to the control, and `{...}` is a hash that contains any HTML settings you want for the text field, such as `{"size" => 30}`. Tying the data in a control to your model makes it easier to store the user-entered data in your model.

Try It Out   Tie a Text Field to a Model

To tie a text field to a model, follow these steps:

1. Create a new application named `textfields3`:

```
C:\rubydev\ch05>Rails textfields3
```

2. Change directories to the textfields3 directory:

```
C:\rubydev\ch05>cd textfields3
C:\rubydev\ch05\textfields3>
```

3. Add a controller named `look`:

```
C:\rubydev\ch05\textfields3>ruby script/generate controller Look
```

4. Edit rubydev\ch05\textfields3\app\controllers\look_controller.rb, adding this code:

```ruby
class LookController < ApplicationController
  def at
    @data_hash = params[:cruncher]
    @cruncher = Cruncher.new(@data_hash[:crunch])

    @data = @cruncher.crunch
  end

  def input
  end
end
```

5. Create a new file, rubydev\ch05\textfields3\app\models\cruncher.rb, placing this code in that file:

```ruby
class Cruncher
  attr_reader :crunch
  attr_writer :crunch

  def initialize(data)
    @crunch = data
  end

end
```

6. Create a new view template for the application, rubydev\ch05\textfields3\app\views\look\input.rhtml:

```html
<html>
  <head>
    <title>Using Text Fields</title>
  </head>
  <body>
    <h1>Working With Text Fields</h1>
    This Ruby on Rails application lets you read data from text fields.
    <br>
    <%= start_form_tag ({:action => "at"}, {:method => "post"}) %>
      Please enter your name.
      <br>
      <%= text_field ("cruncher", "crunch", {"size" => 30}) %>
      <br>
      <br>
      <input type="submit"/>
    <%= end_form_tag %>
  </body>
</html>
```

7. Create another new view template for the application, rubydev\ch05\textfields3\app\views\look\at.rhtml:

```html
<html>
  <head>
    <title>Using HTML Control Shortcuts</title>
  </head>

  <body>
    <h1>Using HTML Control Shortcuts</h1>
    This application uses Rails HTML control shortcuts.
    <br>
    <br>
    Your name is <%= @data %>.
    <br>
    <br>
  </body>
</html>
```

8. Start the WEBrick server:

```
C:\rubydev\ch05\modeler>ruby script/server
```

9. Navigate to `http://localhost:3000/input.html`. You'll see a page much like the one in Figure 5-15.

10. Enter your name and click the Submit Query button. Your name is echoed, as in Figure 5-16.

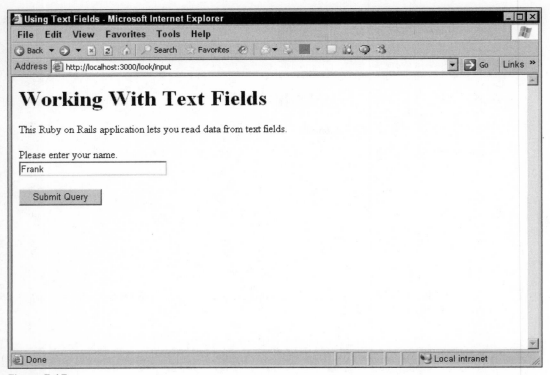

Figure 5-15

How It Works

This example has a model class named `Cruncher`, which supports an attribute named `crunch`:

```ruby
class Cruncher
  attr_reader :crunch
  attr_writer :crunch

  def initialize(data)
    @crunch = data
  end
```

Now you can tie the data in a text field to the `crunch` attribute using an object named `cruncher` like this in the view, rubydev\ch05\textfields3\app\views\look\input.rhtml:

```
<%= text_field ("cruncher", "crunch", {"size" => 30}) %>
```

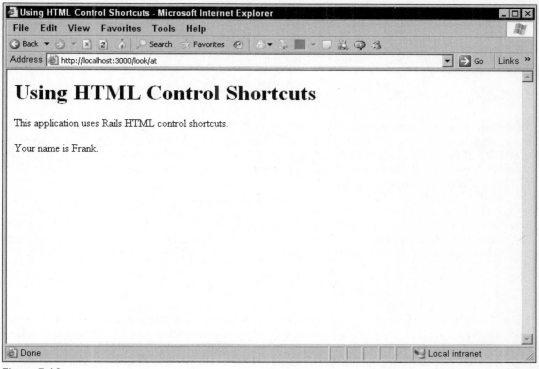

Figure 5-16

The data from this text field is passed back in a hash under the parameter name `:cruncher`, and you can access that hash in the `at` action:

```
def at
  @data_hash = params[:cruncher]
      .
      .
      .
end
```

`@data_hash` holds the data from the text field under the key `:crunch`, so you can initialize a new model object this way:

```
def at
  @data_hash = params[:cruncher]
  @cruncher = Cruncher.new(@data_hash[:crunch])
      .
      .
      .
end
```

Having loaded the model object from the text field, you can access its data like this:

```
def at
  @data_hash = params[:cruncher]
  @cruncher = Cruncher.new(@data_hash[:crunch])

  @data = @cruncher.crunch
end
```

That's how it works. Being able to store data from HTML controls in a hash is going to make life much easier when you want to handle the data from many controls in the same web page—you can store all that data in a single hash and pass that single hash to the model's constructor, as you're going to see in the next chapter. Connecting all the data from an entire web page to a model object is going to take only two lines of code, not dozens.

You can work with other HTML controls—including check_box, radio_button, and text_area— just as easily as text fields. Just pass the name of the model object, the attribute of the model object, and your HTML options in a hash. Then fill the model object using the data you get in the controller:

```
@data_hash = params[:cruncher]
@cruncher = Cruncher.new(@data_hash[:crunch])
```

The only aspect that takes a little extra consideration is when you're dealing with multiple data items from a control, as when you're working with a multiple-selection select control. The key to handling that is ensuring that the control is given a name with [] at the end to let Rails know it's dealing with an array. However, specifying both the model object name and the model attribute name like this:

```
<%= text_field ("cruncher", "crunch", {"size" => 30}) %>
```

results in naming the control cruncher[crunch], which does not end in []. One way to fix that is to omit the attribute when creating the multiple-select control:

```
<html>
  <head>
    <title>Using Select Controls</title>
  </head>
  <body>
    <h1>Working With Select Controls</h1>
    This Ruby on Rails application lets you read data from select controls.
    <br>
    <%= start_form_tag ({:action => "at"}) %>
      Select your new car's color.
      <br>
      <br>
      <%= select ("cruncher", "", {'red' => 'red', 'green' => 'green',
        'blue' => 'blue'}, {}, {:multiple => true, :size => 3}) %>
      <br>
      <br>
      <input type="submit"/>
    <%= end_form_tag %>
  </body>
</html>
```

This creates the name you need, `cruncher[]`:

```
<select id="cruncher_" multiple="multiple" name="cruncher[]" size="3">
  <option value="green">green</option>
  <option value="blue">blue</option>
  <option value="red">red</option>
</select>
```

And makes Rails pass you an array holding the multiple selections the user makes in the select control. You can get that array from the `params` hash, using the key `:cruncher`:

```
def at
  @data_array = params[:cruncher]

      .
      .
      .

end
```

Then you can pass that array to the model's constructor:

```
def at
  @data_array = params[:cruncher]
  @cruncher = Cruncher.new(@data_array)

  @data = @cruncher.crunch
end
```

And you're in business — you're able to handle multiple selections this way, as shown in the `selects3` application.

Initializing Data in Controls

Tying HTML controls to a model object has another benefit — you can initialize the data displayed in those controls the first time they appear in the browser. You do that simply by initializing the model object that's tied to the control. Try it yourself in the following exercise.

Try It Out   **Initialize Data in an HTML Control**

To initialize the text in the text field in the `textfields3` application you just developed, follow these steps:

1.   Edit rubydev\ch05\textfields3\app\controllers\look_controller.rb, adding this code:

```
class LookController < ApplicationController
  def at
    @data_hash = params[:cruncher]
    @cruncher = Cruncher.new(@data_hash[:crunch])

    @data = @cruncher.crunch
  end

  def input
```

```
      @cruncher = Cruncher.new("Steve")
    end
  end
```

2. Start the WEBrick server:

```
C:\rubydev\ch05\modeler>ruby script/server
```

3. Navigate to `http://localhost:3000/input.html`. The web page opens with the text field already initialized, as shown in Figure 5-17.

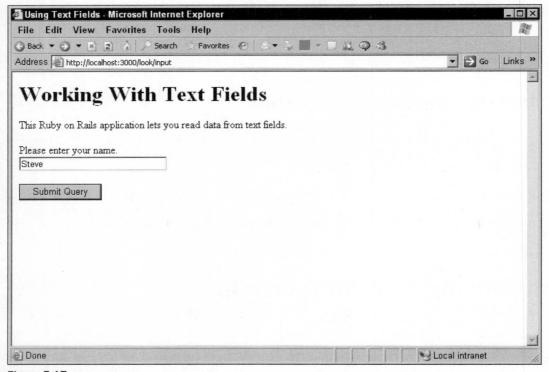

Figure 5-17

How It Works

In this example, the text field is tied to a model object named `cruncher`, and an attribute of that object named `crunch`:

```
<%= text_field ("cruncher", "crunch", {"size" => 30}) %>
```

You create an object named `crunch` with a `crunch` attribute in the action that displays the page containing the text field, and Rails uses the value of that attribute to initialize the text field. Here's how to create the model object that initializes the `crunch` attribute:

```
    def input
      @cruncher = Cruncher.new("Steve")
    end
```

Here's the code for the model — note the `crunch` attribute:

```
class Cruncher
  attr_reader :crunch
  attr_writer :crunch

  def initialize(data)
    @crunch = data
  end

end
```

Storing Data in Sessions

All this data handling in web pages brings up a crucial point — what happens to your data between web page accesses? That's important because by default, web applications are stateless — a fancy word that means your data isn't stored at all. Each time you call a new action, the data in your application is initialized back to its original values.

That can be a problem — what if you need to check whether the user has logged in, for example, or need to store his shopping cart selections? Fortunately, you can store data in *sessions*. A session is made up of memory on the server, and you access that memory using the hash named `session`.

To store a data item in the session, you just place it in the `session` hash using a key:

```
session[:data] = @data
```

Then, when you want to recover that data when the same — or another — action is called in your web application, you recover your data this way:

```
@data = session[:data]
```

For example, you can create a counter variable in which you might store the number of page accesses; storing that variable's value in the session makes sure that that value is accessible to you every time the page is refreshed.

> The data in a session isn't permanent. By default it times out after 15 minutes of inactivity on the user's part.

Try your hand at using a session hash in the following exercise.

Try It Out   Store Data in a Session

To store data in a session, follow these steps:

1. Create a new application named `sessions`:

```
C:\rubydev\ch05>Rails sessions
```

2. Change directories to the sessions directory:

```
C:\rubydev\ch05>cd sessions
C:\rubydev\ch05\sessions>
```

3. Add a controller named `look`:

```
C:\rubydev\ch05\sessions>ruby script/generate controller Look
```

4. Edit rubydev\ch05\sessions\app\controllers\look_controller.rb, adding this code:

```
class LookController < ApplicationController
  def at
    @counter1 = 1


    if(session[:counter2])
      @counter2 = session[:counter2]
      @counter2 += 1
      session[:counter2] = @counter2
    else
      @counter2 = 1
      session[:counter2] = @counter2
    end
  end
end
```

5. Create a new view template for the application, rubydev\ch05\textfields2\app\views\look\input.rhtml:

```
<html>
  <head>
    <title>Using Sessions</title>
  </head>
  <body>
    <h1>Working With Sessions</h1>
    This Ruby on Rails application lets you store data in sessions.
    <%= start_form_tag ({:action => "at"}, {:method => "post"}) %>
      <br>
      Counter 1: <%= @counter1 %>.
      <br>
      Counter 2: <%= @counter2 %>.
      <br>
      <br>
      <input type="submit"/>
```

```
        <%= end_form_tag %>
    </body>
</html>
```

6. Start the WEBrick server:

```
C:\rubydev\ch05\modeler>ruby script/server
```

7. Navigate to `http://localhost:3000/look/input`. The application displays the values of two counters in the web page (see Figure 5-18). Counter 1 is not stored in a session, and Counter 2 is.

Figure 5-18

8. Click the Submit Query button. The result (see Figure 5-19) is that Counter 1 displays the same value it had before, but Counter 2 is incremented.

How It Works

This example displays two counters and increments their values each time the action is called. The application stores the value of Counter 2 in the session. Counter 1 is not stored in the session, and so it's created anew every time:

```
def at
  @counter1 = 1
```

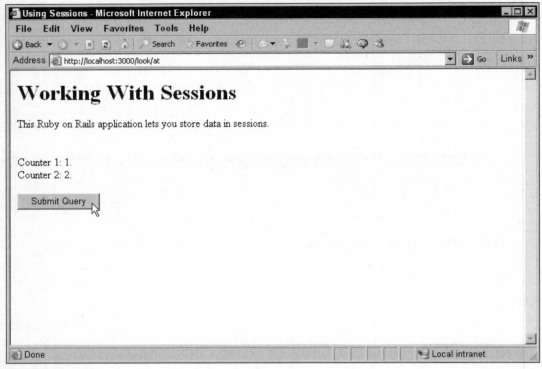

Figure 5-19

But Counter 2 is stored in the session, so its value is preserved between calls to the action:

```
if(session[:counter2])
   @counter2 = session[:counter2]
   @counter2 += 1
   session[:counter2] = @counter2
else
   @counter2 = 1
   session[:counter2] = @counter2
```

The result is as you see in Figures 5-17 and 5-18 — Counter 1 is reinitialized each time you call the action, whereas Counter 2's value is preserved, and it increments as it should.

Storing data in a session can be a good idea when you want to preserve that data between calls to actions. But what about when the user walks away? In that case, you want to store the data on the server's hard drive; as you're going to see in the next chapter, Rails is especially set up to let you work with and store data in databases on the server.

Summary

In this chapter, you got some important points about Rails applications down, including learning how to:

❑ Read data from text fields, checkboxes, radio buttons, and select controls created with `<input>` and `<select>` elements.

❑ Employ Rails shortcuts, such as `text_field_tag` and `check_box_tag`, to create HTML controls.

❑ Work with models by placing an `.rb` file for the model's class in the models directory of your application.

❑ Connect controls to models using Rails methods such as `text_field`, `select`, and `check_box`.

❑ Initialize data in HTML controls so they display that data the first time they appear.

❑ Store and retrieve data in sessions.

In the next chapter, you work with databases in Rails applications. First, though, try the exercises that follow to test your understanding of the material covered in this chapter. The solutions are in Appendix A.

Exercises

1. Add a second text field to the `textfields` example (which uses `<input>` elements to create a text field) to get the user's age, and then display that age.

2. Add a second text field to the `textfields2` example (which uses the `text_field_tag` method to create a text field) to get the user's age, and then display that age.

3. Add a second text field to the `textfields3` example (which uses the `text_field` method to create a text field) to get the user's age, and then display that age.

Connecting to Databases

Web applications often store data online on a server. And most often, they use databases to store that information. Ruby on Rails is especially built to handle databases online easily.

What is a database? If you already know, you can skip the following tutorial and continue reading the next topic, "Creating a Data-Aware Rails Application." If you're not sure you know all about databases, just read through the tutorial as a refresher.

Tutorial on Databases

If you're teaching a Ruby on Rails class and want to keep track of your students' grades, you might write those grades down in a table on a sheet of paper, something like Figure 6-1.

Name	Grade	ID
Tom	A	1
Carol	B	2
Frank	B	3
Anne	A	4
Sam	A	5
Nancy	B	6
Pat	C	7

Figure 6-1

This is actually a paper version of what is called a *table* in a database. Database tables work just like the tables you've probably written out on paper many times. In this instance, you divide your data into columns (see Figure 6-2), such as Name, Grade, and ID in the students table.

Column 1   Column 2   Column 3

Name	Grade	ID
Tom	A	1
Carol	B	2
Frank	B	3
Anne	A	4
Sam	A	5
Nancy	B	6
Pat	C	7

Figure 6-2

Each student gets a *record* in the table. A record is a row in the table, as shown in Figure 6-3, and it contains all of the columns' information for a particular student: name, grade, and ID.

Name	Grade	ID	
Tom	A	1	← Row 1
Carol	B	2	← Row 2
Frank	B	3	← Row 3
Anne	A	4	← Row 4
Sam	A	5	← Row 5
Nancy	B	6	← Row 6
Pat	C	7	← Row 7

Figure 6-3

That's the way it works — you create a table in a database simply by putting together the columns and rows of that table. (The intersection of a column and a row is called a *field*; a row in this example has three fields: Name, Grade, and ID.)

Databases can contain many tables, and in a *relational* database, you can relate those tables together. For example, you may also want to keep track of how much money each student owes you in addition to the students table information. This new table might be called fees, and it might look like Figure 6-4.

ID	Owes
1	20,005.00
2	19,005.00
3	23,005.00
4	21,005.00
5	22,005.00
6	20,005.00
7	21,005.00

Figure 6-4

The `fees` table keeps track of the amount each student owes by ID. If you wanted to know how much the student named Tom owed, but didn't have his ID handy, you could look up Tom in the `students` table, find his ID, and use it in the `fees` table. In other words, the records in the `students` and `fees` tables are tied together by the `ID` field, as Figure 6-5 shows.

Name	Grade	ID		ID	Owes
Tom	A	1	←→	1	20,005.00
Carol	B	2	←→	2	19,005.00
Frank	B	3	←→	3	23,005.00
Anne	A	4	←→	4	21,005.00
Sam	A	5	←→	5	22,005.00
Nancy	B	6	←→	6	20,005.00
Pat	C	7	←→	7	21,005.00

Figure 6-5

You can store these two tables, `students` and `fees`, in a single database, and relate them, record by record, using the `ID` field. A field that you use to connect records in a table to records in another table is called a *primary key*. The `ID` field in the `students` table is that table's primary key. The primary key is the main data item you use to index records in a table. You're going to need an ID column in tables you use with Rails applications — actually, Rails needs `id`, not `ID` — and case is important. Each table should have a column named `id`.

OK, you've got all you need to start working with databases — that wasn't hard, was it? The next step is to transfer all this knowledge to creating Rails applications.

Creating a Data-Aware Rails Application

It's time to see how Rails applications interface with databases. Rails applications are configured by default to work with the MySQL database server, which you can download for free from `http://dev`
`.mysql.com`. This book uses the MySQL database server because that's by far the most common option for use with Ruby on Rails, but you can use Ruby on Rails with many other database servers, too — see the instructions that come with Rails.

To work through the database projects in this book, download and install MySQL — generally, it's easy; just follow the instructions. One caveat: make sure you remember the password you create during installation, because you're going to need that for your database work with Rails.

> **Remember the MySQL password you create.**

You're going to see how to construct an online store in this chapter and the next. You need two controllers — the management controller used to update the online database with what's in stock and set prices, and the customer controller used to let people buy from the store.

Begin by creating the `store` application itself. In the book's code, this application is placed in the ch06 directory:

```
C:\rubydev\ch06>rails store
```

OK, that gives you the application framework. In the next section you'll set it up with a database.

Creating the Database

After installing MySQL, it'll be up and running when you boot your machine. To create the database for the `store` application to use, start the MySQL monitor on the command line like this:

```
C:\rubydev\ch06>mysql -u root -p
```

This command gives `root` as the username and tells the MySQL monitor to ask for a password. Enter the password you set during MySQL installation at the prompt:

```
C:\rubydev\ch06>mysql -u root -p
Enter password: ********
```

That logs you on as root, the most powerful of the MySQL logins. (You don't need to log in as root, of course; if you've set up a MySQL account — see the MySQL documentation — you can log in using that account.) After you've entered your password, the MySQL monitor prints out a greeting and displays a prompt, `mysql>`:

```
C:\rubydev\ch06>mysql -u root -p
Enter password: ********
```

```
Welcome to the MySQL monitor.  Commands end with ; or \g.
Your MySQL connection id is 1 to server version: 5.0.19-nt

Type 'help;' or '\h' for help. Type '\c' to clear the buffer.

mysql>
```

Your goal is to create a database to hold the items for sale in your online store. In fact, establish three databases — one for development, one for testing, and one for production. Name them `store_development`, `store_test`, and `store_production`, and create them using the `create database` command in the MySQL monitor:

```
mysql> create database store_development;
Query OK, 1 row affected (0.06 sec)

mysql> create database store_test;
Query OK, 1 row affected (0.01 sec)

mysql> create database store_production;
Query OK, 1 row affected (0.00 sec)
```

Because everything's in the development phase now, it's best to work with the development database, `store_development`, at this point. To make MySQL work with that database, enter the `use` command and the name of the database to use, `store_development`:

```
mysql> use store_development
Database changed
mysql>
```

Now create a table in the `store_development` database. This table will hold the items for sale in your online store, so a good name for this table is simply `items`. You can create a new table named `items` in the `store_development` database with the `create table` command:

```
mysql> create table items (
```

You need to create the columns for this new table, too, which means there'll be too much to fit on a single line, so press Enter to break to the next line. When the MySQL monitor sees that you haven't ended the command with a semicolon (`;`), it displays a prompt, `->`, for you to keep going:

```
mysql> create table items (
    ->
```

This is the table that will keep track of the items you have for sale, so you should store at least the items' names and descriptions. You'll also need an `id` field in each record for Rails to use. And you should keep track of each item's price as well, making the whole table look like Figure 6-6.

The `id` field has to be an integer field, and you can make it an auto-increment field that will start with 1 and increase automatically each time you add a new record (it's not necessary to make this field an auto-increment field):

```
mysql> create table items (
    -> id          int      not null       auto_increment,
```

id	name	description	price

Figure 6-6

You can make the name field 80 characters long with varchar(80):

```
mysql> create table items (
    -> id       int     not null        auto_increment,
    -> name     varchar(80)     not null,
```

The description is just plain text, so you can set up that field this way:

```
mysql> create table items (
    -> id       int     not null        auto_increment,
    -> name     varchar(80)     not null,
    -> description      text    not null,
```

Finally, the price field is a decimal number — you can make it, say, 8 digits long with two decimal places using decimal(8, 2):

```
mysql> create table items (
    -> id       int     not null        auto_increment,
    -> name     varchar(80)     not null,
    -> description      text    not null,
    -> price    decimal(8, 2)   not null,
```

Finally, you can use the id field as the primary key and inform MySQL of that fact, as well as close the parentheses and add a semicolon:

```
mysql> create table items (
    -> id       int     not null        auto_increment,
    -> name     varchar(80)     not null,
    -> description      text    not null,
    -> price    decimal(8, 2)   not null,
    -> primary key(id)
    -> );
```

MySQL responds with:

```
Query OK, 0 rows affected (0.06 sec)
```

That's because this is a SQL (Standard Query Language) command, and although it doesn't look like a query, that's the official name. You're done creating the `store` database and the `items` table in it, so just exit MySQL:

```
mysql> exit
Bye
```

OK, you've set up the database part of things, even though you haven't stored any data in it yet — that's what the Rails application you're going to work on will do. Next you'll connect the database to your application.

Configuring Database Access

In the `rubydev\ch06\store\config` directory, you'll find a file named `database.yml`. It lets you connect your application to your database. Here's what the file looks like currently:

What's a `.yml` file? It's a YAML file. YAML, a recursive acronym for YAML Ain't Markup Language, is a data serialization language. The creators of Rails are proud of the fact that they don't use XML or other markup languages for configuration purposes, as most other online application frameworks do, hence "YAML."

```
# MySQL (default setup).  Versions 4.1 and 5.0 are recommended.
#
# Install the MySQL driver:
#   gem install mysql
# On MacOS X:
#   gem install mysql -- --include=/usr/local/lib
# On Windows:
#   There is no gem for Windows.  Install mysql.so from RubyForApache.
#   http://rubyforge.org/projects/rubyforapache
#
# And be sure to use new-style password hashing:
#   http://dev.mysql.com/doc/refman/5.0/en/old-client.html
development:
  adapter: mysql
  database: store_development
  username: root
  password:
  host: localhost

# Warning: The database defined as 'test' will be erased and
# re-generated from your development database when you run 'rake'.
# Do not set this db to the same as development or production.
test:
  adapter: mysql
  database: store_test
  username: root
  password:
```

```
      host: localhost

production:
   adapter: mysql
   database: store_production
   username: root
   password:
   host: localhost
```

Note that there is a database set up for each of the databases you created: `store_development`, `store_test`, and `store_production`. That's not a coincidence; when you use Rails to create a new application, those databases are set up automatically in the config directory's `database.yml` file, using the new application's name (that's `store` here). So in the `store` application, `store_development`, `store_test`, and `store_production` are automatically listed in `database.yml`.

By default, Rails uses the development database, `store_development` — the database you added the `items` table to. To let Rails connect to the databases listed in `database.yml`, you have to fill in the username and password fields, editing the `.yml` file directly. The username field comes with `root` already in place, and this example leaves it set to `root`, although you can use the username of any account you've set up with your database server. Add the password you've set up for your account — for example, say that for the `root` account, you use a password that's `open_sesame`; that would look like this:

```
development:
   ...
   username: root
   password: open_sesame
   ...
   ...
test:
   ...
   username: root
   password: open_sesame
   ...
   ...
production:
   username: root
   password: open_sesame
```

Storing your passwords in a file this way might not seem the most secure way of doing things, but it is fairly secure. On an online web server, you should set up the `database.yml`'s protection so that it can't be accessed by the public at large. The problem is that Rails is going to need those passwords to connect to your database server — there's no way around it. So unless you want to physically type in those passwords each time you start Rails, storing them in a `.yml` file is a reasonable alternative.

OK, you've let Rails connect to your database server — theoretically, at least. The next step is to connect your model to your database. That sounds like it could be quite a chore — and it could be. Fortunately, Rails comes to the rescue with a utility called `scaffold`.

Creating the Controller and Model

Actually connecting the database to your code could be tough, but Rails has a utility named `scaffold` that makes the process easy. The purpose of `scaffold` is much as it sounds: to create a scaffold for your application — that is, a framework that you can fill in, or not, as you decide.

You can use the `scaffold` utility to build a model and controller for data-aware applications. Here's how you'd do so:

1. Change directories to the rubydev\ch06\store directory:

```
C:\>cd \rubydev\ch06\store>ruby
C:\rubydev\ch06\store>
```

2. Create a model named `Item` and a controller named `Manage` this way:

```
C:\rubydev\ch06\store>ruby script/generate scaffold Item Manage
```

3. Rails creates the controller and model:

```
C:\rubydev\ch06\store>ruby script/generate scaffold Item Manage
      exists  app/controllers/
      exists  app/helpers/
      create  app/views/manage
      exists  test/functional/
  dependency  model
      exists    app/models/
      exists    test/unit/
      exists    test/fixtures/
      create    app/models/item.rb
      create    test/unit/item_test.rb
      create    test/fixtures/items.yml
      create  app/views/manage/_form.rhtml
      create  app/views/manage/list.rhtml
      create  app/views/manage/show.rhtml
      create  app/views/manage/new.rhtml
      create  app/views/manage/edit.rhtml
      create  app/controllers/manage_controller.rb
      create  test/functional/manage_controller_test.rb
      create  app/helpers/manage_helper.rb
      create  app/views/layouts/manage.rhtml
      create  public/stylesheets/scaffold.css
```

Rails' `scaffold` utility builds the application's model and controller. The model is named `item.rb`, and it contains a new class named `Item`, inherited from `ActiveRecord::Base`:

```
class Item < ActiveRecord::Base
end
```

`ActiveRecord` is the module that contains the Rails support for working with databases, and the `Base` class is the primary class on which you base database-aware models. You're going to see considerably more about `ActiveRecord` and `ActiveRecord::Base` in this book — they are what connect to your database.

Naming the Model

The name of the model, `Item`, was specially chosen. As you may recall, the database created for the `store` application was named `store_development`, and the table contained inside that database was named `items`. The two names — `Item` and `items` — are tied together.

This is an important point. The database table you're working with when you create a Rails application using `scaffold` should have a plural name, and the model should be the same as that name, except that it's singular and initial capped. That's the Rails convention.

That means that if you create a database table named `books`, your model should be named `Book`, and be stored in a file named `book.rb`. This singular/plural convention is a significant one to keep in mind when you create database-aware Rails applications. It's a little irksome — there's no reason the database table and model can't share the same name — but there it is.

You might ask: doesn't this sort of paint `scaffold` into a corner? After all, it has to figure out the plural of the name you specify for the model. That's not a problem if you specify an easy name like `Item` — `scaffold` can figure out that the table it should work with is going to be named `items` (and recall that by default, Rails applications connect to a database named using the name of the application followed by `_development`, which makes the database this application will use by default `store_development`).

But what if you wanted to keep track of a set of people, and so specified a model named `Person`? Wouldn't the table scaffold expect to find `persons`? Actually, no. To support the Rails convention of singular/plural model/table naming, the Rails developers added code to `scaffold` to find the right plurals for many words. In this case, for example, `scaffold` will write code to connect to the database table named `people`, not `persons`. Obviously, though, `scaffold` can't handle all possible plurals, so be careful when using offbeat names (a little caution might be indicated when you track those `hippopotami`, for instance).

Another thing to know is how Rails handles underscores; if a table is named, say, `my_items`, then the model to connect to it should be named `MyItems`. That's the Rails convention.

Naming the Controller

You can choose the name of the controller with more freedom. In the example application, the controller is to be used when managing the online store — adding new items for sale, listing the prices, and so on, so the controller is simply named `Manage`.

That creates a controller class named `ManageController`, inherited from `ApplicationController`, just as the controllers you saw earlier. However, `scaffold` stocks this controller with code, as you see here in `manager_controller.rb`:

```
class ManageController < ApplicationController
  def index
    list
    render :action => 'list'
  end

  # GETs should be safe (see http://www.w3.org/2001/tag/doc/whenToUseGet.html)
  verify :method => :post, :only => [ :destroy, :create, :update ],
```

```
                          :redirect_to => { :action => :list }

        def list
          @item_pages, @items = paginate :items, :per_page => 10
        end

        def show
          @item = Item.find(params[:id])
        end

        def new
          @item = Item.new
        end

        def create
          @item = Item.new(params[:item])
          if @item.save
            flash[:notice] = 'Item was successfully created.'
            redirect_to :action => 'list'
          else
            render :action => 'new'
          end
        end

        def edit
          @item = Item.find(params[:id])
        end

        def update
          @item = Item.find(params[:id])
          if @item.update_attributes(params[:item])
            flash[:notice] = 'Item was successfully updated.'
            redirect_to :action => 'show', :id => @item
          else
            render :action => 'edit'
          end
        end

        def destroy
          Item.find(params[:id]).destroy
          redirect_to :action => 'list'
        end
      end
```

As you can see, a number of actions have already been built into the Manage controller. How about taking a look at them in action?

Running the store Application

Change directories to the rubydev\ch06\store directory and run WEBrick to start the store application like this:

```
C:\rubydev\ch06\store>ruby script/server
=> Booting WEBrick...
=> Rails application started on http://0.0.0.0:3000
=> Ctrl-C to shutdown server; call with --help for options
[2006-05-30 11:23:26] INFO  WEBrick 1.3.1
[2006-05-30 11:23:26] INFO  ruby 1.8.2 (2004-12-25) [i386-mswin32]
[2006-05-30 11:23:26] INFO  WEBrick::HTTPServer#start: pid=1252 port=3000
```

Now navigate to `http://localhost:3000/manage`, as shown in Figure 6-7. You see the titles of the fields in the items table — Name, Description, and Price. In other words, the model was successful in connecting to the `items` database table. (The `id` field isn't shown because it's an auto-increment field.)

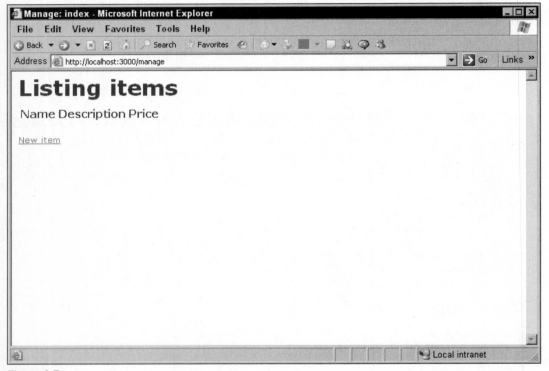

Figure 6-7

By entering simply the name of the controller, without an action, in the URL (`http://localhost:3000/manage`), you called the default `index` action, which looks like this in the `manage_controller.rb` file:

```
class ManageController < ApplicationController
  def index
    list
    render :action => 'list'
  end
end
```

This method calls the `list` action, which loads the current items in the `items` table into `@item_pages` and `@items`:

```
def list
  @item_pages, @items = paginate :items, :per_page => 10
end
```

The `index` action then calls `render :action => 'list'` to render the view associated with the `list` action, which is rubydev\ch06\store\app\views\manage\list.rhtml. The list view lists the current records in the `items` table. However, there are no records to display yet. Change that by adding some. Just click the New Item link you see in Figure 6-7.

Adding a Record to the store Application

The New Item link links to `http://localhost:3000/manage/new`, bringing up the page shown in Figure 6-8. This is the page that lets you create new records by entering data into various HTML controls—a text field for the name of the new item you're creating in the store's database, a text area for its description, and so on.

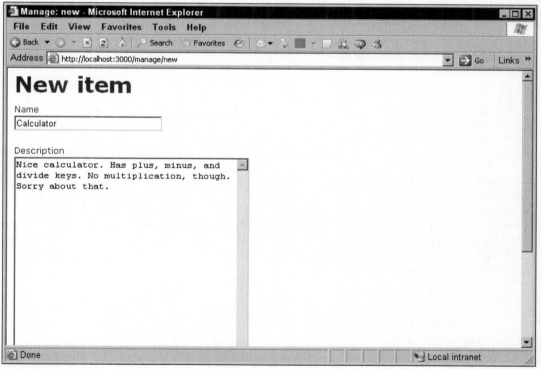

Figure 6-8

The New Item link accesses the `new` action to display the page you see in Figure 6-8, which creates a new record using the model class, `Item`:

```
  def new
    @item = Item.new
  end
```

The view for the `new` action, rubydev\ch06\store\app\views\manage\new.rhtml, looks like this:

```
<h1>New item</h1>

<%= start_form_tag :action => 'create' %>
  <%= render :partial => 'form' %>
  <%= submit_tag "Create" %>
<%= end_form_tag %>

<%= link_to 'Back', :action => 'list' %>
```

There are a few things to note here. First, this view includes an HTML form tied to the `create` action, which does the actual creation of the new record. Where is the HTML for the Name text field, the Description text area, and so on? That's in another view, which is accessed with `render :partial => 'form'` this way:

```
<h1>New item</h1>

<%= start_form_tag :action => 'create' %>
  <%= render :partial => 'form' %>
  <%= submit_tag "Create" %>
<%= end_form_tag %>

<%= link_to 'Back', :action => 'list' %>
```

You already know about the `render` method — that's the method that lets you display a view in the browser. When you render a partial view, you render it in-place — that is, inside the current view. So `render :partial => 'form'` really means "display the form view at this location in the current view."

Partial rendering is great when you want to construct a composite view, built up using other views. In this case, the form view will display the needed HTML controls to let you enter data for new records in the `items` table. Partial view templates are considered special in Rails, however, so the form view isn't simply stored in a file whose name is `form.rhtml` — it's `_form.rhtml`, with a leading underscore. You'll find that view template, `_form.rhtml`, as rubydev\ch06\store\app\views\manage_form.rhtml. This template just includes the HTML controls needed to get the data for each new record (you'll see the `error_messages_for` method in Chapter 7):

```
<%= error_messages_for 'item' %>

<!--[form:item]-->
<p><label for="item_name">Name</label><br/>
<%= text_field 'item', 'name'  %></p>

<p><label for="item_description">Description</label><br/>
<%= text_area 'item', 'description'  %></p>

<p><label for="item_price">Price</label><br/>
<%= text_field 'item', 'price'  %></p>
<!--[eoform:item]-->
```

This view template, _form.rhtml, is inserted into the view for the new action, inside the HTML form connected to the create action:

```
<h1>New item</h1>

<%= start_form_tag :action => 'create' %>
  <%= render :partial => 'form' %>
  <%= submit_tag "Create" %>
<%= end_form_tag %>

<%= link_to 'Back', :action => 'list' %>
```

When you fill out the controls in this view with the data for the new record and click the Create button, you navigate to the create action, which looks like this in the manage controller:

```
def create
  @item = Item.new(params[:item])
  if @item.save
    flash[:notice] = 'Item was successfully created.'
    redirect_to :action => 'list'
  else
    render :action => 'new'
  end
end
```

This is where the new record is created. As you saw, the data you entered was stored in a form connected to a model object named item, with name, description, and price accessors in _form.rhtml:

```
<p><label for="item_name">Name</label><br/>
<%= text_field 'item', 'name'  %></p>

<p><label for="item_description">Description</label><br/>
<%= text_area 'item', 'description'  %></p>

<p><label for="item_price">Price</label><br/>
<%= text_field 'item', 'price'  %></p>
```

In the create action, Rails uses the information entered into the _form view to create a new model object like this:

```
def create
  @item = Item.new(params[:item])
    .
    .
    .
end
```

Then the create action attempts to save the new record in the database, using the model's save method (built into ActiveRecord::Base, the class from which the Item class inherits) this way:

```
def create
  @item = Item.new(params[:item])
```

```
      if @item.save
          .
          .
          .
      end
  end
```

If the `save` operation is successful, the `save` method returns a value of true, and the `create` action executes this code:

```
def create
  @item = Item.new(params[:item])
  if @item.save
    flash[:notice] = 'Item was successfully created.'
    redirect_to :action => 'list'
        .
        .
        .
  end
end
```

It's easy enough to understand the `redirect_to` method — it redirects the browser to the `list` action, which lists all the records in the `items` table in the browser. But what's the line `flash[:notice] = 'Item was successfully created.'`?

The Rails `flash` is a hash that lets you store data temporarily in the session, and it's deleted automatically in the next action. You use the `flash` to pass data to a new action after redirecting the user to that new action. This is one of those tricky things that online programming sometimes excels at. You need to store data in a `flash` in this case, because you're redirecting the browser to a new action:

```
flash[:notice] = 'Item was successfully created.'
redirect_to :action => 'list'
```

The `redirect` action doesn't take place on the server — it takes place in the browser. That means the online application loses control of execution because the control is passed to the browser. The browser then calls the `new` action, and in that action you can retrieve the message that was stored in the `flash` (using the key `:notice` here), and display it. So using a `flash` is just a technique for passing data on to the next action after using a `redirect`.

In this case, the new item has been successfully created, so the message passed on to the `list` action is `'Item was successfully created.'`. If the new item had not been successfully created, the code renders the `new` action so you can try to create the item again:

```
def create
  @item = Item.new(params[:item])
  if @item.save
    flash[:notice] = 'Item was successfully created.'
    redirect_to :action => 'list'
  else
    render :action => 'new'
  end
end
```

Fill in the data for a new item for sale, a calculator. As shown in Figure 6-8, give it the name Calculator, the description "Nice calculator. Has plus, minus, and divide keys. No multiplication, though. Sorry about that.", and the price $200.99. Then click the Create button to create the new record.

At this point, the `create` action creates the new item and, if successful, redirects the browser to the `list` action, which displays the new record in the browser.

Displaying a New Record

Here's what `list.rhtml` looks like:

```
<h1>Listing items</h1>

<table>
  <tr>
  <% for column in Item.content_columns %>
    <th><%= column.human_name %></th>
  <% end %>
  </tr>

<% for item in @items %>
  <tr>
  <% for column in Item.content_columns %>
    <td><%=h item.send(column.name) %></td>
  <% end %>
    <td><%= link_to 'Show', :action => 'show', :id => item %></td>
    <td><%= link_to 'Edit', :action => 'edit', :id => item %></td>
    <td><%= link_to 'Destroy', { :action => 'destroy', :id => item }, :confirm =>
'Are you sure?', :post => true %></td>
  </tr>
<% end %>
</table>

<%= link_to 'Previous page', { :page => @item_pages.current.previous } if
@item_pages.current.previous %>
<%= link_to 'Next page', { :page => @item_pages.current.next } if
@item_pages.current.next %>

<br />

<%= link_to 'New item', :action => 'new' %>
```

This is the template for the page that presents the records in the `items` table using an HTML table.

Before taking this view apart and seeing what makes it tick, however, note one important point. Remember that the message `'Item was successfully created.'` was supposed to be passed on to this view and displayed? Well, look through the code—you won't find any mention of a `flash` or `flash[:notice]`. Why is that? Take a look at Figure 6-9, where you see the newly created record displayed in the view connected to the `list` action. And the message `'Item was successfully created.'` is clearly visible at the top of the page. How is that possible with no mention of `flash[:notice]` in `list.rhtml`?

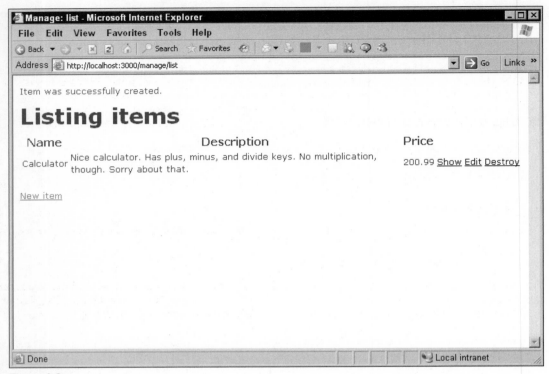

Figure 6-9

It's possible because this application uses a Rails *layout*. Layouts are templates that views are inserted into automatically. Using a layout gives your application a consistent feel across many different views, because you can create standard headers and footers for each web page, as well as use a standard stylesheet, and more.

Using a Layout

The layout for all the actions in the `manage` controller in the `store` application is in the file `manage` `.rhtml`, stored as rubydev\store\ch06\app\views\layouts\manage.rhml, and here's what it looks like:

```
<html>
<head>
  <title>Manage: <%= controller.action_name %></title>
  <%= stylesheet_link_tag 'scaffold' %>
</head>
<body>

<p style="color: green"><%= flash[:notice] %></p>

<%= @content_for_layout %>

</body>
</html>
```

Here's where the message stored in `flash[:notice]` is displayed:

```
<p style="color: green"><%= flash[:notice] %></p>
```

That explains how the message 'Item was successfully created.' appears in Figure 6-9. But how does the list view appear in that page too, listing all the records in the `items` table? Whenever you display a view connected to an action in the `manage` controller, Rails stores the content for that view in a variable named `@content_for_layout`, and then uses the layout `manage.rhtml`. In `manage.rhtml`, the contents of the `@content_for_layout` variable are simply popped into the web page like this:

```
<%= @content_for_layout %>
```

And that's how the `manage.rhtml` layout works.

Using a Stylesheet

Note the `stylesheet_link_tag` method in `manage.rhtml`, which links to the stylesheet `scaffold.css`:

```
<%= stylesheet_link_tag 'scaffold' %>
```

This stylesheet, rubydev\store\ch06\public\stylesheets\scaffold.css, specifies the cascading style sheet (CSS) styles used in the layout, and, therefore, in all the views displayed using the layout. Here's what `scaffold.css` looks like—you won't have to know CSS styles to work with this book:

```
body { background-color: #fff; color: #333; }

body, p, ol, ul, td {
  font-family: verdana, arial, helvetica, sans-serif;
  font-size:    13px;
  line-height: 18px;
}

pre {
  background-color: #eee;
  padding: 10px;
  font-size: 11px;
}

a { color: #000; }
a:visited { color: #666; }
a:hover { color: #fff; background-color:#000; }

.fieldWithErrors {
  padding: 2px;
  background-color: red;
  display: table;
}

#errorExplanation {
  width: 400px;
  border: 2px solid red;
  padding: 7px;
  padding-bottom: 12px;
  margin-bottom: 20px;
```

```
    background-color: #f0f0f0;
  }

#errorExplanation h2 {
  text-align: left;
  font-weight: bold;
  padding: 5px 5px 5px 15px;
  font-size: 12px;
  margin: -7px;
  background-color: #c00;
  color: #fff;
}

#errorExplanation p {
  color: #333;
  margin-bottom: 0;
  padding: 5px;
}

#errorExplanation ul li {
  font-size: 12px;
  list-style: square;
}

div.uploadStatus {
  margin: 5px;
}

div.progressBar {
  margin: 5px;
}

div.progressBar div.border {
  background-color: #fff;
  border: 1px solid grey;
  width: 100%;
}

div.progressBar div.background {
  background-color: #333;
  height: 18px;
  width: 0%;
}
```

Now you know how layouts work—they're templates into which views are inserted. For example, the list view is displayed after you create a new record in the `items` table.

Displaying Records

The list view displays all the records in the `items` table in an HTML table. That HTML table is created using embedded Ruby to call the `Item` model's `content_columns` class method to get the names of the columns in the `items` table, and to display them by calling each column object's `human_name` method (which, in this case, just returns the column's name in the `items` table):

```
<table>
  <tr>
  <% for column in Item.content_columns %>
    <th><%= column.human_name %></th>
  <% end %>
  </tr>
      .
      .
      .
</table>
```

The HTML table continues by looping over the item records in @items, and displaying the content of the various fields in those records. The content of each record is displayed using an inner loop over the record's fields (that is, the columns). Note the use of the send method of a record to access the fields in that record:

```
<table>
  <tr>
  <% for column in Item.content_columns %>
    <th><%= column.human_name %></th>
  <% end %>
  </tr>
```

```
<% for item in @items %>
  <tr>
  <% for column in Item.content_columns %>
    <td><%=h item.send(column.name) %></td>
  <% end %>
      .
      .
      .
</table>
```

In addition, three hyperlinks are created for each record (Show, Edit, and Destroy), each tied to an action of the same name:

```
<table>
  <tr>
  <% for column in Item.content_columns %>
    <th><%= column.human_name %></th>
  <% end %>
  </tr>
```

```
<% for item in @items %>
  <tr>
  <% for column in Item.content_columns %>
    <td><%=h item.send(column.name) %></td>
  <% end %>
    <td><%= link_to 'Show', :action => 'show', :id => item %></td>
    <td><%= link_to 'Edit', :action => 'edit', :id => item %></td>
    <td><%= link_to 'Destroy', { :action => 'destroy', :id => item }, :confirm =>
'Are you sure?', :post => true %></td>
  </tr>
<% end %>
</table>
```

Note the key/value pair :id => item; that's actually short for :id => item.id, because the id field is the default field. So as this code loops over the item objects in @items (created in the list action and holding all the records in the items table), each link references a specific record by id.

And you can see the results in Figure 6-9, where the newly created record is displayed.

Was a new record really created and stored in the MySQL database store_development? What better way to check than to ask MySQL itself? Start up the MySQL monitor at the command line, and enter your password:

```
C:\rubydev>mysql -u root -p
Enter password: ********
Welcome to the MySQL monitor.  Commands end with ; or \g.
Your MySQL connection id is 4 to server version: 5.0.19-nt

Type 'help;' or '\h' for help. Type '\c' to clear the buffer.

mysql>
```

To work with the store_development database, enter the use command at the MySQL prompt:

```
mysql> use store_development
Database changed
```

To see the contents of the items table, enter the SQL command select * from items;, which selects and displays all records in the items table. Here's the result—despite the word wrap, you can see that your new record is indeed there in the items table:

```
mysql> select * from items;
+----+------------+-----------------------------------------------------------
------------------------------------+--------+
| id | name       | description
                                     | price  |
+----+------------+-----------------------------------------------------------
------------------------------------+--------+
| 1  | Calculator | Nice calculator. Has plus, minus, and divide keys. No multip
lication, though. Sorry about that. | 200.99 |
+----+------------+-----------------------------------------------------------
------------------------------------+--------+
1 row in set (0.00 sec)
```

Adding Another Record

To create another new record, just navigate to http://localhost:3000/manage. As you recall, the manage controller's default action is the index action, which renders the list action like this in the manage controller:

```
def index
  list
  render :action => 'list'
end
```

When you're in the list view, it's easy to create new records, as you'll do in the following Try It Out.

Try It Out Create an Additional Record

To create a new record, follow these steps:

1. Start the WEBrick server:

```
C:\rubydev\ch06\store>ruby script/server
```

2. Navigate to `http://localhost:3000/manage`.

3. In the list view, click the New Item link to get to the `http://localhost:3000/manage/new` page.

4. Create a new item for sale, as shown in Figure 6-10, giving it the name clock, the description "A nice digital clock. Contains all you would expect—and the alarm is not too loud!", and the price $14.99.

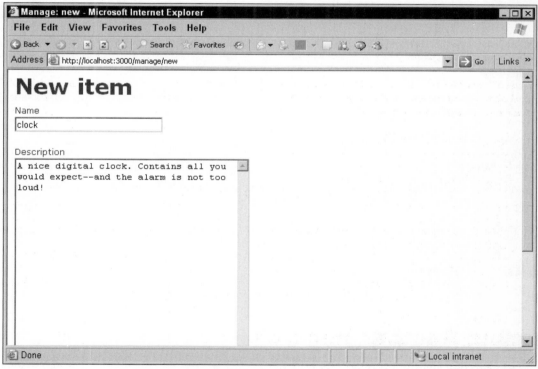

Figure 6-10

5. Click the Create button on the page (`http://localhost:3000/manage/new`). The new item is created and your browser is redirected to the `http://localhost:3000/manage/list` page, as shown in Figure 6-11.

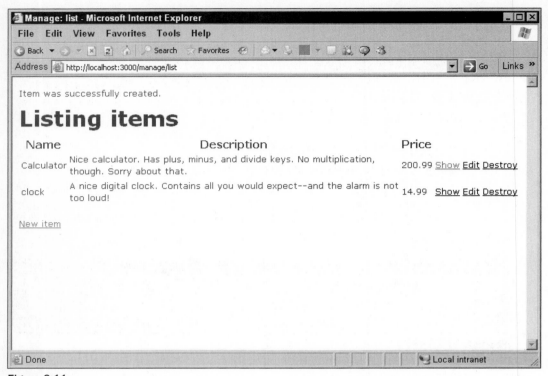

Figure 6-11

How It Works

Just like the first record created earlier in the chapter, this record is stored in the `items` table of the `store_development` database. You can add as many records as you like.

But what about maintaining the data in those records? What if you have to change it?

Editing Records

Making changes to records is no problem with the `manage` controller — just click the Edit link. In the following exercise you update the price of alarm clocks in your database.

Edit a Record

To edit a record, follow these steps:

1. Start the WEBrick server:

```
C:\rubydev\ch06\store>ruby script/server
```

2. Navigate to `http://localhost:3000/manage/`.

3. Click the Edit link for the alarm clock.

4. Change the price of the alarm clock to $15.99, as shown in Figure 6-12.

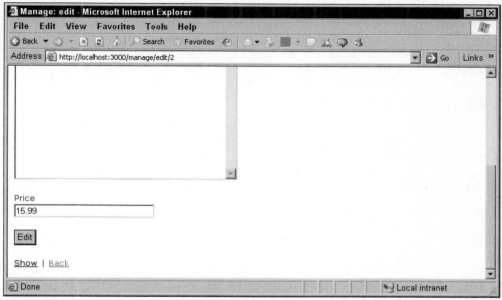

Figure 6-12

5. Click the Edit button. The alarm clock's record is updated, and the new data is displayed, as shown in Figure 6-13.

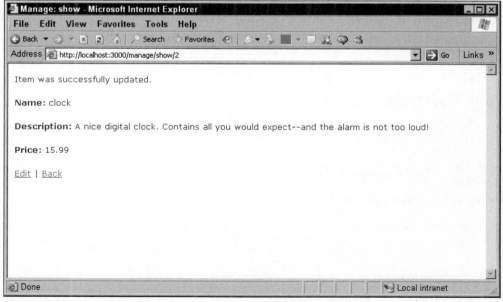

Figure 6-13

6. Click the Back link at the bottom of the clock record to return to list view (see Figure 6-14). As you can see in that view, the price of the alarm clock has indeed been updated.

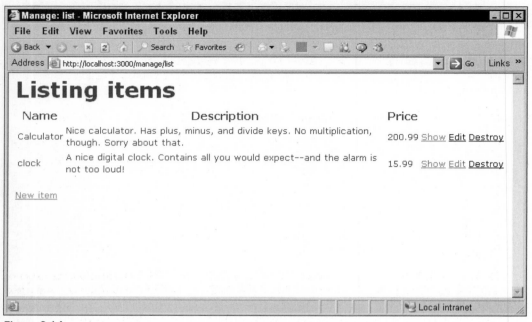

Figure 6-14

How It Works

You start off in the list view, which displays each record, along with an Edit link:

```
<h1>Listing items</h1>

<table>
  <tr>
  <% for column in Item.content_columns %>
    <th><%= column.human_name %></th>
  <% end %>
  </tr>

<% for item in @items %>
  <tr>
  <% for column in Item.content_columns %>
    <td><%=h item.send(column.name) %></td>
  <% end %>
    <td><%= link_to 'Show', :action => 'show', :id => item %></td>
    <td><%= link_to 'Edit', :action => 'edit', :id => item %></td>
      .
      .
      .
```

This link connects to the edit action, passing the id of the current record to that action. Here's what the edit action looks like in the controller:

```
def edit
  @item = Item.find(params[:id])
end
```

The code relies on the ActiveRecord::Base class's find method, which looks up records for you. In this case, params[:id] identifies the record to find, and the find method finds it, and returns a model object holding that record.

Control then passes to the edit view, rubydev\store\ch06\app\views\manage\edit.rhml:

```
<h1>Editing item</h1>

<%= start_form_tag :action => 'update', :id => @item %>
  <%= render :partial => 'form' %>
  <%= submit_tag 'Edit' %>
<%= end_form_tag %>

<%= link_to 'Show', :action => 'show', :id => @item %> |
<%= link_to 'Back', :action => 'list' %>
```

The edit view renders _form.rhtml, which, as you know, displays the HTML controls corresponding to the various fields in a record — a text field for the name, a text area for the description, and a text field for the price. Those controls are tied to the model object @item, whose three attributes — name, description, and price — display the data already in the record about to be edited:

```
<%= error_messages_for 'item' %>

<!--[form:item]-->
<p><label for="item_name">Name</label><br/>
<%= text_field 'item', 'name'  %></p>

<p><label for="item_description">Description</label><br/>
<%= text_area 'item', 'description'  %></p>

<p><label for="item_price">Price</label><br/>
<%= text_field 'item', 'price'  %></p>
<!--[eoform:item]-->
```

The form action — that is, the action that the data in the form will be sent to — in edit.rhtml is the update action, so after the user edits the displayed data for the record being edited and clicks the Edit button, the update action gets control. update starts by creating a model object that contains the object being edited:

```
def update
  @item = Item.find(params[:id])
        .
        .
        .
end
```

Then the code grabs the new data for the item using the :item symbol from _form.rhtml, passing that new data to the model object's update_attributes method:

```
def update
  @item = Item.find(params[:id])
  if @item.update_attributes(params[:item])
       .
       .
       .
  end
end
```

If update_attributes returns a value of true, the record's data in the items table has been updated. In that case, the code passes the message "Item was successfully updated." using the flash hash to the show action:

```
def update
  @item = Item.find(params[:id])
  if @item.update_attributes(params[:item])
    flash[:notice] = 'Item was successfully updated.'
    redirect_to :action => 'show', :id => @item
       .
       .
       .
  end
end
```

show simply grabs the newly updated record from the items table:

```
def show
  @item = Item.find(params[:id])
end
```

and displays it in the show view:

```
<% for column in Item.content_columns %>
<p>
  <b><%= column.human_name %>:</b> <%=h @item.send(column.name) %>
</p>
<% end %>

<%= link_to 'Edit', :action => 'edit', :id => @item %> |
<%= link_to 'Back', :action => 'list' %>
```

You can see what the show view looks like in Figure 6-13.

On the other hand, if update_attributes returns a value of false, control is sent back to the edit view for another try at editing the record:

```
def update
  @item = Item.find(params[:id])
  if @item.update_attributes(params[:item])
```

```
        flash[:notice] = 'Item was successfully updated.'
        redirect_to :action => 'show', :id => @item
    else
        render :action => 'edit'
    end
end
```

And that's the way you edit records.

Beautifying the Display

Bear in mind that you have control over what all these views look like — the scaffold utility generates template files, and it's up to you to customize them as you want. For example, you might want to beautify the display of the list view.

To do so, you could follow these steps:

1. Add background0 and background1 style classes to rubydev\ch06\store\public\stylesheets\ scaffold.css:

```
body { background-color: #fff; color: #333; }
    .
    .
    .
.fieldWithErrors {
  padding: 2px;
  background-color: red;
  display: table;
}

.background0 {
  background-color: coral;
}

.background1 {
  background-color: white;
}
    .
    .
    .
```

2. Modify rubydev\ch06\store\app\views\manage\list.rhtml, adding this code:

```
<h1>Listing items</h1>

<table>
  <tr>
  <% for column in Item.content_columns %>
    <th><%= column.human_name %></th>
  <% end %>
```

```
        </tr>

<%
even_odd = 0
for item in @items
even_odd = 1 - even_odd
%>
    <tr class="background<%= even_odd %>">
    <% for column in Item.content_columns %>
      <td><%=h item.send(column.name) %></td>
    <% end %>
      <td><%= link_to 'Show', :action => 'show', :id => item %></td>
      <td><%= link_to 'Edit', :action => 'edit', :id => item %></td>
      <td><%= link_to 'Destroy', { :action => 'destroy', :id => item }, :confirm =>
'Are you sure?', :post => true %></td>
    </tr>
<% end %>
</table>
```

Now start the WEBrick server and navigate to `http://localhost:3000/manage/list`. The page (see Figure 6-15) shows the new list view with a number of additional records.

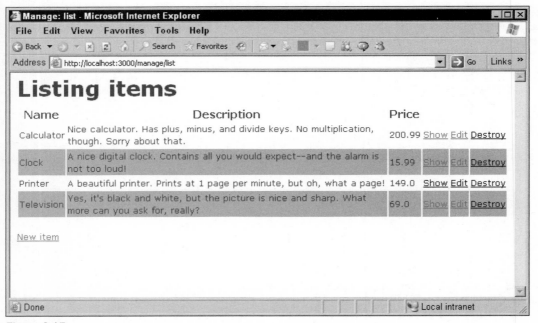

Figure 6-15

Summary

In this chapter, you got some important points about databases and Rails applications down. You learned the following:

- ❑ What a database and a database table are and how to create them.
- ❑ How to configure database access using the `database.yml` file.
- ❑ How to use the `scaffold` utility to create a controller and a model.
- ❑ How to add and edit records in a database-aware application.

In the next chapter, you learn to create the user interface to the `store` application. Before proceeding, though, try the exercises that follow to test your understanding of the material covered in this chapter. You can find the solutions to these exercises in Appendix A.

Exercises

1. Configure a Rails application to connect to a database server with the username `orson_welles` and the password `rosebud`.

2. Use the `scaffold` utility to create a model named `item` and a controller named `merchandise`.

3. If you know CSS, set the font size of `scaffold`-generated views to 16 points.

Working with Databases

With your database set up, it's time to look at things from the user's point of view — how to display your items to users, and how to get their purchases in a cart.

It all starts by presenting what you have to sell to the user.

> Copy the `store` application from rubydev\ch06\store to rubydev\ch07\store before working with the code in this chapter. That just means copying the store folder from rubydev\ch06 to rubydev\ch07. After you do that, you'll be keeping track of the changes made to the `store` application in this chapter, instead of working on the Chapter 6 version.

Displaying Items to the Customer

The `manage` controller, as you saw in the preceding chapter, is used to control the `store` application's connection to the database. You need a second controller if you want to let users peruse the store — obviously, they shouldn't have access to the administrative part of the store. The following exercise leads you through the creation of another controller.

Try It Out   Create a Second Controller

To create a second controller for the `store` application, follow these steps:

1. Change directories to the rubydev\ch07\store directory:

```
C:\>cd \rubydev\ch07\store>ruby
C:\rubydev\ch07\store>
```

2. Create the second controller, named `buy`, like this:

```
C:\>cd \rubydev\ch07\store>ruby script/generate controller Buy index
```

3. Start the WEBrick server:

```
C:\rubydev\ch07\store>ruby script/server
```

4. Navigate to `http://localhost:3000/buy`, as shown in Figure 7-1.

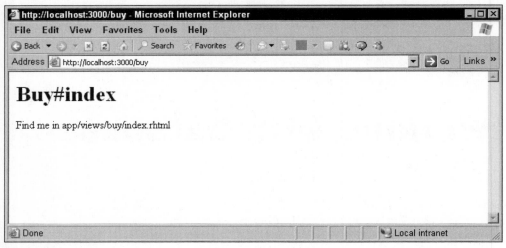

Figure 7-1

How It Works

The command

```
C:\>cd \rubydev\ch07\store>ruby script/generate controller Buy index
```

creates the `buy` controller and the action named `index`. Because you've named the action `index`, it'll be the default action, executed if the user navigates to `http://localhost:3000/buy`. Figure 7-1 showed the results of navigating to that URL.

That's a good start, but the goal here is to grab the items for sale and display them when the user navigates to the `buy` controller. There's still work to do.

Getting the Items for Sale

You used the `scaffold` utility in Chapter 6, so this time you'll handle the coding yourself. Fortunately, that's not hard. How do you get the records from the `items` table?

You can create a class method in the model, rubydev\ch07\store\app\models\item.rb, named, say, `return_items`, like this:

```
class Item < ActiveRecord::Base
  def self.return_items
      .
      .
      .
  end
end
```

When you call `return_items` from an action, it supplies an array of all the records in the `items` table. How does that work?

You call `find(:all)` in `return_items` in the model class, rubydev\ch07\store\app\models\item.rb:

```ruby
class Item < ActiveRecord::Base
  def self.return_items
    find(:all)
  end
end
```

There are actually three ways to call `find`:

❑ `find(:id)` — Finds a record by ID

❑ `find(:first)` — Finds the first record

❑ `find(:all)` — Returns all the records in the table

In fact, you can specify other requirements in hash form following `:id`, `:first`, or `:all`. Here's an example that finds items less than or equal to $20.00, and orders the found records by name, and if the name is the same, by description:

```ruby
class Item < ActiveRecord::Base
  def self.return_items
    find(:all,
      :order => "name description",
      :conditions => "price <= 20.00"
    )
  end
end
```

Those other requirements are SQL-oriented; if you know SQL, here they are:

Ruby	SQL Information
`:conditions`	SQL code indicating a condition or conditions to match.
`:group`	Specifies an attribute indicating how the result should be grouped, making use of the SQL GROUP BY clause.
`:include`	Specifies associations to be included using SQL LEFT OUTER JOINs.
`:joins`	Specifies additional SQL joins.
`:limit`	Specifies an integer setting the upper limit of the number of rows to be returned.
`:offset`	Specifies an integer indicating the offset from where the rows should be returned.
`:order`	Lets you specify the fields to set the order of returned records.
`:readonly`	Marks the returned records read-only.
`:select`	A SQL SELECT statement, as in SELECT * FROM items.

OK, a new class method in the `Item` model, `return_items`, returns the full set of records in the `items` table. To start the process of displaying the items for sale when the `buy` controller's `index` action is called, you call `return_items` in the `index` action:

```
class BuyController < ApplicationController

  def index
    @items = Item.return_items
  end
end
```

You're making progress — you've loaded all the records from the `items` table into the `@items` array. Now you've got to display them.

Showing the Items for Sale

Displaying the records is the job of the view connected to the `index` action, rubydev\ch07\store\app\views\buy\index.rhtml, which currently looks like this:

```
<h1>Buy#index</h1>
<p>Find me in app/views/buy/index.rhtml</p>
```

That's the web page that appears in Figure 7-1, and the one you're going to adapt to display the items for sale.

Try It Out   Show Database Items in a Web Page

To show the database items stored in the `@items` array in a web page, follow these steps:

1. Create a new web page:

```
<html>
  <head>
    <title>The Store</title>
  </head>

  <body>
    <h1>Buy From Our Store!</h1>
    <b>Welcome to the store.</b>
    <br>
    <b><i>Please buy a lot of items, thank you.</i></b>
    <br>
    <br>
       .
       .
       .
  </body>
</html>
```

2. You can display the items for sale in an HTML table, so add that as well:

```
<html>
  <head>
```

```
    <title>The Store</title>
  </head>

  <body>
    <h1>Buy From Our Store!</h1>
    <b>Welcome to the store.</b>
    <br>
    <b><i>Please buy a lot of items, thank you.</i></b>
    <br>
    <br>
    <table cellpadding="6">
        .
        .
        .
    </table>
  </body>
</html>
```

3. Add a loop over the items in the @items array:

```
<html>
  <head>
    <title>The Store</title>
  </head>

  <body>
    <h1>Buy From Our Store!</h1>
    <b>Welcome to the store.</b>
    <br>
    <b><i>Please buy a lot of items, thank you.</i></b>
    <br>
    <br>
    <table cellpadding="6">
      <% for item in @items %>
        .
        .
        .
      <% end %>
    </table>
  </body>
</html>
```

4. Display the name and description of each item, row by row in the table:

```
<table cellpadding="6">
  <% for item in @items %>
  <tr>
    <td><b><%=h item.name %></b></td>
    <td><%=h item.description %></td>
    .
    .
    .
  </tr>
  <% end %>
</table>
```

5. Finally, add a link that lets the user add each item to the shopping cart:

```
<table cellpadding="6">
  <% for item in @items %>
  <tr>
    <td><b><%=h item.name %></b></td>
    <td><%=h item.description %></td>
    <td><%= link_to 'Add to cart', :action => 'add', :id => item %></td>
  </tr>
  <% end %>
</table>
```

6. Start the WEBrick server:

```
C:\rubydev\ch07\store>ruby script/server
```

7. Navigate to `http://localhost:3000/buy` to see the result, as shown in Figure 7-2.

Figure 7-2

How It Works

As you can see in Figure 7-2, this works — you've recovered all the records in the `items` table and displayed them to the user. Very cool.

If you wanted to, you could use a layout here as well. To create a layout, you just have to name it ruby-dev\ch07\store\app\views\layout\buy.rhtml, something like the following (note the crucial <%= @content_for_layout %>, where the view is inserted):

```
<html>
  <head>
    <title>Buy From Us</title>
```

```
      <%= stylesheet_link_tag 'scaffold' %>
    </head>

    <body>
      <p style="color: green"><%= flash[:notice] %></p>

      <%= @content_for_layout %>

    </body>
  </html>
```

That finishes the display of the items for sale. You can beautify the display by using CSS formatting, if you like, and work on polishing the HTML for the item display. But the point's been made — you know how to grab data from a database table and display it.

Of course, the purpose of displaying the items is so users will buy them. You need to start building a shopping cart so that can happen.

Creating a Shopping Cart

Users are presented with all items in the store in the index.rhtml view. If they want to buy an item, they click the Add to Cart link that you created in step 5 of the preceding Try It Out:

```
<tr>
  <td><b><%=h item.name %></b></td>
  <td><%=h item.description %></td>
  <td><%= link_to 'Add to cart', :action => 'add', :id => item %></td>
</tr>
```

That link connects to the add action in the buy controller.

Designing the Shopping Cart

The session hash is going to be involved with the shopping cart because it's a good place to store the customer's purchases. Theoretically, you could just set up some arrays to store the names of the items the customer has purchased, their descriptions, and their prices, and store that in the session hash. Then when you need that data, you simply fetch it from the session.

That's certainly one way to handle the shopping cart data. However, for this book, you want your data handled by a model in Rails applications. Rails data-handling is model-centric, and your code is made easier if you use models (for instance, you can access all your data as @model_object.name, @model_object.id, @model_price, and so on). Storing data with a model in this example will also point out some new aspects of database-handling in Rails.

Here's the plan: create a new model named Purchase to hold a single item that the customer has purchased. The model will be tied to a table named purchases in the store_development, with the following fields: id, item_id (this is the item's id in the items table), quantity, and price. So Figure 7-3 shows how you store a single purchase as a record in the purchases table.

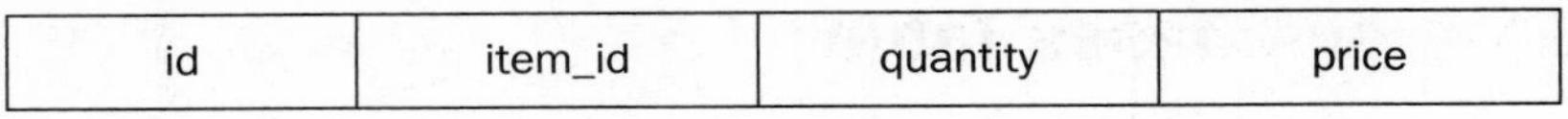

id	item_id	quantity	price

Figure 7-3

Hopefully, the customer will buy many items, as illustrated in Figure 7-4.

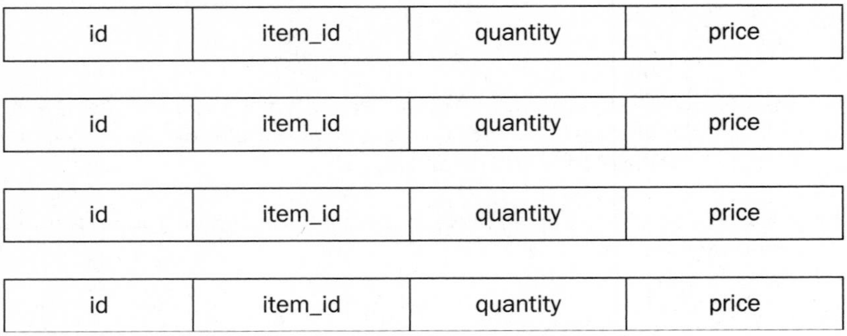

id	item_id	quantity	price

id	item_id	quantity	price

id	item_id	quantity	price

id	item_id	quantity	price

Figure 7-4

To corral these purchases, store them in an array in an object of a new class, the Cart class, as shown in Figure 7-5.

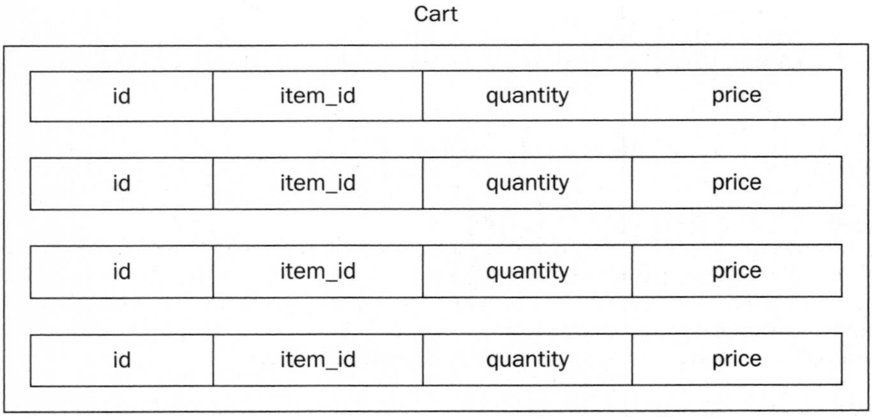

Cart

id	item_id	quantity	price
id	item_id	quantity	price
id	item_id	quantity	price
id	item_id	quantity	price

Figure 7-5

So you need two new classes — the Purchase class to keep track of individual purchases, and the Cart class to keep track of the many Purchase objects a customer creates as he shops.

Creating the purchases Table

The Purchase class is a model tied to a database table, the purchases table, so first create that table. Just follow these steps:

1. Start the MySQL monitor:

```
C:\rubydev\ch07\store>mysql -u root -p
   .
   .
   .
mysql>
```

2. Switch to the store_development database:

```
mysql> use store_development
Database changed
```

3. Create the purchases table:

```
mysql> create table purchases (
    -> id        int       not null        auto_increment,
    -> item_id   int       not null,
    -> quantity  int       not null        default 0,
    -> price     decimal(8, 2)   not null,
    -> constraint purchases_items foreign key (item_id) references items(id),
    -> primary key (id)
    -> );
Query OK, 0 rows affected (0.05 sec)

mysql>
```

4. Exit the MySQL monitor:

```
mysql> exit
Bye
```

Creating the purchases table was much like you've done before, with two differences: First, this line sets a default value for the quantity field:

```
mysql> create table purchases (
    -> id        int       not null        auto_increment,
    -> item_id   int       not null,
    -> quantity  int       not null        default 0,
    -> price     decimal(8, 2)   not null,
    -> constraint purchases_items foreign key (item_id) references items(id),
    -> primary key (id)
    -> );
```

And second, the table sets up a connection to another table, the items table:

```
mysql> create table purchases (
    -> id        int       not null        auto_increment,
    -> item_id   int       not null,
```

```
        -> quantity int      not null          default 0,
        -> price      decimal(8, 2)    not null,
        -> constraint purchases_items foreign key (item_id) references items(id),
        -> primary key (id)
        -> );
```

Recall from the previous chapter that the `items` table stores the items for sale. Like the `purchases` table, the `items` table has an `id` value for each record. The preceding line of SQL says that the `item_id` field in the `purchases` table holds the `id` value of the item in the `items` table. That is, `item_id` is a foreign (not primary) key. Foreign keys can be used to relate tables — if you want to look up a purchase in the `items` table, for instance, you can do that using the `item_id` value in the `purchases` table.

Creating the Purchase Model

The `purchases` table, each record of which will hold a purchase by the customer, now needs to be tied to a model in the `store` application. To do that, change directories to rubydev\ch07\store, and then create the new model like this:

```
C:\rubydev\ch07\store>ruby script/generate model Purchase
```

Excellent. Now when the user makes a purchase, you'll catch that item, create a `Purchase` object from it, and then store that object in the cart.

Here's the new model, `purchase.rb`:

```
class Purchase < ActiveRecord::Base
end
```

Not too exciting. But you're not yet done with creating this class — you still have to tell Rails about the foreign key connection to the `items` table:

```
mysql> create table purchases (
    -> id        int      not null          auto_increment,
    -> item_id   int      not null,
    -> quantity int      not null          default 0,
    -> price     decimal(8, 2)    not null,
    -> constraint purchases_items foreign key (item_id) references items(id),
    -> primary key (id)
    -> );
```

The Rails core development team set things up so that you have to tell Rails about foreign keys yourself. That's because not all database servers let you work with foreign keys. You tell Rails about your `item_id` foreign key with the `belongs_to` method in the `purchase.rb`. model. The syntax looks like this:

```
class Purchase < ActiveRecord::Base
  belongs_to :item
  .
  .
  .
end
```

That connects the `purchases` and `items` tables as far as Rails is concerned. You're going to need the `belongs_to` method each time you want to connect database tables using foreign keys.

You also need some way of producing new `Purchase` objects when the user buys something. How does that work? You might create a new class method named `buy_one` that you can pass an item (from the `items` table) to when the user purchases that item:

```
class Purchase < ActiveRecord::Base
  belongs_to :item

  def self.buy_one(item)
      .
      .
      .
  end
end
```

So when the user buys a displayed item, you can pass that item to the `Purchase` class's `buy_one` method to create a `Purchase` object from that item. That means that when you call the `buy_one` method, you start by creating a new `Purchase` object:

```
class Purchase < ActiveRecord::Base
  belongs_to :item

  def self.buy_one(item)
    purchase = self.new
        .
        .
        .

  end
end
```

To make life easier for yourself, you can store the purchased item inside the new `Purchase` object like this:

```
class Purchase < ActiveRecord::Base
  belongs_to :item

  def self.buy_one(item)
    purchase = self.new
    purchase.item = item
        .
        .
        .
  end
end
```

Now when you create a new `Purchase` object, you'll have access to the actual `Item` object that was purchased, which means you can access its name, description, and so on.

Next, you can store the quantity of the item purchased in the `Purchase` object, enabling the user to purchase multiple items:

```
class Purchase < ActiveRecord::Base
  belongs_to :item

  def self.buy_one(item)
    purchase = self.new
    purchase.item = item
    purchase.quantity = 1
        .
        .
        .
  end
end
```

You also create a new field for the Purchase object named price, holding the price of the item:

```
class Purchase < ActiveRecord::Base
  belongs_to :item

  def self.buy_one(item)
    purchase = self.new
    purchase.item = item
    purchase.quantity = 1
    purchase.price = item.price
        .
        .
        .
  end
end
```

Finally, you just return the new Purchase object from the buy_one method:

```
class Purchase < ActiveRecord::Base
  belongs_to :item

  def self.buy_one(item)
    purchase = self.new
    purchase.item = item
    purchase.quantity = 1
    purchase.price = item.price
    return purchase
  end
end
```

OK, the Purchase class is ready to go — when the user buys one of the displayed items, all you have to do is to fetch the item from the items table and pass it to the Purchase class's buy_one method to create a new Purchase object.

That new Purchase object should go into the shopping cart — which means you've got to create a Cart class next.

Creating the Cart

The Cart class exists to keep track of the purchases the user makes — which means keeping track of Purchase objects as they're created. What better way to do that than in an array? Here's how you might start writing the Cart class, by creating an empty Purchases array named @purchases in the ini-tialize constructor:

```
class Cart

  def initialize
      @purchases = []
        .
        .
        .
  end

end
```

The cart should also keep track of the total price of all the purchased items, so you might add an attribute named price to the Cart class, setting it to 0.0 when the cart is first created:

```
class Cart

  def initialize
      @purchases = []
      @total = 0.0
  end

end
```

You can make the purchases and price attributes available publicly by using attr_reader:

```
class Cart
  attr_reader :purchases
  attr_reader :total

  def initialize
      @purchases = []
      @total = 0.0
  end

end
```

Next, you're going to need a way to add new purchases to the cart. A convenient means to do that is to add a new method, add_purchase, to the Cart class. It's easiest to set this method up to accept items as the user purchases:

```
class Cart
  attr_reader :purchases
  attr_reader :total

  def initialize
```

```
          @purchases = []
          @total = 0.0
      end

      def add_purchase(item)
          .
            .
              .
      end

end
```

When you pass a new item to the add_purchase method, you can use that item to create a new Purchase object, and add that new object to the purchases array using the array append operator, <<:

```
class Cart
    attr_reader :purchases
    attr_reader :total

    def initialize
        @purchases = []
        @total = 0.0
    end

    def add_purchase(item)
        @purchases << Purchase.buy_one(item)
            .
              .
                .
    end

end
```

And when you add a new purchase to the cart, update the total attribute of the cart by adding the price of the new item to the total:

```
class Cart
    attr_reader :purchases
    attr_reader :total

    def initialize
        @purchases = []
        @total = 0.0
    end

    def add_purchase(item)
        @purchases << Purchase.buy_one(item)
        @total += item.price
    end

end
```

That's the Cart class, which is stored in cart.rb. You can place it with the other models in rubydev\ ch07\store\app\models\cart.rb. The Cart class is not derived from the ActiveRecord::Base class, but it's as much a model as the other two models in this example (item.rb and purchase.rb).

Now you need to make some provision for storing the cart and keeping it available between page accesses. That's the whole point of the cart — to let you store the purchases made by the customer. And because control goes back and forth between the server and the browser as the customer buys items, you have to find someplace to store the cart between times the server gets control — and what better place to store the cart than the session?

Storing the Cart in a Session

As the customer navigates from page to page, the server is going to lose control of the application, which means all your data will be reset to its initialization values. To store the purchases in the cart, you've got to store the whole cart in the session.

To make accessing the cart easy, create a helper method in the controller, get_cart:

```
class BuyController < ApplicationController

  def index
    @items = Item.return_items
  end

  private
    def get_cart
        .
        .
        .
    end
end
```

This helper method is private, which means Rails won't make it into an action. Private methods in the controller stay private to the controller and are not accessible as public actions.

When get_cart is called, it should first check if the cart was already stored in the session and if so, it should return the cart:

```
class BuyController < ApplicationController

  def index
    @items = Item.return_items
  end

  private
    def get_cart
      if session[:shopping_cart]
        return session[:shopping_cart]
        .
        .
        .
      end
    end
end
```

If the cart doesn't exist in the session, the `get_cart` method should create a new `Cart` object and return that:

```
class BuyController < ApplicationController

  def index
    @items = Item.return_items
  end

private
  def get_cart
    if session[:shopping_cart]
      return session[:shopping_cart]
    else
      return Cart.new
    end
  end
end
```

You're almost all set up to store the cart in the session, but there's one more precaution you might take. Because Rails loads classes only as it needs them, you might conceivably get into a situation where you're requesting Rails to read the cart from the session before it knows about the `Cart` class, and that would cause an error. That's not going to happen with the code in this example as it's written, but it's worth knowing that you can head off that kind of trouble — where Rails is expected to retrieve an object from the session without first knowing what kind of object it is — by forcing Rails to load classes early on. For example, if you load the `Cart` and `Purchase` classes early on, Rails will know all about them when it's asked to retrieve objects of those classes from the session.

You can pre-load classes in Rails by editing the `application.rb` file in the application's controller directory. You may have wondered what that file is there for; it's to handle *context issues*, such as pre-loading classes so that Rails knows about them. The `application.rb` file is run first so you can initialize your application. To make the `store` application pre-load the `Cart` and `Purchase` classes, add the following code to rubydev\ch07\store\app\controllers\application.rb:

```
class ApplicationController < ActionController::Base
  model :cart
  model :purchase
end
```

The next step is to put the cart to use and handle a purchase.

Handling a Purchase

When the user navigates to the store, http://localhost:3000/buy, he sees the buy page (which you saw in Figure 7-2) that displays the items available. When the user clicks an item's Add to Cart link, that item's ID is sent to the controller.

Now you define a new action named `add` to tell the controller it's time to add that item to the cart.

Add a Purchase to the Cart

To add a purchase to the cart, follow these steps:

1.   Edit the rubydev\ch07\store\app\controllers\buy_controller.rb, adding the add action:

```
class BuyController < ApplicationController

  def index
    @items = Item.return_items
  end

  def add
    .
    .
    .
  end

private
  def get_cart
    if session[:shopping_cart]
      return session[:shopping_cart]
    else
      return Cart.new
    end
  end
end
```

2.   Add this code to the add action:

```
def add
  item = Item.find(params[:id])
  @cart = get_cart
  @cart.add_purchase(item)
  session[:shopping_cart] = @cart
  redirect_to(:action => 'display_cart')
end
```

How It Works

The add action you added to the controller lets the customer add an item to the shopping cart. When the user clicks an Add to Cart link in the http://localhost:3000/buy page, the ID of the clicked item is sent to the controller. The http://localhost:3000/buy page was created from the items table, so the ID is the ID of the purchased item in that table. You retrieve the item using the Item model's find method:

```
def add
  item = Item.find(params[:id])
    .
    .
    .
end
```

Next you convert that item into a `Purchase` object and add that purchase to the cart. That starts by calling the `get_cart` method to fetch the cart from the session if it's been stored there, or by creating a new cart:

```
def add
  item = Item.find(params[:id])
  @cart = get_cart
     .
     .
     .

end
```

```
private
  def get_cart
    if session[:shopping_cart]
      return session[:shopping_cart]
    else
      return Cart.new
    end
  end
end
```

Now you can add the newly purchased item to the cart with the cart's `add_purchase` method:

```
def add
  item = Item.find(params[:id])
  @cart = get_cart
  @cart.add_purchase(item)
     .
     .
     .
end
```

That adds the new purchase to the cart. To update the cart and save it for future operations, you store it in the session:

```
def add
  item = Item.find(params[:id])
  @cart = get_cart
  @cart.add_purchase(item)
  session[:shopping_cart] = @cart
     .
     .
     .
end
```

Now you need some way of displaying the results to the customer. To do that, you redirect to a new action, `display_cart`:

```
def add
  item = Item.find(params[:id])
  @cart = get_cart
  @cart.add_purchase(item)
  session[:shopping_cart] = @cart
  redirect_to(:action => 'display_cart')
end
```

Displaying the Cart

The `display_cart` action displays the cart, so add that action to rubydev\ch07\store\app\controllers\buy_controller.rb now:

```ruby
class BuyController < ApplicationController

  def index
    @items = Item.return_items
  end

  def display_cart
    .
    .
    .
  end

private
  def get_cart
    if session[:shopping_cart]
      return session[:shopping_cart]
    else
      return Cart.new
    end
  end
end
```

`display_cart` simply needs to set up the data to be displayed in the accompanying view, so you start by getting the cart from the session, using the `get_cart` method, and load two instance variables: `@purchases` with the array of purchases and `@total` with the total of the purchases, like this:

```ruby
def display_cart
  @cart = get_cart
  @purchases = @cart.purchases
  @total = @cart.total
end
```

That makes the data in the cart accessible to the `display_cart` view.

In that view, rubydev\ch07\app\views\buy\display_cart.rhtml, you need to display both the purchases the user made and the total. That's most easily done with an HTML table, so set one up in the `display_cart` view:

```html
<html>
  <head>
    <title>Your Cart</title>
  </head>

  <body>
    <h1>Your Shopping Cart</h1>
    <b>Here are the items in your cart:</b>
    <br>
    <br>
```

```
<table cellpadding="6">
      .
      .
      .
</table>
<br>
</body>
</html>
```

For column headers in this table, use the columns for each item as given in the items table, this way:

```
<table cellpadding="6">
  <tr>
    <% for column in Item.content_columns %>
      <th><%= column.human_name %></th>
    <% end %>
  </tr>
    .
    .
    .
</table>
```

Then loop over the purchases:

```
<table cellpadding="6">
  <tr>
    <% for column in Item.content_columns %>
      <th><%= column.human_name %></th>
    <% end %>
  </tr>
  <% for purchase in @purchases
       item = purchase.item
  %>
    .
    .
    .
  <% end %>
</table>
```

For each purchase, list the purchased item's name, description, and price:

```
<table cellpadding="6">
  <tr>
    <% for column in Item.content_columns %>
      <th><%= column.human_name %></th>
    <% end %>
  </tr>
  <% for purchase in @purchases
       item = purchase.item
  %>
  <tr>
    <td><b><%=h item.name %></b></td>
    <td><%=h item.description %></td>
    <td><%=h item.price %></td>
  </tr>
```

```
    <% end %>
  </table>      .
```

And add the total of all purchases, which you can recover from the cart, this way:

```
    <table cellpadding="6">
      <tr>
        <% for column in Item.content_columns %>
          <th><%= column.human_name %></th>
        <% end %>
      </tr>
      <% for purchase in @purchases
           item = purchase.item
      %>
      <tr>
        <td><b><%=h item.name %></b></td>
        <td><%=h item.description %></td>
        <td><%=h item.price %></td>
      </tr>
      <% end %>
    </table>
    <br>
    <b>Total: $<%=h @total %></b>
  </body>
</html>
```

Is anything missing? How about a link back to the page that lists all the items for sale so the customer can keep on shopping? Here's that link:

```
    <table cellpadding="6">
           .
           .
           .
    </table>
    <br>
    <b>Total: $<%=h @total %></b>
    <br>
    <br>
    <%= link_to 'Shop some more!', :action => 'index' %>
  </body>
</html>
```

Figure 7-6 shows the result after the user makes some purchases by clicking the Add to Cart link. As you see, the purchased items appear in the cart, and the total cost of all the items appears at the bottom of the page.

Not bad — you've now been able to let the customer select items to buy, and have displayed his shopping cart as he adds items to it.

But what if a customer wants to purchase *two* calculators? You'd end up with the situation shown in Figure 7-7, where you have two single entries for calculators — clearly, that would make customers blink. How about combining purchases as they're made?

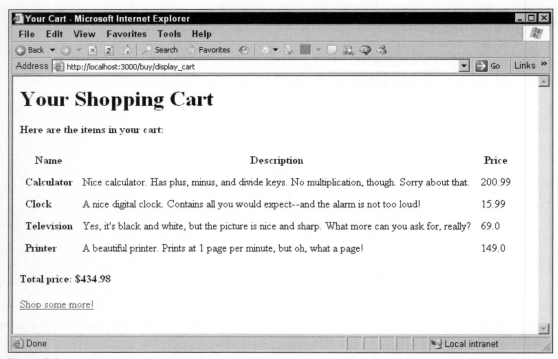

Figure 7-6

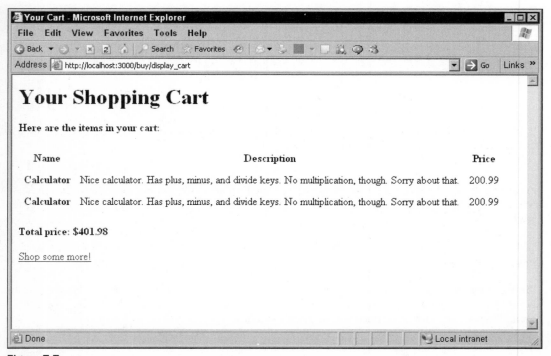

Figure 7-7

Combining Purchases in the Cart

To combine purchases in the cart, you have to modify `cart.rb`—specifically, the `add_purchase` method, which simply (and naively) adds new items to the `@purchases` array:

```
def add_purchase(item)
  @purchases << Purchase.buy_one(item)
  @total += item.price
end
```

You need to check whether the item being added to the `@purchases` array is already in that array. To do so, loop over the array:

```
def add_purchase(item)

  for purchase in @purchases
      .
      .
      .
  end

end
```

It's easy enough to compare the ID of the new item to the items already in the `@purchases` array, this way:

```
def add_purchase(item)

  for purchase in @purchases
    if (item.id == purchase.item.id)
      .
      .
      .
    end
  end

end
```

If the item already exists in the `@purchases` array, you can set a true/false flag, `appendFlag`, to false, indicating that the item should not be appended to the array:

```
def add_purchase(item)
  appendFlag = true
  for purchase in @purchases
    if (item.id == purchase.item.id)
      appendFlag = false
      .
      .
      .
    end
  end

end
```

If the item already exists in the `@purchases` array, all you need to do is to increase the quantity of the item by one:

```
def add_purchase(item)
  appendFlag = true
  for purchase in @purchases
    if (item.id == purchase.item.id)
      appendFlag = false
      purchase.quantity += 1
    end

  end
```

If the item doesn't already exist in the array, you create a new element in `@purchases`. In either case, you update the total with the new item's price, as before:

```
def add_purchase(item)
  appendFlag = true
  for purchase in @purchases
    if (item.id == purchase.item.id)
      appendFlag = false
      purchase.quantity += 1
    end
  end

  if(appendFlag)
    @purchases << Purchase.buy_one(item)
  end

  @total += item.price
end
```

Now the code does the right thing with the `@purchases` array when the customer purchases multiple items. To display that array correctly, you need to modify `display_cart.rhtml`. Start by adding a new column to the display of purchased items — the quantity of each item purchased:

```
<html>
  <head>
    <title>Your Cart</title>
  </head>

  <body>
    <h1>Your Shopping Cart</h1>
    <b>Here are the items in your cart:</b>
    <br>
    <br>
    <table cellpadding="6">
      <tr>
        <% for column in Item.content_columns %>
          <th><%= column.human_name %></th>
        <% end %>
        <th>Quantity</th>
      </tr>
        .
```

```
     .
     .
     .
  </body>
</html>
```

Then display the actual quantity of each purchased item:

```
<table cellpadding="6">
  <tr>
    <% for column in Item.content_columns %>
      <th><%= column.human_name %></th>
    <% end %>
    <th>Quantity</th>
  </tr>
  <% for purchase in @purchases
       item = purchase.item
  %>
  <tr>
    <td><b><%=h item.name %></b></td>
    <td><%=h item.description %></td>
    <td><%=h item.price %></td>
    <td><%=h purchase.quantity %></td>
  </tr>
  <% end %>
</table>
```

And there you have it—now when the customer buys several of the same items, the store application handles the situation correctly by displaying the quantity of each item in the display_cart.rhtml view, as you see in Figure 7-8.

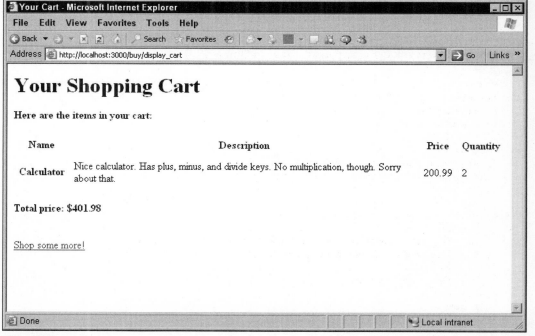

Figure 7-8

There's one more refinement you could make: letting the customer clear the cart if he wants to.

Clearing the Cart

As a convenience, you might let the customer clear the cart when he wants to. To do that, add a link in the display_cart.rhtml file with the text Clear cart, connected to the action clear_cart:

```
<html>
  <head>
    <title>Your Cart</title>
  </head>

  <body>
    <h1>Your Shopping Cart</h1>
    <b>Here are the items in your cart:</b>
    <br>
    <br>
    <table cellpadding="6">
        .
        .
        .
    </table>
    <br>
    <b>Total: $<%=h @total %></b>
    <br>
    <br>
    <%= link_to 'Clear cart', :action => 'clear_cart' %>
    <br>
    <%= link_to 'Shop some more!', :action => 'index' %>
  </body>
</html>
```

You can see this new link in the display cart page in Figure 7-9.

When the user clicks that link, control is transferred to the clear_cart action, which calls the initialize method of the Cart object to clear the cart:

```
class BuyController < ApplicationController

  def index
    @items = Item.return_items
  end
    .
    .
    .
  def clear_cart
    @cart = get_cart
    @cart.initializeinitialize
  end

private
  def get_cart
    if session[:shopping_cart]
```

```
          return session[:shopping_cart]
        else
          return Cart.new
        end
      end
    end
  end
```

In `cart.rb`, add the `clear` method to reset the `@purchases` array and set the current total price to `0.0`:

```
class Cart
  attr_reader :purchases
  attr_reader :price

  def initialize
    @purchases = []
    @price = 0.0
  end

  def clear
    @purchases = []
    @price = 0.0
  end
      .
      .
      .
end
```

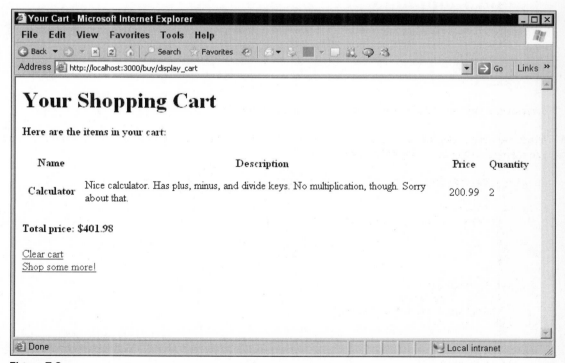

Figure 7-9

All that's left is to tell the customer that the cart has indeed been cleared. You can do so by displaying a new page, `clear_cart.rhtml`, connected to the `clear_cart` action, like this:

```html
<html>
  <head>
    <title>Your Cart</title>
  </head>

  <body>
    <h1>Your Shopping Cart</h1>
    <b>There are no items in your cart:</b>
    <br>
    <br>
    <%= link_to 'Shop some more!', :action => 'index' %>
  </body>
</html>
```

Figure 7-10 shows the page that comes up after the user clears the cart. Very nice.

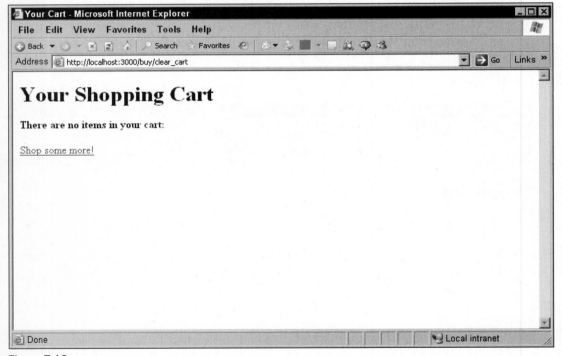

Figure 7-10

There's one more thing to add to this project.

Letting the User View the Cart Anytime

As a final refinement, let the user view his cart at anytime. To do that, just add a link, See your cart, to the index.rhtml page that displays the items for sale:

```
<html>
  <head>
    <title>The Store</title>
  </head>

  <body>
    <h1>Buy From Our Store!</h1>
    <b>Welcome to the store.</b>
    <br>
    <b><i>Please buy a lot of items, thank you.</i></b>
    <br>
    <br>
    <table cellpadding="6">
      <% for item in @items %>
      <tr>
        <td><b><%=h item.name %></b></td>
        <td><%=h item.description %></td>
        <td><%= link_to 'Add to cart', :action => 'add', :id => item %></td>
      </tr>
      <% end %>
    </table>
    <br>
    <%= link_to 'See your cart', :action => 'display_cart' %>
  </body>
</html>
```

Figure 7-11 shows the new link on the page.

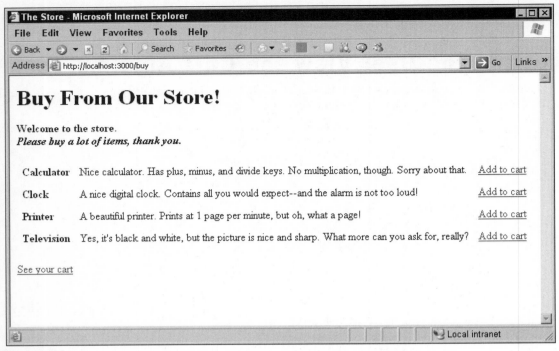

Figure 7-11

Letting the customer view the cart at any time means that the cart could be empty, so it'd be a problem trying to loop over the @purchases array in the display_cart.rhtml view. To head that off, check to see if @purchases is empty in display_cart.rhtml, and if so, display a message that the cart is empty, like this:

```
<html>
  <head>
    <title>Your Cart</title>
  </head>

  <body>
    <h1>Your Shopping Cart</h1>
    <% if (@purchases == []) %>
      <b>There are no items in your cart:</b>
      <br>
      <br>
      <%= link_to 'Shop some more!', :action => 'index' %>
    <% else %>
      <b>Here are the items in your cart:</b>
      <br>
      <br>
      <table cellpadding="6">
        <tr>
```

```
      <% for column in Item.content_columns %>
        <th><%= column.human_name %></th>
      <% end %>
      <th>Quantity</th>
    </tr>
    <% for purchase in @purchases
        item = purchase.item
    %>
      <tr>
      <td><b><%=h item.name %></b></td>
      <td><%=h item.description %></td>
      <td><%=h item.price %></td>
      <td><%=h purchase.quantity %></td>
    </tr>
    <% end %>
  </table>
  <br>
  <b>Total: $<%=h @total %></b>
  <br>
  <br>
  <%= link_to 'Clear cart', :action => 'clear_cart' %>
  <br>
  <%= link_to 'Shop some more!', :action => 'index' %>
  <% end %>
  </body>
</html>
```

And that's it — you've created a full, multi-page shopping cart demonstration application. Congratulations!

Summary

In this chapter, you got some important points about creating shopping cart applications, including how to:

- ❑ Create and work with a second controller.
- ❑ Use `find(:all)` to get all the records in a table.
- ❑ Add items to a shopping cart.
- ❑ Create a foreign key, and to let Rails know about it.
- ❑ Store a shopping cart in the session.
- ❑ Make Rails pre-load class definitions to avoid problems.
- ❑ Create private helper functions in controllers.

In the next chapter, you continue behind the scenes with Rails. First, though, try the exercises that follow to test your understanding of the material covered in this chapter. The solutions are in Appendix A.

Exercises

1. Add a text field and a Submit button to the display cart view asking for the user's name so that he can check out.

2. Add a `checkout` action to the `buy` controller that recovers the customer's name and the amount he owes.

3. Add a `checkout` view that displays the user's name and how much he owes to let him check out.

Validating and Testing

When you're working with online applications, validating the data the user sends you can be important, especially in release versions of your application. And Rails is up to the task, giving you easy ways to check the data. Was data entered? Was it a number? Was it an email address? Rails can check all of that, as you'll see in this chapter.

Besides validating data, it's important to keep testing your application as you develop it. Agile development is one of the bywords of Rails work, and one of its primary points is to continue testing as you write. Rails comes to the rescue here in two ways: it supports an easy testing framework, and it builds that framework into every Rails application.

Let's start by validating the data the user enters into your online application.

Validating the Presence of Data

The `store` application contains a controller named `manage` that lets managers enter new items for sale in the `items` database. What if the manager makes an error? For instance, what if he forgets to enter the name of the new item?

Rails to the rescue.

Copy your `store` *application from rubydev\ch07\store to rubydev\ch08\store before working with the code in this chapter. That just means copying the store folder from rubydev\ch07 to rubydev\ch08. After you do that, you'll be keeping track of the changes made to the* `store` *application in this chapter, instead of working on the Chapter 7 version.*

Try It Out   Make Sure Data Is Present

To make sure that data is present in the `manage` view, follow these steps:

1. Edit the rubydev\ch08\store\app\models\item.rb file, adding this line:

```
class Item < ActiveRecord::Base
  validates_presence_of :name, :description, :price
```

```
  def self.return_items
    find(:all)
  end
end
```

2. Start the WEBrick server:

```
C:\rubydev\ch06\store>ruby script/server
```

3. Navigate to `http://localhost:3000/manage`, as shown in Figure 8-1.

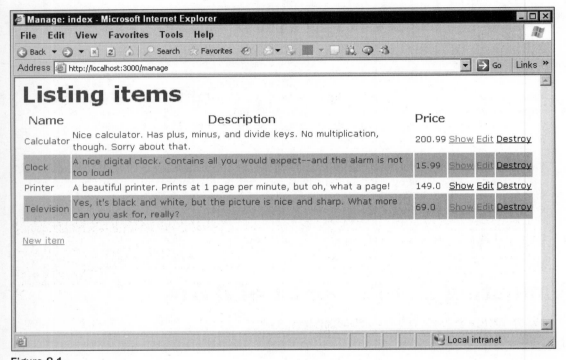

Figure 8-1

4. Click the New Item link, taking you to `http://localhost:3000/manage/new`, as shown in Figure 8-2.

5. Create a new phone item, but do not enter a name for the item. Enter the text **"This nice phone will never let you down."** in the Description box, and **19.99** in the Price box, leaving the Name box blank.

6. Click the Create button. You'll see an error, as shown in Figure 8-3.

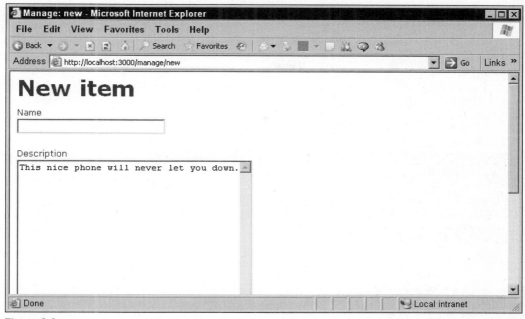

Figure 8-2

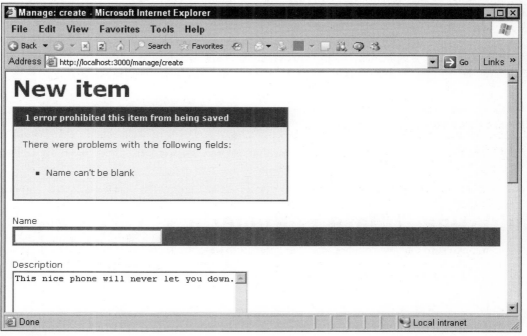

Figure 8-3

How It Works

In this example, you just needed one line of code, using the `validates_presence_of` method:

```
validates_presence_of :name, :description, :price
```

That makes sure that the user enters data in the Name, Description, and Price fields of `http://local-host:3000/manage/new`. Very cool — you enforced the presence of those items with a single line of code.

> Please insert HIW end rule. Thanks.

You can also specify options when you use `validates_presence_of`, like this:

```
class Item < ActiveRecord::Base
  validates_presence_of :name, :message => "is blank", :if => test()
  def self.return_items
    find(:all)
  end
end
```

Here are the possible options and what they mean:

Option	Description
message	An error message; the default is: `"can't be blank"`.
on	Indicates when this validation should be checked; the default is `:save`, and other options are `:create` and `:update`.
if	Specifies a method or symbol to check to determine if the validation should occur. The method or symbol should evaluate to true or false.

When you see validation problems, as in Figure 8-3, you can simply correct those problems and click the Submit (or Create or Update) button.

Rails has other validation methods, such as one that lets you check if data entered is a number, coming up next.

Validating if Data Is Numeric

You can make sure that the data the manager enters into the Price field is actually a number. A manager entering a non-number when the database is expecting a number could cause a serious error. Once again, Rails to the rescue.

Try It Out   Make Sure Data Is Numeric

To make sure that data is numeric, follow these steps:

1.   Edit the rubydev\ch08\store\app\models\item.rb file, adding this line:

```
class Item < ActiveRecord::Base
  validates_presence_of :name, :description, :price
  validates_numericality_of :price
  def self.return_items
    find(:all)
  end
end
```

2.   Start the WEBrick server:

```
C:\rubydev\ch06\store>ruby script/server
```

3.   Navigate to `http://localhost:3000/manage`.

4.   Click the New Item link, taking you to `http://localhost:3000/manage/new`.

5.   Create a new phone item, but enter **twelve** for the price of the item, as shown in Figure 8-4.

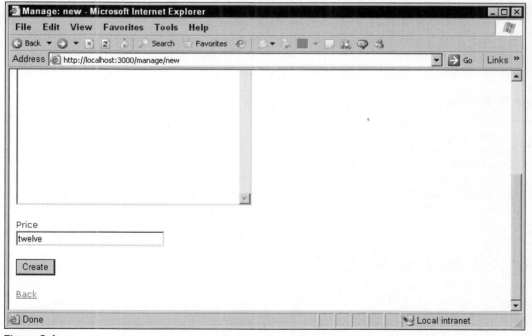

Figure 8-4

6. Click the Create button. You'll see an error, as shown in Figure 8-5.

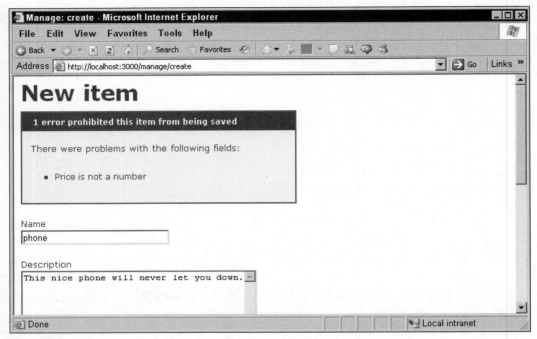

Figure 8-5

How It Works

In this case, you also needed just one line of code, putting the `validates_numericality_of` (good name, huh?) method to work:

```
class Item < ActiveRecord::Base
  validates_presence_of :name, :description, :price
  validates_numericality_of :price
  def self.return_items
    find(:all)
  end
end
```

You can also specify options when you use `validates_numericality_of`, like this:

```
class Item < ActiveRecord::Base
  validates_presence_of :name, :description, :price
  validates_numericality_of :price, :message => "is not numeric", :if => test()
  def self.return_items
    find(:all)
  end
end
```

Here are the possible options and what they mean:

Option	Description
message	An error message; the default is: `"is not a number"`.
on	Indicates when this validation should be checked; the default is `:save`, and other options are `:create` and `:update`.
only_integer	Indicates if the checked value has to be an integer; the default is false.
allow_nil	Rails skips this validation if the attribute is nil; the default is false.
if	Specifies a method or symbol to check to determine if the validation should occur. The method or symbol should evaluate to true or false.

Rails also lets you check if your data is unique.

Validating if Data Is Unique

You probably don't want to enter data that overrides existing data because their names are the same. In other words, you want to ensure that the data is unique. You can check that with the `validates_uniqueness_of` method. The following Try It Out shows you how.

Try It Out   **Make Sure Data Is Unique**

To make sure that an item is unique, follow these steps:

1. Edit the rubydev\ch08\store\app\models\item.rb file, adding this line:

```
class Item < ActiveRecord::Base
  validates_presence_of :name, :description, :price
  validates_numericality_of :price
  validates_uniqueness_of :name

  def self.return_items
    find(:all)
  end
end
```

2. Start the WEBrick server:

```
C:\rubydev\ch06\store>ruby script/server
```

3. Navigate to `http://localhost:3000/manage` and click the New Item link, taking you to `http://localhost:3000/manage/new`.

4. Try to create a new printer item, as shown in Figure 8-6.

5. Click the Create button. You'll see an error, as shown in Figure 8-7, indicating that that name has already been taken. This fails because the `items` table already contains a printer item.

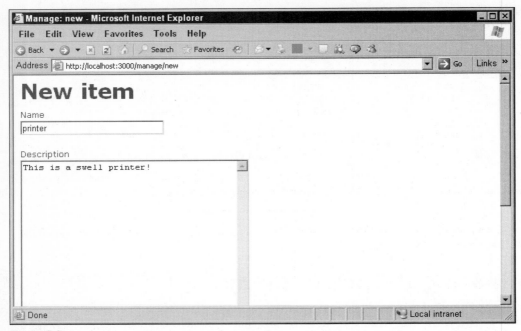

Figure 8-6

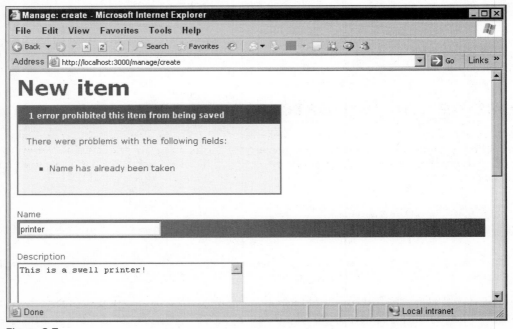

Figure 8-7

How It Works

As before, you need just one line of code, `validates_uniqueness_of :name`, to make this work:

```
class Item < ActiveRecord::Base
  validates_presence_of :name, :description, :price
  validates_numericality_of :price
  validates_uniqueness_of :name

  def self.return_items
    find(:all)
  end
end
```

That's all it takes to verify that the data in a field is unique.

You can also specify options when you use `validates_numericality_of`. The following table describes those options.

Option	Description
message	An error message; the default is: `"has already been taken"`.
scope	Specifies one or more columns to limit the scope of the uniqueness check.
if	Specifies a method or symbol to determine if the validation should occur. The method or symbol should evaluate to true or false.

There are other validation methods available to you in Rails as well, but you've taken the `store` application about as far as it can go here, so it's time to create a new application: the `Validator`.

Creating the Validator Application

To check out the other validation methods available, create a new application, `Validator`. This application is simply going to accept text tied to a database table named `fields`, and it will show how to work with validation methods not appropriate for the `store` application (such as validating email addresses, for example).

Start by creating the `Validator` application:

```
C:\rubydev\ch08>rails validator
    .
    .
    .
```

Next, add your username and password to the `validator_development` database information in ruby-dev\ch08\validator\config\database.yml:

```
# MySQL (default setup).  Versions 4.1 and 5.0 are recommended.
#
# Install the MySQL driver:
#   gem install mysql
# On MacOS X:
#   gem install mysql -- --include=/usr/local/lib
# On Windows:
#   There is no gem for Windows.  Install mysql.so from RubyForApache.
#   http://rubyforge.org/projects/rubyforapache
#
# And be sure to use new-style password hashing:
#   http://dev.mysql.com/doc/refman/5.0/en/old-client.html
development:
  adapter: mysql
  database: validator_development
  username: root
  password: *********
  host: localhost
     .
     .
     .
```

Now create the `validator_development` database, giving it a table named `fields`, and giving that table a single column, `data`:

```
C:\rubydev\ch08>mysql -u root -p
Enter password: ********
     .
     .
     .

mysql> create database validator_development;
Query OK, 1 row affected (0.00 sec)

mysql> use validator_development
Database changed

mysql> create table fields (
    -> data text not null);
Query OK, 0 rows affected (0.03 sec)

mysql> exit
Bye
```

Next, use the `scaffold` utility to create a model named `field` and a controller named `manage`:

```
C:\rubydev\ch08\validator>ruby script/generate scaffold Field Manage
     .
     .
     .
```

Okay, that gives you the `Validator` application. Let's put it to work.

Validating the Format of Data

In Rails, validation techniques can extend as far as using regular expressions — you can validate data only if it matches a regular expression, for example. A regular expression gives you a way of matching text — the syntax of regular expressions is too complex for a full discussion here, but if you're not familiar with them, you might take a look at http://perldoc.perl.org/perlre.html for all the details. You won't need to know how to use regular expressions in this book, but they're useful for such things as validating that the user has entered an email address.

Try It Out   Validate an Email Address

To validate an email address, follow these steps:

1. Add this line of code to rubydev\ch08\validator\app\models\field.rb:

```
class Field < ActiveRecord::Base
  validates_format_of :data, :with => /^([^@\s]+)@((?:[-a-z0-9]+\.)+[a-z]{2,})$/i,
  :message => "is not a valid email address"
end
```

2. Change this line in rubydev\ch08\validator\app\views\manage_form.rhtml:

```
<%= error_messages_for 'field' %>

<!--[form:field]-->
<p><label for="field_data">Data</label><br/>
<%= text_area 'field', 'data', "rows" => 4  %></p>
<!--[eoform:field]-->
```

to this:

```
<%= error_messages_for 'field' %>

<!--[form:field]-->
<p><label for="field_data">Your email</label><br/>
<%= text_area 'field', 'data', "rows" => 4  %></p>
<!--[eoform:field]-->
```

3. Start the WEBrick server:

```
C:\rubydev\ch06\store>ruby script/server
```

4. Navigate to http://localhost:3000/manage and click the New Field link.

5. Enter a non-email address into the Your email control, as shown in Figure 8-8, and click the Create button.

6. The result, shown in Figure 8-9, is an error pointing out that the text you entered is not a valid email address.

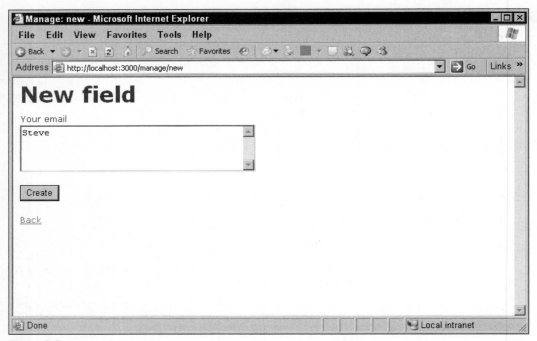

Figure 8-8

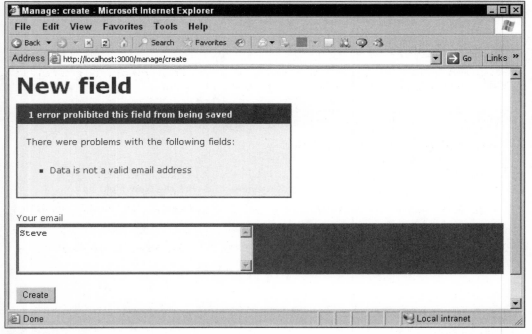

Figure 8-9

How It Works

In this example, you use the `validates_format_of` method to check the email address the user entered against a regular expression that matches email addresses:

```
validates_format_of :data, :with => /^([^@\s]+)@((?:[-a-z0-9]+\.)+[a-z]{2,})$/i,
:message => "is not a valid email address"
```

If it doesn't match, an error message displays.

You can also use various options with `validates_format_of`. Those options are described in the following table.

Option	Description
message	An error message; the default is: `"is invalid"`.
with	Specifies the regular expression used.
on	Indicates when this validation should be checked; the default is `:save`, and other options are `:create` and `:update`.
if	Specifies a method or symbol to check to determine if the validation should occur. The method or symbol should evaluate to true or false.

Besides checking data against regular expressions, you can also check it against a list of items, coming up next.

Validating against Inclusion in a List

You can use the `validates_inclusion_of` method to check whether the data the user has entered is in a list of items that you supply. The following exercise shows you how.

Try It Out **Validate against Inclusion in a List**

To validate against inclusion in a list, follow these steps:

1. Add this line of code to rubydev\ch08\validator\app\models\field.rb:

```
class Field < ActiveRecord::Base
  validates_inclusion_of :data, :in=> 1..99, :message => "is out of bounds"
end
```

2. Change this line in rubydev\ch08\validator\app\views\manage_form.rhtml:

```
<%= error_messages_for 'field' %>

<!--[form:field]-->
<p><label for="field_data">Your email</label><br/>
<%= text_area 'field', 'data', "rows" => 4  %></p>
<!--[eoform:field]-->
```

to this:

```
<%= error_messages_for 'field' %>

<!--[form:field]-->
<p><label for="field_data">Your age</label><br/>
<%= text_area 'field', 'data', "rows" => 4  %></p>
<!--[eoform:field]-->
```

3. Start the WEBrick server:

```
C:\rubydev\ch06\store>ruby script/server
```

4. Navigate to `http://localhost:3000/manage` and click the New Field link.

5. Enter an age that's outside the range `1..99`, as shown in Figure 8-10, and click the Create button.

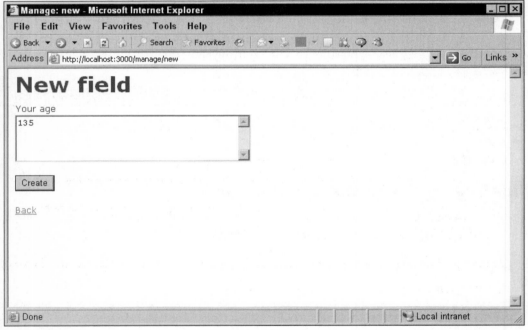

Figure 8-10

6. An error points out that the age you entered is not valid, as shown in Figure 8-11.

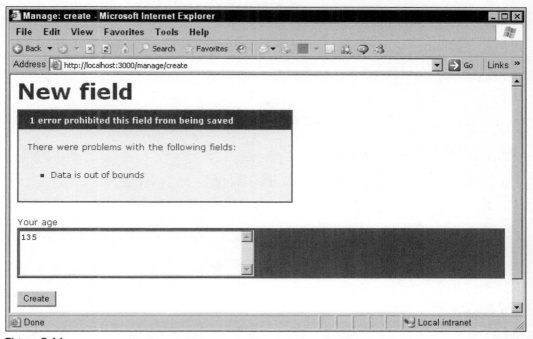

Figure 8-11

How It Works

The `validates_inclusion_of` method checks the age the user enters against the range 1..99:

```
validates_inclusion_of :data, :in=> 1..99, :message => "is out of bounds"
```

If the data doesn't fit into this range, an error displays.

The various options that can be used with `validates_inclusion_of` are described in the following table.

Option	Description
in	Specifies an enumerable object containing allowed items.
message	An error message; the default is: `"is not included in the list"`.
allow_nil	If true, skips this check if the attribute is null.
if	Specifies a method or symbol to check to determine if the validation should occur. The method or symbol should evaluate to true or false.

In addition to `validates_inclusion_of`, there's also `validates_exclusion_of`, which validates only if the data is *not* in a specified range. For example, you might want to exclude underage customers like this:

```ruby
class Field < ActiveRecord::Base
  validates_exclusion_of :data, :in=> 1..18, :message => "Customer is underage."
end
```

The options you can use with `validates_exclusion_of` are described in the following table.

Option	Description
in	Specifies an enumerable object containing unallowed items.
message	An error message; the default is: `"is reserved"`.
allow_nil	If true, skips this check if the attribute is null.
if	Specifies a method or symbol to check to determine if the validation should occur. The method or symbol should evaluate to true or false.

You can also validate against whether the user checked a confirmation checkbox.

Validating That the User Clicked a Checkbox

There are several situations in which you would to make sure that the user has checked a specific check-box. The most common is when you want to ensure that a user has checked a box indicating acceptance of an End User License Agreement (EULA). You can use the `validates_acceptance_of` method to verify whether a checkbox has been checked. Try it for yourself in the following exercise.

Try It Out   **Validate Using Checkboxes**

To validate using a checkbox, follow these steps:

1.   Add this line of code to rubydev\ch08\validator\app\models\field.rb:

```ruby
class Field < ActiveRecord::Base
  validates_acceptance_of :check1, :message => "was not checked"
end
```

2.   Add two lines to rubydev\ch08\validator\app\views\manage_form.rhtml:

```erb
<%= error_messages_for 'field' %>

<!--[form:field]-->
<p><label for="field_data">Your age</label><br/>
<%= text_area 'field', 'data', "rows" => 4  %></p>
Do you accept the End User License Agreement?
<p><%= check_box "field", "check1" %>Yes</p>
<!--[eoform:field]-->
```

3. Start the WEBrick server:

```
C:\rubydev\ch06\store>ruby script/server
```

4. Navigate to `http://localhost:3000/manage` and click the New Field link.

5. Do not check the checkbox, and click the Create button shown in Figure 8-12.

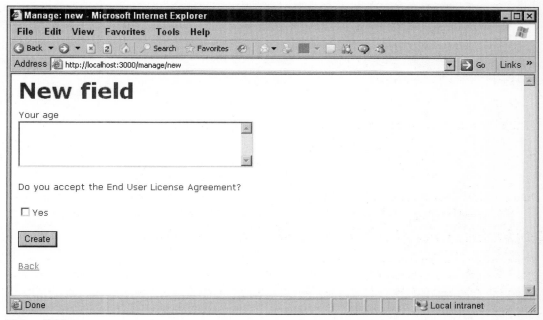

Figure 8-12

6. An error displays, pointing out that you didn't check the checkbox, as shown in Figure 8-13.

How It Works

In this example, you used the `validates_acceptance_of` method to determine whether the user checked a checkbox:

```
validates_acceptance_of :check1, :message => "was not checked"
```

The two lines of code you added in step 2 create the checkbox:

```
Do you accept the End User License Agreement?
<p><%= check_box "field", "check1" %>Yes</p>
```

There's a little going on behind the scenes that you should know about here. By default, the `check_box` method creates a checkbox with a value of `'1'`, and, also by default, that's the value the `validates_acceptance_of` method looks for.

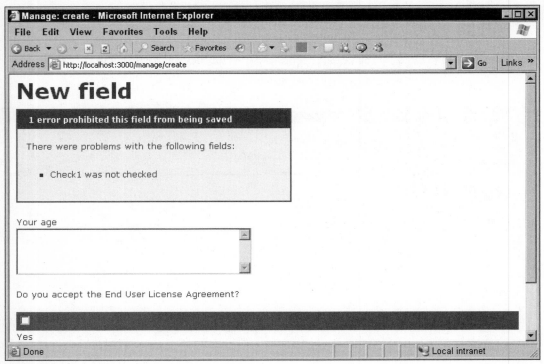

Figure 8-13

The following table describes the options you can set with `validates_acceptance_of`.

Option	Description
accept	Indicates the checkbox value that is acceptable. The default value is `'1'`.
message	An error message; the default is: `"must be accepted"`.
on	Specifies when this validation is operative; the default is `:save`, and the other options are `:create` and `:update`.
if	Specifies a method or symbol to check to determine if the validation should occur. The method or symbol should evaluate to true or false.

Validating Confirmation of Passwords

You know those double text fields where you're asked to enter your password and then type it again to confirm it? You can do that in Rails, too, using `validates_confirmation_of`. All you need is a control named, say, `password`, and a second control named the same way, but with `_confirmation` appended, such as `password_confirmation`.

Try It Out   **Validate Password Confirmations**

To validate password confirmations, follow these steps:

1.   Add this line of code to rubydev\ch08\validator\app\models\field.rb:

```
class Field < ActiveRecord::Base
  validates_confirmation_of :data, :message => "should match confirmation"
end
```

2.   Change rubydev\ch08\validator\app\views\manage_form.rhtml to this:

```
<%= error_messages_for 'field' %>

<!--[form:field]-->
<p><label for="field_data">Your password</label><br/>
<%= text_area 'field', 'data', "rows" => 4  %></p>
<p><label for="field_data_confirmation">Confirm your password</label><br/>
<%= text_area 'field', 'data_confirmation', "rows" => 4  %></p>

<!--[eoform:field]-->
```

3.   Start the WEBrick server:

```
C:\rubydev\ch06\store>ruby script/server
```

4.   Navigate to `http://localhost:3000/manage` and click the New Field link.

5.   Enter two different passwords and click the Create button shown in Figure 8-14.

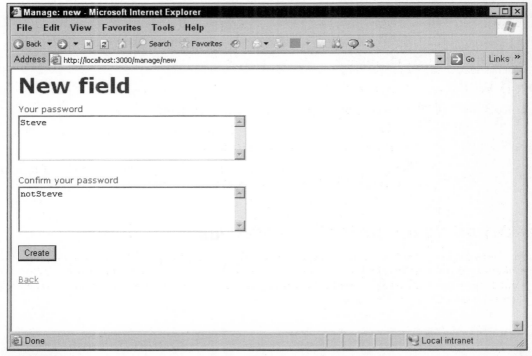

Figure 8-14

6. When the confirmation password fails to match the original, an error displays, as shown in Figure 8-15.

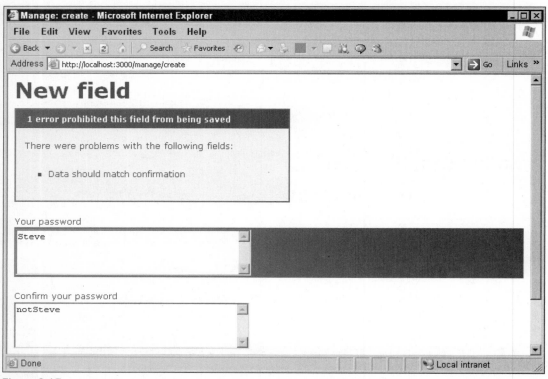

Figure 8-15

How It Works

To check whether the passwords match, all you need to do is to use the `validates_confirmation_of` method in the model:

```
validates_confirmation_of :data, :message => "should match confirmation"
```

The code you added in step 2 creates the confirmation control:

```
<%= error_messages_for 'field' %>

<!--[form:field]-->
<p><label for="field_data">Your password</label><br/>
<%= text_area 'field', 'data', "rows" => 4 %></p>
<p><label for="field_data_confirmation">Confirm your password</label><br/>
<%= text_area 'field', 'data_confirmation', "rows" => 4 %></p>

<!--[eoform:field]-->
```

You can set three options with `validates_confirmation_of`, and they're described in the following table.

Option	Description
message	An error message; the default is: `"doesn't match confirmation"`.
on	Specifies when this validation is operative; the default is `:save`, and the other options are `:create` and `:update`.
if	Specifies a method or symbol to check to determine if the validation should occur. The method or symbol should evaluate to true or false.

Validating Length of Text

You can also validate on the length of text, such as when you want a password that's between four and eight characters, inclusive. You can validate that kind of data with the `validates_length_of` method, which you'll use in this exercise.

Try It Out   **Validate on Text Length**

To validate on text length, follow these steps:

1.   Add these lines of code to rubydev\ch08\validator\app\models\field.rb:

```
class Field < ActiveRecord::Base
  validates_length_of :data, :maximum => 8, :message => "is too long"
  validates_length_of :data, :minimum => 4, :message => "is too short"
end
```

2.   Change rubydev\ch08\validator\app\views\manage_form.rhtml to this:

```
<%= error_messages_for 'field' %>

<!--[form:field]-->
<p><label for="field_data">Your password (4-8 letters)</label><br/>
<%= text_area 'field', 'data', "rows" => 4  %></p>

<!--[eoform:field]-->
```

3.   Start the WEBrick server:

```
C:\rubydev\ch06\store>ruby script/server
```

4.   Navigate to `http://localhost:3000/manage` and click the New Field link.

5.   Enter an overly long password and click the Create button shown in Figure 8-16.

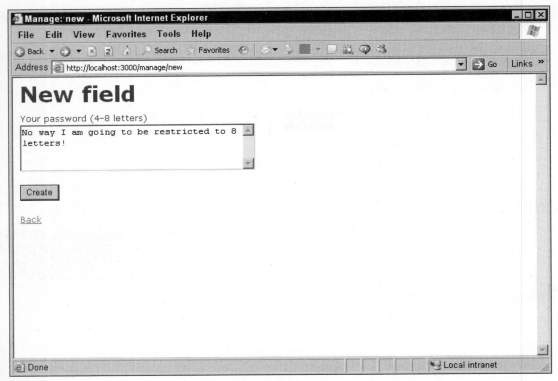

Figure 8-16

6. A password longer than eight characters fails validation and the error shown in Figure 8-17 displays.

How It Works

To check whether the entered password is too long or too short, you add two tests to the model:

```
validates_length_of :data, :maximum => 8, :message => "is too long"
validates_length_of :data, :minimum => 4, :message => "is too short"
```

You can't combine a test using :minimum and :maximum together—you need two separate tests. (The :within option allows a single test. It's described in the next options table.)

Then you only have to indicate the minimum and maximum lengths you'll accept for your password in the view:

```
<p><label for="field_data">Your password (4-8 letters)</label><br/>
```

And that's all there is to it.

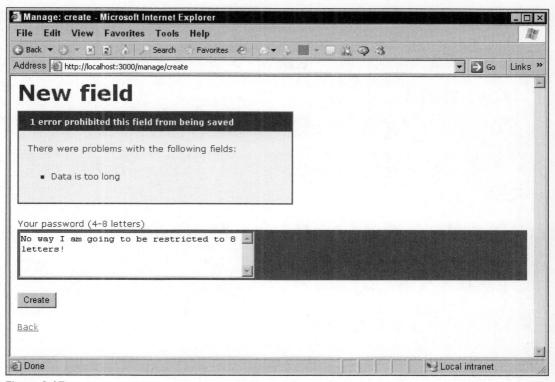

Figure 8-17

The following table describes the various options you can set with `validates_confirmation_of`.

Option	Description
minimum	Specifies the minimum size of the attribute's data.
maximum	Specifies the maximum size of the attribute's data.
is	Specifies the exact size of the attribute.
within	Specifies a range holding the minimum and maximum size of the attribute's data.
in	Same as `:within`.
allow_nil	If true, skips this check if the attribute is null.
message	An error message for `:maximum`, `:minimum`, or `:is`; the default is `"doesn't match confirmation"`.
on	Specifies when this validation is operative; the default is `:save`, and the other options are `:create` and `:update`.

Option	Description
too_long	Specifies the error message if the attribute's data is over the maximum; the default is `"is too long (maximum is xxx characters)"`.
too_short	Specifies the error message if the attribute is under the minimum; the default is `"is too short (min is xxx characters)"`.
wrong_length	Specifies the error message for the `:is` method; the default is `"is the wrong length (should be xxx characters)"`.
if	Specifies a method or symbol to check to determine if the validation should occur. The method or symbol should evaluate to true or false.

Writing Your Own Validate Method

Haven't seen the kind of validation you'd like to do? You can write your own validate method, which Rails will call. If there's an error, you can add a message to the list of errors that will be displayed by Rails. The following exercise is an example of a custom method.

Try It Out   **Write a Custom Validate Method**

These steps lead you through writing a custom validate method:

1.   Add these lines of code to rubydev\ch08\validator\app\models\field.rb:

```
class Field < ActiveRecord::Base
  protected
  def validate
    errors.add(:data, "is not 'Steve'") unless data == "Steve"
  end
end
```

2.   Change rubydev\ch08\validator\app\views\manage_form.rhtml to this:

```
<%= error_messages_for 'field' %>

<!--[form:field]-->
<p><label for="field_data">Your name</label><br/>
<%= text_area 'field', 'data', "rows" => 4  %></p>

<!--[eoform:field]-->
<%= error_messages_for 'field' %>
```

3.   Start the WEBrick server:

```
C:\rubydev\ch06\store>ruby script/server
```

4.   Navigate to `http://localhost:3000/manage` and click the New Field link.

5.   Enter any name except Steve, and click the Create button shown in Figure 8-18.

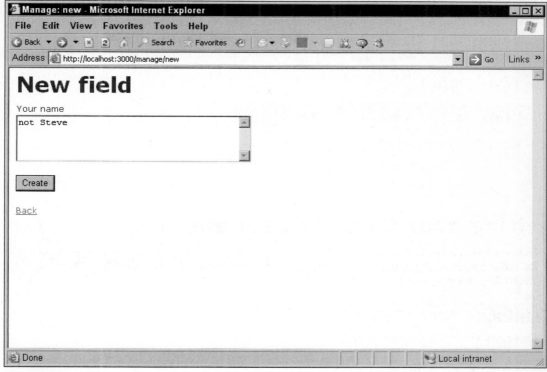

Figure 8-18

6. An error indicates that your entered name is not Steve, as shown in Figure 8-19.

How It Works

You can write your own custom validation method. Make it protected so that Rails doesn't think it's an attribute of the model:

```
protected
def validate
      .
      .
      .
end
```

To add an error to the errors list displayed by Rails, you call the `errors.add` method, passing it the attribute the error is associated with and the message you want to connect to that attribute. Here's the code that registers an error if the `:data` attribute's data isn't `'Steve'`:

```
errors.add(:data, "is not 'Steve'") unless data == "Steve"
```

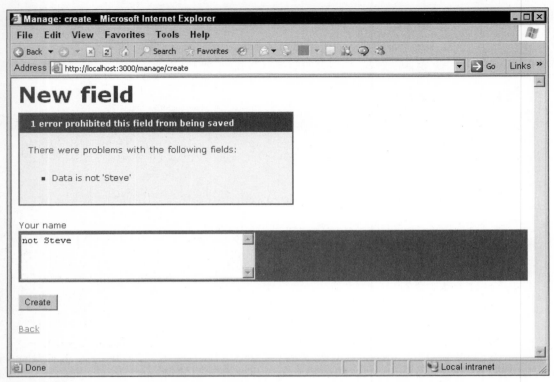

Figure 8-19

In addition to validation, Rails gives you some built-in support for testing your applications as you develop them. You explore that in the next section.

Testing Your Model

Testing is built into the Rails framework, and when it creates an application for you, it adds a test directory full of good stuff. Here are the subdirectories of the rubydev\ch08\store\test directory:

```
store
|__test
   |__fixtures
   |__functional
   |__integration
   |__mocks
   |__unit
```

It's a Rails convention to call model tests *unit tests*, and to call controller tests *functional tests*. To start, you might take a look at the unit tests that test the model in rubydev\ch08\store\test\unit:

```
store
|__test
  |__fixtures
  |__functional
  |__integration
  |__mocks
  |__unit
      |__item_test.rb
      |__purchase_test.rb
```

The two pre-built files — `item_test.rb` and `purchase_test.rb` — correspond to the two models you have in the `store` application: `Item` and `Purchase`. Take a look at the rubydev\ch08\store\test\unit\item_test.rb file:

```ruby
require File.dirname(__FILE__) + '/../test_helper'

class ItemTest < Test::Unit::TestCase
  fixtures :items

  # Replace this with your real tests.
  def test_truth
    assert true
  end
end
```

This shows the general form of a test — a method that starts with `test_`. To get things started, how about testing the model to see if it supports the right kind of `Item` objects? This test will check whether the model is working and connected to a database table.

Try It Out   Test the Model

To test the model of the `store` application, follow these steps:

1. Edit rubydev\ch08\store\test\unit\item_test.rb, making these changes, including renaming the `test_truth` method to `test_model`:

```ruby
require File.dirname(__FILE__) + '/../test_helper'

class ItemTest < Test::Unit::TestCase
  fixtures :items

  def setup
    @item = Item.find(1)
  end

  # Replace this with your real tests.
  def test_model
    assert_kind_of Item, @item
  end
end
```

2. Run `item_test.rb` from the command line:

```
C:\rubydev\ch08\store>ruby test/unit/item_test.rb
Loaded suite test/unit/item_test
Started
EE
Finished in 0.078 seconds.

  1) Error:
test_truth(ItemTest):
ActiveRecord::StatementInvalid: Mysql::Error: #42S02Table 'store_test.items' doe
sn't exist: DELETE FROM items
    c:/ruby/lib/ruby/gems/1.8/gems/activerecord-1.14.2/lib/active_record/connect
ion_adapters/abstract_adapter.rb:120:in `log'
    c:/ruby/lib/ruby/gems/1.8/gems/activerecord-1.14.2/lib/active_record/connect
ion_adapters/mysql_adapter.rb:185:in `execute'
    c:/ruby/lib/ruby/gems/1.8/gems/activerecord-1.14.2/lib/active_record/connect

       .
       .
       .

  2) Error:
test_truth(ItemTest):
NoMethodError: You have a nil object when you didn't expect it!
You might have expected an instance of Array.
The error occured while evaluating nil.-
    c:/ruby/lib/ruby/gems/1.8/gems/activerecord-1.14.2/lib/active_record/transac
tions.rb:112:in `unlock_mutex'
    c:/ruby/lib/ruby/gems/1.8/gems/activerecord-1.14.2/lib/active_record/fixture
s.rb:534:in `teardown'

1 tests, 0 assertions, 0 failures, 2 errors
```

This doesn't look so good. It turns out that you need to create the `store_test` database to be able to test the model.

3. Use this command to clone the `store_development` database into the `store_test` database:

```
C:\rubydev\ch08\store>rake clone_structure_to_test
(in C:/rubydev/ch08/store)
```

4. Edit rubydev\ch08\store\test\fixtures\items.yml from this:

```
# Read about fixtures at http://ar.rubyonrails.org/classes/Fixtures.html
first:
  id: 1
another:
  id: 2
```

to this:

```
# Read about fixtures at http://ar.rubyonrails.org/classes/Fixtures.html
first:
  id: 1
  name: Calculator
  description: A nice calculator.
  price: 19.99
second:
  id: 2
```

```
name: Printer
description: A nice printer.
price: 29.99
```

5. Rerun the test:

```
C:\rubydev\ch08\store>ruby test/unit/item_test.rb
Loaded suite test/unit/item_test
Started
.
Finished in 0.11 seconds.

1 tests, 1 assertions, 0 failures, 0 errors
```

6. The test succeeded. Excellent.

How It Works

You first added a `setup` method to the file rubydev\ch08\store\test\unit\item_test.rb:

```
require File.dirname(__FILE__) + '/../test_helper'

class ItemTest < Test::Unit::TestCase
  fixtures :items

  def setup
    @item = Item.find(1)
  end

  # Replace this with your real tests.
  def test_truth
    assert true
  end
end
```

`setup` runs before the tests are run, so you can use it for initialization. In this case, the code reads an item from the `items` table and stores it in `@item` for use in the following tests.

In the `test_model` method, you used the `assert_kind_of` method to assert that `@item` contains an object of class `Item` to make sure the model is working okay:

```
def test_model
  assert_kind_of Item, @item
```

That's the way you create tests — with *assertions*. You assert something is true or false, and when the test runs, Rails lets you know whether your assertion was correct.

That's how it works. You can create as many tests as you like; each one is a method starting with `test_`. Inside each method, you use assertions to perform the actual tests.

Clean Up with teardown

You can also add a `teardown` method in rubydev\ch08\store\test\unit\item_test.rb to perform cleanup:

```
require File.dirname(__FILE__) + '/../test_helper'

class ItemTest < Test::Unit::TestCase
  fixtures :items

  def setup
    @item = Item.find(1)
  end

  def teardown
    #perform cleanup
  end

  # Replace this with your real tests.
  def test_truth
    assert true
  end
end
```

It's worth noting that you won't usually have to clean up databases with the `teardown` method — even if you've modified them when you run your tests — because Rails re-creates your test database from scratch each time you run your tests in a way you'll see in a minute.

To test the model fully, you need to set up a database for testing — and that's the `store_test` database (unlike the `store_development` database you've been using by default so far). You could go to the trouble of creating the whole `store_test` database — or you could use a shortcut, using the `rake` utility this way:

```
C:\rubydev\ch08\store>rake clone_structure_to_test
(in C:/rubydev/ch08/store)
```

This creates the `store_test` database for you, copying the structure from `store_development` — a handy thing to know.

You still have to stock that new database with data, and you do that with a *fixture*, which, in Rails, simply means the initial contents of a model for testing (the word fixture means different things in different languages' testing frameworks, but that's what it means in Rails). You'll find the test fixture for the store's items model in rubydev\ch08\store\test\fixtures\items.yml, which starts off looking like this:

```
# Read about fixtures at http://ar.rubyonrails.org/classes/Fixtures.html
first:
  id: 1
another:
  id: 2
```

And you edit that file, adding two records to the `store_test` database:

```
# Read about fixtures at http://ar.rubyonrails.org/classes/Fixtures.html
first:
  id: 1
  name: Calculator
  description: A nice calculator.
  price: 19.99
second:
  id: 2
  name: Printer
  description: A nice printer.
  price: 29.99
```

These records will be installed in the `store_test` database each time you run your tests. That means you start off with a fresh copy of that database each time you execute your test application. How does Ruby know which fixture to use when you run your tests? That's where the `fixtures :items` line in `item_test.rb` comes in — it tells Ruby to use `items.yml` as a fixture:

```
fixtures :items
```

After editing the fixture file `items.yml`, you can run the test like this:

```
C:\rubydev\ch08\store>ruby test/unit/item_test.rb
Loaded suite test/unit/item_test
Started
.
Finished in 0.11 seconds.

1 tests, 1 assertions, 0 failures, 0 errors
```

As you see here, the test assertion was a success — which means that your model is working as it should, at least as far as holding objects of the `Item` class goes. How about adding some more in-depth tests?

Using Equality Assertions

You can use the `assert_equal` method to test for equality. For example, the first record in `store_test`'s `items` table should have the ID 1 and the name Calculator, and you can test that by adding these two lines to rubydev\ch08\store\test\unit\item_test.rb:

```
require File.dirname(__FILE__) + '/../test_helper'

class ItemTest < Test::Unit::TestCase
  fixtures :items

  def setup
    @item = Item.find(1)
  end

  # Replace this with your real tests.
  def test_model
    assert_kind_of Item, @item
```

```
      assert_equal 1, @item.id
      assert_equal "Calculator", @item.name
    end
end
```

Will that work? Check it out:

```
C:\rubydev\ch08\store>ruby test/unit/item_test.rb
Loaded suite test/unit/item_test
Started
.
Finished in 0.859 seconds.

1 tests, 3 assertions, 0 failures, 0 errors
```

Yes, that works.

Using General Assertions

In addition to using assertion methods like `assert_kind_of`, `assert_equal`, and `assert_not_equal`, you can create your own test conditions and test them with the `assert` method in rubydev\ch08\ store\test\unit\item_test.rb. If the condition you pass to the `assert` method is true, the assertion passes; otherwise, it doesn't. Here's an example, where the code tests that `@item.price` equals 19.99, as it should:

```
require File.dirname(__FILE__) + '/../test_helper'

class ItemTest < Test::Unit::TestCase
  fixtures :items

  def setup
    @item = Item.find(1)
  end

  # Replace this with your real tests.
  def test_model
    assert_kind_of Item, @item
    assert_equal 1, @item.id
    assert_equal "Calculator", @item.name
    assert @item.price == 19.99
  end
end
```

Does this work? Take a look:

```
C:\rubydev\ch08\store>ruby test/unit/item_test.rb
Loaded suite test/unit/item_test
Started
.
Finished in 0.109 seconds.

1 tests, 4 assertions, 0 failures, 0 errors
```

You bet.

Using Different Records

You set up two fixtures in rubydev\ch08\store\test\fixtures\items.yml, `first` and `second`:

```
first:
  id: 1
  name: Calculator
  description: A nice calculator.
  price: 19.99
second:
  id: 2
  name: Printer
  description: A nice printer.
  price: 29.99
```

So far, you've been working only with the first fixture. You can you work with the second one by referencing it by name, which is `second`, like this: `items(:second)` — that's the name of the set of fixtures, `items`, and the individual fixture to use, `:second`. So here's how you could use the `second` fixture:

```ruby
require File.dirname(__FILE__) + '/../test_helper'

class ItemTest < Test::Unit::TestCase
  fixtures :items

  def setup
    @item = Item.find(1)
  end

  # Replace this with your real tests.
  def test_model
    assert_kind_of Item, @item
    assert_equal 1, @item.id
    assert_equal "Calculator", @item.name
    assert @item.price == 19.99
    assert_equal 2, items(:second).id
  end
end
```

And that works fine:

```
C:\rubydev\ch08\store>ruby test/unit/item_test.rb
Loaded suite test/unit/item_test
Started
.
Finished in 0.094 seconds.

1 tests, 5 assertions, 0 failures, 0 errors
```

There's also a shortcut here — change this line in rubydev\ch08\store\test\test_helper.rb:

```ruby
self.use_instantiated_fixtures  = false
```

to this:

```ruby
self.use_instantiated_fixtures  = true
```

Doing so allows you to refer to fixtures by name, as @first and @second. Then, for example, you could use @second by changing this line:

```
assert_equal 2, items(:second).id
```

to this:

```
assert_equal 2, @second.id
```

As you can see, it's not hard testing the model.

You've used both the store_development *and* store_test *databases; how do you use the* store_production *database when you've finished developing your application? You can do that on startup this way:* ruby script/server -e production. *Or, if you're running on a commercial server and can't start the server yourself, you can uncomment the line* # ENV['RAILS_ENV'] ||= 'production' *in rubydev\ch08\store\config\environment.rb.*

Testing Your Controller

As it happens, Rails knows all about your controller and has already created a great set of tests for you in rubydev\ch08\store\test\functional. There are two test files in that directory—buy_controller_test.rb and manage_controller_test.rb—one for each of the controllers in the store application. Take a look at manage_controller_test.rb and note all the excellent tests already built in, one for each of the controller's actions:

```
require File.dirname(__FILE__) + '/../test_helper'
require 'manage_controller'

# Re-raise errors caught by the controller.
class ManageController; def rescue_action(e) raise e end; end

class ManageControllerTest < Test::Unit::TestCase
  fixtures :items

  def setup
    @controller = ManageController.new
    @request    = ActionController::TestRequest.new
    @response   = ActionController::TestResponse.new
  end

  def test_index
    get :index
    assert_response :success
    assert_template 'list'
  end

  def test_list
    get :list

    assert_response :success
```

```
    assert_template 'list'

    assert_not_nil assigns(:items)
  end

  def test_show
    get :show, :id => 1

    assert_response :success
    assert_template 'show'

    assert_not_nil assigns(:item)
    assert assigns(:item).valid?
  end

  def test_new
    get :new

    assert_response :success
    assert_template 'new'

    assert_not_nil assigns(:item)
  end

  def test_create
    num_items = Item.count

    post :create, :item => {}

    assert_response :redirect
    assert_redirected_to :action => 'list'

    assert_equal num_items + 1, Item.count
  end

  def test_edit
    get :edit, :id => 1

    assert_response :success
    assert_template 'edit'

    assert_not_nil assigns(:item)
    assert assigns(:item).valid?
  end

  def test_update
    post :update, :id => 1
    assert_response :redirect
    assert_redirected_to :action => 'show', :id => 1
  end

  def test_destroy
    assert_not_nil Item.find(1)

    post :destroy, :id => 1
```

```
      assert_response :redirect
      assert_redirected_to :action => 'list'

      assert_raise(ActiveRecord::RecordNotFound) {
        Item.find(1)
      }
   end
end
```

Notice the kinds of tests you can perform when testing controllers — you can check the type of response:

```
      assert_response :redirect
```

You can check that the browser was redirected to a specific action like this:

```
      assert_redirected_to :action => 'list'
```

You can check the current view template:

```
      assert_template 'list'
```

And so on. There are many tests here; will they all work? Here goes, where the file manage_controller_test.rb will create a manage controller and test it:

```
C:\rubydev\ch08\store>ruby test/functional/manage_controller_test.rb
Loaded suite test/functional/manage_controller_test
Started
F.......
Finished in 0.406 seconds.

  1) Failure:
test_create(ManageControllerTest) [test/functional/manage_controller_test.rb:55]
:
Expected response to be a <:redirect>, but was <200>

8 tests, 25 assertions, 1 failures, 0 errors
```

Not too bad — only one test failed. The test that failed was test_create, which creates a dummy empty record in the items table using the post method:

```
   def test_create
     num_items = Item.count

     post :create, :item => {}

     assert_response :redirect
     assert_redirected_to :action => 'list'

     assert_equal num_items + 1, Item.count
   end
```

That this test failed isn't surprising — it tried to create an empty record, and the `items` table was specifically written to make sure that all fields in all records are not null, something that Rails couldn't know when it created this test.

And that's it — as you can see, the framework for testing the controller has already been built for you, and it's ready to use. If you want to customize it you can, but often there's no need — the testing framework Rails builds for you provides a good test of your application's work flow.

Summary

In this chapter, you learned important information about testing and validating, including how to:

- ❑ Use `validates_presence_of` to determine if the user filled in a field.
- ❑ Use `validates_numericality_of` to determine if a field's data is numeric, and `validates_uniqueness_of` to validate that a field's data is unique.
- ❑ Validate using regular expressions with `validates_format_of`.
- ❑ Validate against lists of items with `validates_inclusion_of` or `validates_exclusion_of`.
- ❑ Validate that the user checked a checkbox with `validates_acceptance_of`.
- ❑ Validate confirmation of passwords with `validates_confirmation_of`.
- ❑ Validate the length of text with `validates_length_of`.
- ❑ Write your own validate method.
- ❑ Test models and test controllers.

Before you head to the next chapter, where you'll continue behind the scenes with Rails, try the exercises that follow to test your understanding of the material covered in this chapter. The solutions to these exercises are in Appendix A.

Exercises

1. Say you added a field named `subtitle` to the `items` table. Validate that the manager supplies some data for that field when creating new records.

2. Make sure that the `subtitle` field, created in the preceding exercise, holds unique data.

3. Now say that you add another field, `number`, which holds the number of the current item in stock, to the `items` table. Make sure the manager enters a numeric value for this field.

Controlling the Action with the Action Controller

The previous two chapters were on the model part of Rails applications, ActiveRecord. This chapter is on the controller, ActionController. You've already seen how to add actions to controllers, simply by adding a method to the controller class. That's just a drop in the bucket, however, and in this chapter, you're going to get the bigger picture.

Routing Refinements

One of the main things Rails controllers handle is routing requests, and you've already seen the default way that works. If you've got a controller named `look` and want to handle URLs like `http://yourisp.com/look/at`, you only have to add an action named `at` to the `look` controller, like this:

```
class LookController < ApplicationController
  def at
    @id = @params[:id]
  end
end
```

And this action is automatically connected to a view template named `at.rhtml`.

It turns out there's more to the story: you can set the routing of requests yourself, using a file named config\routes.rb — in fact, you can tailor the routing completely. To see this at work, take a look at an example that routes URLs where you specify the date, such as `http://yourisp.com/look/at/25/12/2007`. Being able to handle routing requests like this is part of understanding what controllers are all about in Rails applications.

Try It Out   Perform Custom Routing

To perform custom routing, follow these steps:

1.   Create a new application, `router`, in the rubydev\ch09 directory:

```
C:\rubydev\ch09>rails router
     create
     create    app/controllers
     create    app/helpers
     create    app/models
     create    app/views/layouts
     create    config/environments
     create    components
     create    db
     create    doc
     create    lib
        .
        .
        .
     create    public/javascripts/prototype.js
     create    public/javascripts/effects.js
     create    public/javascripts/dragdrop.js
     create    public/javascripts/controls.js
     create    public/javascripts/application.js
     create    doc/README_FOR_APP
     create    log/server.log
     create    log/production.log
     create    log/development.log
     create    log/test.log
```

2.   Change directories to the router directory:

```
C:\rubydev\ch09>cd router
```

3.   Create a controller named `Look` for the router directory:

```
C:\rubydev\ch09\router>ruby script/generate controller Look
     exists    app/controllers/
     exists    app/helpers/
     create    app/views/look
     exists    test/functional/
     create    app/controllers/look_controller.rb
     create    test/functional/look_controller_test.rb
     create    app/helpers/look_helper.rb
```

4.   Edit rubydev\ch09\router\config\routes.rb, which currently looks like this:

```
ActionController::Routing::Routes.draw do |map|
  # The priority is based upon order of creation: first created -> highest priority.

  # Sample of regular route:
  # map.connect 'products/:id', :controller => 'catalog', :action => 'view'
  # Keep in mind you can assign values other than :controller and :action

  # Sample of named route:
```

```
  # map.purchase 'products/:id/purchase', :controller => 'catalog', :action =>
'purchase'
  # This route can be invoked with purchase_url(:id => product.id)

  # You can have the root of your site routed by hooking up ''
  # -- just remember to delete public/index.html.
  # map.connect '', :controller => "welcome"

  # Allow downloading Web Service WSDL as a file with an extension
  # instead of a file named 'wsdl'
  map.connect ':controller/service.wsdl', :action => 'wsdl'

  # Install the default route as the lowest priority.
  map.connect ':controller/:action/:id'
end
```

to this:

```
ActionController::Routing::Routes.draw do |map|
  # The priority is based upon order of creation: first created -> highest
priority.

  # Sample of regular route:
  # map.connect 'products/:id', :controller => 'catalog', :action => 'view'
  # Keep in mind you can assign values other than :controller and :action

  # Sample of named route:
  # map.purchase 'products/:id/purchase', :controller => 'catalog', :action =>
'purchase'
  # This route can be invoked with purchase_url(:id => product.id)

  # You can have the root of your site routed by hooking up ''
  # -- just remember to delete public/index.html.
  # map.connect '', :controller => "welcome"

  # Allow downloading Web Service WSDL as a file with an extension
  # instead of a file named 'wsdl'
  map.connect ':controller/service.wsdl', :action => 'wsdl'

  # Install the default route as the lowest priority.
  map.connect ':controller/:action/:id'

  map.connect "look/at/:day/:month/:year",
    :controller => "look",
    :action     => "at",
    :requirements => {:year => /(19|20)\d\d/}

  map.connect "anything",
    :controller => "look",
    :action     => "unknown_request"
end
```

5. Edit rubydev\ch09\router\app\controllers\look_controller.rb, adding this code to create the at action:

```
class LookController < ApplicationController
  def at
    @day = @params[:day]
    @month = @params[:month]
    @year = @params[:year]
  end
end
```

6. Create rubydev\ch09\router\app\views\look\at.rhtml, and place this code in it:

```
<html>
  <head>
    <title>Routing requests</title>
  </head>

  <body>
    <h1>Routing Requests</h1>
    <br>
    Day: <%= @day %>
    <br>
    Month: <%= @month %>
    <br>
    Year: <%= @year %>
    <br>
  </body>
</html>
```

7. Start the WEBrick server:

```
C:\rubydev\ch09\router>ruby script/server
=> Booting WEBrick...
=> Rails application started on http://0.0.0.0:3000
=> Ctrl-C to shutdown server; call with --help for options
[2006-06-12 11:52:40] INFO  WEBrick 1.3.1
[2006-06-12 11:52:40] INFO  ruby 1.8.2 (2004-12-25) [i386-mswin32]
[2006-06-12 11:52:40] INFO  WEBrick::HTTPServer#start: pid=2304 port=3000
```

8. Navigate to http://localhost:3000/look/at/15/11/2007. You should see the date displayed, as shown in Figure 9-1.

How It Works

In this case, you added new routing to routes.rb, which is what sets the routing for a particular request. When you create a Rails application, the default ':controller/:action/:id' routing is already in place:

```
:  # Install the default route as the lowest priority.
   map.connect ':controller/:action/:id'
```

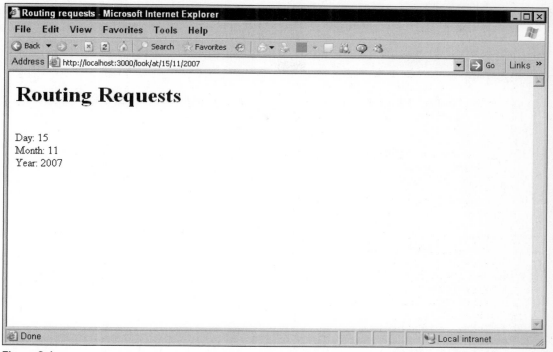

Figure 9-1

To create a routing that will enable you to handle dates, following the pattern `"look/at/:day/:month/:year"`, you can add the following code to config\routes.rb:

```
map.connect "look/at/:day/:month/:year",
  :controller => "look",
  :action     => "at",
  :requirements => {:year => /(19|20)\d\d/}
    .
    .
    .
```

This sets up a unique routing that lets you handle dates in URLs like this: `http://localhost:3000/look/at/15/11/2007`. Each routing handles a unique URL pattern, which is how Rails knows to match routing patterns to actual URLs.

`:requirements` lets you specify a regular expression — or a list of regular expressions, separated by commas — to which the parts of the URL must conform. This example specifies that the year must start with 19 or 20, and be made up of four digits.

You can also use the keyword `"anything"` as a default in case no other routing applies, or you might tie it to the action `"unknown_request"`, which will display an error message:

```
map.connect "look/at/:day/:month/:year",
  :controller => "look",
```

```
    :action     => "at",
    :requirements => {:year => /(19|20)\d\d/}
```

```
  map.connect "anything",
    :controller => "look",
    :action     => "unknown_request"
```

In the `look` controller's at action, you can get the day, month, and year from the @params array:

```
class LookController < ApplicationController
  def at
    @day = @params[:day]
    @month = @params[:month]
    @year = @params[:year]
  end
end
```

And in the at action's view template, rubydev\ch09\router\app\views\look\at.rhtml, you can display the @day, @month, and @year data like this:

```
<html>
  <head>
    <title>Routing requests</title>
  </head>

  <body>
    <h1>Routing Requests</h1>
    <br>
    Day: <%= @day %>
    <br>
    Month: <%= @month %>
    <br>
    Year: <%= @year %>
    <br>
  </body>
</html>
```

And that gives you the result you see in Figure 9-1.

As you can tell, it's not difficult to set up your own custom routing in Rails applications. All you've got to do is to create a unique routing pattern that Rails can understand in `routes.rb`:

```
  map.connect "look/at/:day/:month/:year",
    :controller => "look",
    :action     => "at",
    :requirements => {:year => /(19|20)\d\d/}
```

Creating Cookies

One of the most popular technologies to use with online applications is cookies, those small segments of text that are stored on the user's machine to be read later. You can use cookies to store customer data, user account information, and more. You can greet the user by name, having read that name from a cookie you've stored previously on his machine, or fill in customer fields automatically when they're ready to check out.

Cookies are made up of text, and each cookie is given a name. You can set and read cookies using the `cookies` hash in Rails applications.

Setting a Cookie

To set a cookie, you simply need to assign a value to the `cookies` hash in the application's controller. The only requirement is that you must go back to the browser after having set the cookie in your code before you actually use that cookie. Returning to the browser ensures that the cookie is actually installed in the browser before you use it.

Try It Out   **Set a Cookie**

To set a cookie, follow these steps:

1. Create a new application, `cookies`, in the rubydev\ch09 directory:

```
C:\rubydev\ch09>rails cookies
      create
      create   app/controllers
      create   app/helpers
      create   app/models
      create   app/views/layouts
      create   config/environments
      create   components
      create   db
      create   doc
      create   lib
         .
         .
         .
      create   public/images/rails.png
      create   public/javascripts/prototype.js
      create   public/javascripts/effects.js
      create   public/javascripts/dragdrop.js
      create   public/javascripts/controls.js
      create   public/javascripts/application.js
      create   doc/README_FOR_APP
      create   log/server.log
      create   log/production.log
      create   log/development.log
      create   log/test.log
```

2. Change directories to the cookies directory:

```
C:\rubydev\ch09>cd cookies
```

3. Create a controller named `Look` for the router directory:

```
C:\rubydev\ch09\router>ruby script/generate controller Look
      exists  app/controllers/
      exists  app/helpers/
      create  app/views/look
      exists  test/functional/
      create  app/controllers/look_controller.rb
      create  test/functional/look_controller_test.rb
      create  app/helpers/look_helper.rb
```

4. Edit rubydev\ch09\cookies\app\controllers\look_controller.rb, adding this code to create the `set` action:

```
class LookController < ApplicationController
  def set
    cookies[:customer] = {:value => "Nancy",
                          :expires => 31.days.from_now}
  end
end
```

5. Create rubydev\ch09\cookies\app\views\look\set.rhtml, and place this code in it:

```
<html>
  <head>
    <title>Setting a cookie</title>
  </head>

  <body>
    <h1>Setting a cookie</h1>
    <br>
    The cookie was set.
    <br>
    Click <%= link_to 'here', :action => 'read' %> to read the cookie.
  </body>
</html>
```

6. Start the WEBrick server:

```
C:\rubydev\ch09\router>ruby script/server
=> Booting WEBrick...
=> Rails application started on http://0.0.0.0:3000
=> Ctrl-C to shutdown server; call with --help for options
[2006-06-12 11:52:40] INFO  WEBrick 1.3.1
[2006-06-12 11:52:40] INFO  ruby 1.8.2 (2004-12-25) [i386-mswin32]
[2006-06-12 11:52:40] INFO  WEBrick::HTTPServer#start: pid=2304 port=3000
```

7. Navigate to `http://localhost:3000/look/set`. The cookie has been set, as shown in Figure 9-2.

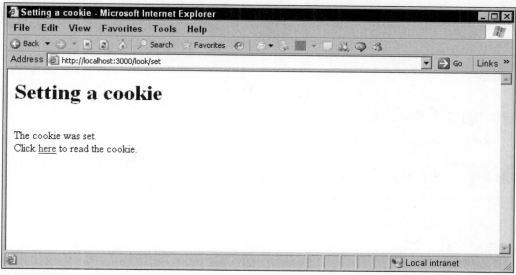

Figure 9-2

How It Works

This example revolves around rubydev\ch09\cookies\app\controllers\look_controller.rb, where you added this code to set the cookie:

```
class LookController < ApplicationController
  def set
    cookies[:customer] = {:value => "Nancy",
                          :expires => 31.days.from_now}
  end
end
```

That sets the cookie named `customer` to the text `"Nancy"` and sets it to expire 31 days from now. If you don't include the `:expires` key, the cookie is permanent and will not be deleted until or if the user deletes all cookies on her machine. If you assign the `:expires` key an empty string— `:expires => ""` —the cookie will be deleted when the current browsing session is over and the user shuts down his browser.

In the view template connected with the `set` action, rubydev\ch09\cookies\app\views\look\set.rhtml, you just need to display a message that the cookie was set, and a link to an action that will read the new cookie's data:

```
<html>
  <head>
    <title>Setting a cookie</title>
  </head>

  <body>
    <h1>Setting a cookie</h1>
```

269

```
      <br>
      The cookie was set.
      <br>
      Click <%= link_to 'here', :action => 'read' %> to read the cookie.
   </body>
</html>
```

Reading a Cookie

The next step? Reading the cookie.

Read a Cookie

To read a cookie, follow these steps:

1. Edit rubydev\ch09\cookies\app\controllers\look_controller.rb, adding this code to create the
read action:

```
class LookController < ApplicationController
  def set
    cookies[:customer] = {:value => "Nancy",
                             :expires => 31.days.from_now}
  end

  def read
    @cookie_data = cookies[:customer]
  end
end
```

2. Create rubydev\ch09\cookies\app\views\look\read.rhtml, and place the following code in it:

```
<html>
  <head>
    <title>Reading a cookie</title>
  </head>

  <body>
    <h1>Reading a cookie</h1>
    <br>
    The cookie says the customer is <%= @cookie_data %>.
  </body>
</html>
```

3. Click the here link in http://localhost:3000/look/set, which takes you to http://
localhost:3000/look/read (see Figure 9-3). Congratulations — you've been able to read
a cookie.

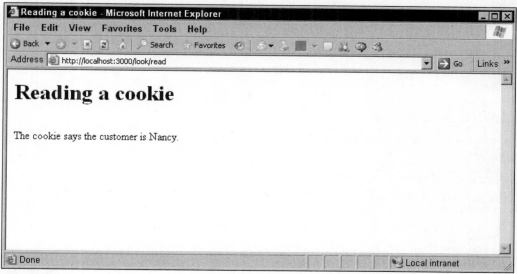

Figure 9-3

How It Works

In the previous section, you set a cookie in rubydev\ch09\cookies\app\controllers\look_controller.rb, using the key :customer like this:

```
class LookController < ApplicationController
  def set
    cookies[:customer] = {:value => "Nancy",
                          :expires => 31.days.from_now}
  end
end
```

After setting the cookie, you displayed a link to the read action to read the cookie:

```
<html>
  <head>
    <title>Setting a cookie</title>
  </head>

  <body>
    <h1>Setting a cookie</h1>
    <br>
    The cookie was set.
    <br>
    Click <%= link_to 'here', :action => 'read' %> to read the cookie.
  </body>
</html>
```

In the `read` action, you recovered the data stored in the `cookies` hash, using the `:customer` key, and stored the cookie's data in an instance variable named `@cookie_data`:

```
class LookController < ApplicationController
  def set
    cookies[:customer] = {:value => "Nancy",
                          :expires => 31.days.from_now}
  end

  def read
    @cookie_data = cookies[:customer]
  end
end
```

In the view template connected with the `read` action, `read.rhtml`, you can display the data recovered from the cookie this way:

```
<html>
  <head>
    <title>Reading a cookie</title>
  </head>

  <body>
    <h1>Reading a cookie</h1>
    <br>
    The cookie says the customer is <%= @cookie_data %>.
  </body>
</html>
```

And you get the results you see in Figure 9-3, where you read the data from the cookie.

You can also use `cookies.size` to determine how many cookies are in the hash:

```
cookies.size => 1
```

And you can also delete specific cookies by name, using `cookies.delete`:

```
cookies.delete :customer
```

And here are the options you can use when setting a cookie — they are all optional:

Option	Description
value	The cookie's value. You can also assign a list of values, such as an array.
path	The application path for which this cookie applies — the cookie won't be available for other paths. The default is the root of the application.
domain	The domain for which this cookie applies; the cookie won't be available for other domains.
expires	Sets the time when the cookie expires. Use a Rails Time object.
secure	Indicates whether the cookie is secure; the default is false. Note: secure cookies are only sent to secure (HTTPS) servers.

If you omit all options when setting a cookie, like this:

```
cookies[:customer] = "Nancy"
```

then you create a cookie under the key :customer with the data "Nancy" — and it expires and is deleted when the user shuts down her browser.

Creating a Filter

You can install filters in controllers in Rails to take control of the flow of control. A filter grabs control either before or after actions do, and you can use them to take control from actions. For example, you might have an online game that you don't want people to play during business hours when they should be working. The following Try It Out shows you how to resolve that issue.

Try It Out   **Filter an Online Game**

To filter an online game, follow these steps:

1. Create a new application, game, in the rubydev\ch09 directory:

```
C:\rubydev\ch09>rails game
        .
        .
        .
```

2. Change directories to the game directory:

```
C:\rubydev\ch09>cd game
```

3. Create a controller named play in the router directory:

```
C:\rubydev\ch09\game>ruby script/generate controller Play
    .
    .
    .
```

4. Edit rubydev\ch09\game\app\controllers\play_controller.rb, adding this code to create a filter named check_time:

```
class PlayController < ApplicationController

private
  def check_time
    if (Time.now.hour >= 9 && Time.now.hour <== 17)
      redirect_to(:action => "not")
    end
  end
end
```

5. Install this new filter as a before filter in the controller, so that it will be run before the various actions:

```
class PlayController < ApplicationController
  before_filter :check_time, :except => :not

private
  def check_time
    if (Time.now.hour >= 9 && Time.now.hour <== 17)
      redirect_to(:action => "not")
    end
  end
end
```

6. Add an empty action named now:

```
class PlayController < ApplicationController
  before_filter :check_time, :except => :not

  def now
  end

private
  def check_time
    if (Time.now.hour >= 9 && Time.now.hour <== 17)
      redirect_to(:action => "not")
    end
  end
end
```

7. Add another action named not:

```
class PlayController < ApplicationController
  before_filter :check_time, :except => :not

  def now
  end

  def not
  end

private
  def check_time
    if (Time.now.hour >= 9 && Time.now.hour <= 17)
      redirect_to(:action => "not")
    end
  end
end
```

8. Add a view template for the now action, rubydev\ch09\game\app\views\play\now.rhtml, which looks like this:

```
<html>
  <head>
    <title>Welcome to the Game</title>
  </head>

  <body>
    <h1>Welcome to the Game</h1>
```

```
        Pretty good game, huh?

    </body>
</html>
```

9. Add a view template for the `not` action, rubydev\ch09\game\app\views\play\not.rhtml, which looks like this:

```html
<html>
  <head>
    <title>Get back to work</title>
  </head>

  <body>
    <h1>Get back to work</h1>

    No playing the game during business hours.

  </body>
</html>
```

10. Start the WEBrick server:

```
C:\rubydev\ch09\game>ruby script/server
=> Booting WEBrick...
=> Rails application started on http://0.0.0.0:3000
=> Ctrl-C to shutdown server; call with --help for options
[2006-06-12 11:52:40] INFO  WEBrick 1.3.1
[2006-06-12 11:52:40] INFO  ruby 1.8.2 (2004-12-25) [i386-mswin32]
[2006-06-12 11:52:40] INFO  WEBrick::HTTPServer#start: pid=2304 port=3000
```

11. Navigate to `http://localhost:3000/play/game`. If you're navigating to this action between 9 and 5, you'll see the admonishing page in Figure 9-4. Otherwise, you'll see the "game" page in Figure 9-5.

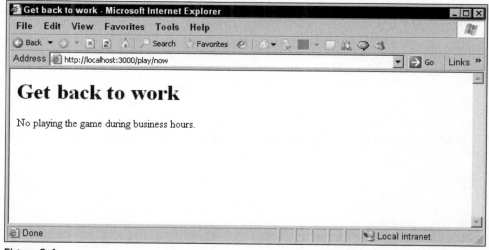

Figure 9-4

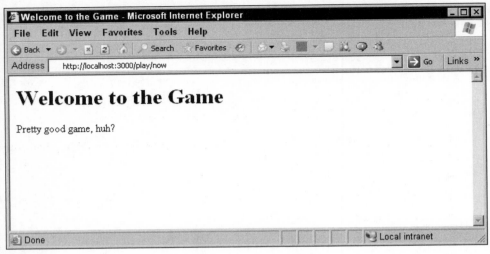

Figure 9-5

How It Works

It all revolves around the controller, rubydev\ch09\game\app\controllers\play_controller.rb. To install a filter, you can use a method (you can also use a new class or a block) like this:

```
class PlayController < ApplicationController
  before_filter :check_time, :except => :not

  def now
  end

  def not
  end

private
  def check_time
    if (Time.now.hour >= 9 && Time.now.hour <= 17)
      redirect_to(:action => "not")
    end
  end
end
```

This method, check_time (you can use any name), checks the current time. If the time is between 9 A.M. and 5 P.M., the method redirects control to the not action, which displays a warning message to get back to work:

```
<html>
  <head>
    <title>Get back to work</title>
  </head>

  <body>
```

```
<h1>Get back to work</h1>

No playing the game during business hours.

  </body>
</html>
```

Remember, to redirect to another controller as well as another action, use syntax like this: `redirect_to(:controller => controller2, :action => "not")`.

How do you actually install this filter so it'll be run before any action gets control? You use `before_filter`, like this:

```
class PlayController < ApplicationController
  before_filter :check_time, :except => :not

  def now
  end

  def not
  end

private
  def check_time
    if (Time.now.hour >= 9 && Time.now.hour <= 17)
      redirect_to(:action => "not")
    end
  end
end
```

That line of code installs the `check_time` method as a filter for all the actions in the current controller—except for the `not` action. Why except the `not` action? If you filtered all actions, including the `not` action, then when you redirected to the `not` action, you'd enter an infinite loop—redirect to the `not` action, filter the `not` action, redirect to the `not` action, filter the `not` action, and so on.

If you're accessing the `now` action outside the hours of 9 a.m. to 5 p.m., you see the game page, as you should:

```
<html>
  <head>
    <title>Welcome to the Game</title>
  </head>

  <body>
    <h1>Welcome to the Game</h1>

    Pretty good game, huh?

  </body>
</html>
```

Before filters run before any action, they're particularly useful for checking logins, which you'll examine next.

Logging in with Filters

Filters are especially useful for ensuring that users log in. Go ahead and tackle this Try It Out.

Try It Out   **Log in Using Filters**

To create a login filter, follow these steps:

1. Create a new application, `login`, in the rubydev\ch09 directory:

```
C:\rubydev\ch09>rails login
      create
      create  app/controllers
      create  app/helpers
      create  app/models
      create  app/views/layouts
      create  config/environments
      create  components
      create  db
      create  doc
      create  lib
        .
        .
        .
      create  public/images/rails.png
      create  public/javascripts/prototype.js
      create  public/javascripts/effects.js
      create  public/javascripts/dragdrop.js
      create  public/javascripts/controls.js
      create  public/javascripts/application.js
      create  doc/README_FOR_APP
      create  log/server.log
      create  log/production.log
      create  log/development.log
      create  log/test.log
```

2. Change directories to the login directory:

```
C:\rubydev\ch09>cd login
```

3. Create a controller named `Look` in the login directory:

```
C:\rubydev\ch09\login>ruby script/generate controller Look
      exists  app/controllers/
      exists  app/helpers/
      create  app/views/look
      exists  test/functional/
      create  app/controllers/look_controller.rb
      create  test/functional/look_controller_test.rb
      create  app/helpers/look_helper.rb
```

4. Edit rubydev\ch09\login\app\controllers\look_controller.rb, adding this code to create a filter named `check_login`:

```
class LookController < ApplicationController

private
  def check_login
    unless session[:user_name]
      redirect_to(:action => "getter")
    end
  end
end
```

5. Install this new filter as a before filter in the controller, so that it will be run for the at action and only for the at action—that's what the keyword :only is for here:

```
class LookController < ApplicationController
  before_filter :check_login, :only => :at

private
  def check_login
    unless session[:user_name]
      redirect_to(:action => "getter")
    end
  end
end
```

6. Add an empty action named getter:

```
class LookController < ApplicationController
  before_filter :check_login, :only => :at

  def getter
  end

private
  def check_login
    unless session[:user_name]
      redirect_to(:action => "getter")
    end
  end
end
```

7. Add a view template for the getter action, rubydev\ch09\login\app\views\look\getter.rhtml:

```
<html>
  <head>
    <title>Log in, please</title>
  </head>
  <body>
    <h1>Log in, please</h1>
    Please enter your username.
    <br>
    <%= start_form_tag ({:action => "got"}, {:method => "post"}) %>
      <br>
      <%= text_field_tag ("text1", "", {"size" => 30}) %>
      <br>
```

```
        <br>
        <input type="submit"/>
      <%= end_form_tag %>
    </body>
  </html>
```

8. Add another action named `got`:

```
class LookController < ApplicationController
  before_filter :check_login, :only => :at

  def getter
  end

  def got
    session[:user_name] = params[:text1]
  end

private
  def check_login
    unless session[:user_name]
      redirect_to(:action => "getter")
    end
  end
end
```

9. Add a view template for the `got` action, rubydev\ch09\login\app\views\look\got.rhtml, which looks like this:

```
<html>
  <head>
    <title>Thanks for logging in</title>
  </head>
  <body>
    <h1>Thanks for logging in</h1>
    You are now logged in.
  </body>
</html>
```

10. Add another action named `at`:

```
class LookController < ApplicationController
  before_filter :check_login, :only => :at

  def getter
  end

  def got
    session[:user_name] = params[:text1]
  end

  def at
  end

private
```

```
      def check_login
        unless session[:user_name]
          redirect_to(:action => "getter")
        end
      end
    end
```

11. Add a view template for the `at` action, rubydev\ch09\login\app\views\look\at.rhtml, which looks like this:

```
<html>
  <head>
    <title>Congratulations</title>
  </head>
  <body>
    <h1>Congratulations</h1>
    If you're seeing this page, you must be logged in.
  </body>
</html>
```

12. Start the WEBrick server:

```
C:\rubydev\ch09\login>ruby script/server
=> Booting WEBrick...
=> Rails application started on http://0.0.0.0:3000
=> Ctrl-C to shutdown server; call with --help for options
[2006-06-12 11:52:40] INFO  WEBrick 1.3.1
[2006-06-12 11:52:40] INFO  ruby 1.8.2 (2004-12-25) [i386-mswin32]
[2006-06-12 11:52:40] INFO  WEBrick::HTTPServer#start: pid=2304 port=3000
```

13. Navigate to `http://localhost:3000/look/at`. You should be asked to log in before viewing that page, as shown in Figure 9-6.

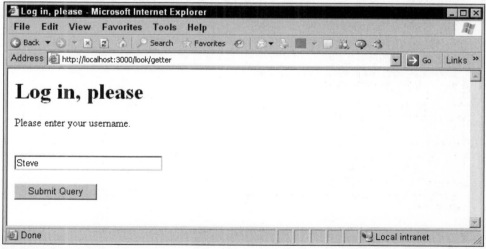

Figure 9-6

14. After you enter your username and click Submit Query, you should see a confirming message indicating that you're logged on, as shown in Figure 9-7.

Figure 9-7

15. Navigate to `http://localhost:3000/look/at` again. Now that you're logged in, you should see a congratulatory page, as shown in Figure 9-8.

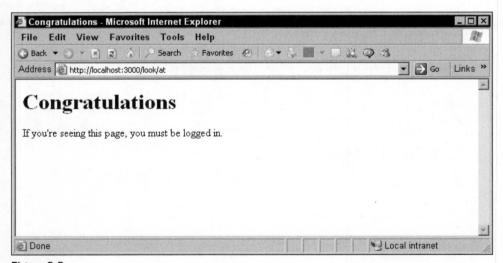

Figure 9-8

How It Works

In this case, you're installing a filter that only filters the :at action, which you need to log in to access —
note the use of the keyword :only here:

```
class LookController < ApplicationController
  before_filter :check_login, :only => :at

  def getter
  end

  def got
    session[:user_name] = params[:text1]
  end

  def at
  end

  private
  def check_login
    unless session[:user_name]
      redirect_to(:action => "getter")
    end
  end
end
```

The filter method, check_login, checks to make sure that the user has entered a username to log in —
because Rails creates one and only one session per user until that session expires, storing the username
in the session makes sense. If the user hasn't logged in, he's redirected to the getter action to do so:

```
class LookController < ApplicationController
  before_filter :check_login, :except => :getter

  def getter
  end

  def got
    session[:user_name] = params[:text1]
  end

  def at
  end

  private
  def check_login
    unless session[:user_name]
      redirect_to(:action => "getter")
    end
  end
end
```

In the `getter` view template, the user logs in, and the data is sent back to the `got` action:

```html
<html>
  <head>
    <title>Log in, please</title>
  </head>
  <body>
    <h1>Log in, please</h1>
    Please enter your username.
    <br>
    <%= start_form_tag ({:action => "got"}, {:method => "post"}) %>
      <br>
      <%= text_field_tag ("text1", "", {"size" => 30}) %>
      <br>
      <br>
      <input type="submit"/>
    <%= end_form_tag %>
  </body>
</html>
```

In the `got` action, the username is stored in the session:

```ruby
class LookController < ApplicationController
  before_filter :check_login, :except => :getter

  def getter
  end

  def got
    session[:user_name] = params[:text1]
  end

  def at
  end

  private
  def check_login
    unless session[:user_name]
      redirect_to(:action => "getter")
    end
  end
end
```

Now that the user is logged in, he can navigate to the `at` action safely — the `check_login` filter will note that he's already logged in and let him pass:

```ruby
class LookController < ApplicationController
  before_filter :check_login, :except => :getter

  def getter
  end

  def got
```

```
      session[:user_name] = params[:text1]
    end

    def at
    end

  private
    def check_login
      unless session[:user_name]
        redirect_to(:action => "getter")
      end
    end
  end
```

Now that the user is logged in, he's directed to at.rhtml, which displays a congratulatory message this way:

```
<html>
  <head>
    <title>Congratulations</title>
  </head>
  <body>
    <h1>Congratulations</h1>
    If you're seeing this page, you must be logged in.
  </body>
</html>
```

Before filters filter actions before they're called. But you can also create after filters, which filter actions after they've run.

Using After Filters

Why would you want to filter an action after it's run? To give you access to whatever the action is returning to the browser. For example, you can add text such as a copyright notice to the end of a web page being sent back to the browser. The following Try It Out shows you how.

Try It Out   **Use an After Filter**

To use an after filter, follow these steps:

1.   Create a new application, copyrighter, in the rubydev\ch09 directory:

```
C:\rubydev\ch09>rails login
      .
      .
      .
```

2.   Change directories to the copyrighter directory:

```
C:\rubydev\ch09>cd copyrighter
```

3. Create a controller named `Look` in the copyrighter directory:

```
C:\rubydev\ch09\copyrighter>ruby script/generate controller Look
   .
   .
   .
```

4. Edit rubydev\ch09\copyrighter\app\controllers\look_controller.rb, adding this code to create a filter named `add_copyright`:

```
class LookController < ApplicationController

private
  def add_copyright
    response.body = response.body + "<br><hr>(c) 2007"
  end
end
```

5. Install this new filter as an after filter in the controller:

```
class LookController < ApplicationController
  after_filter :add_copyright

private
  def add_copyright
    response.body = response.body + "<br><hr>(c) 2007"
  end
end
```

6. Add an action named `at`:

```
class LookController < ApplicationController
  after_filter :add_copyright

  def at
  end

private
  def add_copyright
    response.body = response.body + "<br><hr>(c) 2007"
  end
end
```

7. Add a view template for the `at` action, rubydev\ch09\copyrighter\app\views\look\at.rhtml:

```
<html>
  <head>
    <title>Welcome to my page</title>
  </head>
  <body>
    <h1>Welcome to my page</h1>
    <br>
    Pretty good page, huh?
    <br>
  </body>
</html>
```

8. Add another action named `at2`:

```
class LookController < ApplicationController
  after_filter :add_copyright

  def at
  end

  def at2
  end

private
  def add_copyright
    response.body = response.body + "<br><hr>(c) 2007"
  end
end
```

9. Add a view template for the `at2` action, rubydev\ch09\copyrighter\app\views\look\at2.rhtml, which looks like this:

```
<html>
  <head>
    <title>Welcome to my second page</title>
  </head>
  <body>
    <h1>Welcome to my second page</h1>
    <br>
    Pretty nifty page, huh?
    <br>
  </body>
</html>
```

10. Start the WEBrick server:

```
C:\rubydev\ch09\copyrighter>ruby script/server
=> Booting WEBrick...
=> Rails application started on http://0.0.0.0:3000
=> Ctrl-C to shutdown server; call with --help for options
[2006-06-12 11:52:40] INFO  WEBrick 1.3.1
[2006-06-12 11:52:40] INFO  ruby 1.8.2 (2004-12-25) [i386-mswin32]
[2006-06-12 11:52:40] INFO  WEBrick::HTTPServer#start: pid=2304 port=3000
```

11. Navigate to `http://localhost:3000/look/at`. You should see a copyright notice, as shown in Figure 9-9.

12. Navigate to `http://localhost:3000/look/at2`. You should see another copyright notice at the bottom of the page, as shown in Figure 9-10.

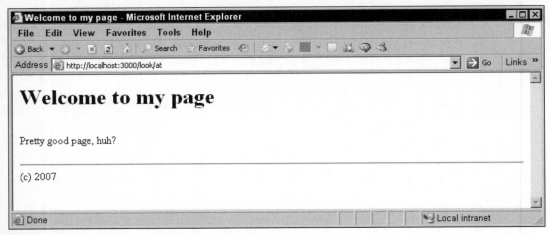

Figure 9-9

Figure 9-10

How It Works

The goal of this after filter example is to add a copyright notice to the end of all web pages in your application. It does that with an after filter named add_copyright:

```
class LookController < ApplicationController
  after_filter :add_copyright

  def at
  end

  def at2
  end
```

```
  private
    def add_copyright
      response.body = response.body + "<br><hr>(c) 2007"
    end
end
```

You can access the response being sent back to the browser as `response.body`, as is done in this filter method. To add the copyright notice, you have only to append `"<br><hr>(c) 2007"` to `response.body`. That's all it takes.

Then you install the `add_copyright` method as an after filter:

```
class LookController < ApplicationController
  after_filter :add_copyright

  def at
  end

  def at2
  end

  private
    def add_copyright
      response.body = response.body + "<br><hr>(c) 2007"
    end
end
```

And you're in business — you've added a copyright notice to the end of every web page displayed on your site with a simple filter. That filter could be updated to display the time and date, for example, and if you want to change it, you only have to change it in one place, not in every view template.

In fact, if you want to, you can rewrite the entire `response.body` being sent back to the browser instead of just appending text to the end of it.

As you can see, filters are handy. You can use them to block access; to log access (you can log access with the `Time.now` object, and you get the user's IP address with the request object's `remote_ip` method like this: `request.remote_ip()`); enforce logins; append data to the end of web pages; and even scan web pages for inappropriate content.

Other useful methods of the request object include `domain()`, *which returns the domain name in the request;* `env`, *which returns the environment of the request, such as* `env("HTTP_ACCEPT_LANGUAGE")`; `method`, *which returns the request method:* `:get`, `:delete`, `:head`, `:post`, *or* `:put`.

You can log text in Rails by using the logger object in actions. You can pass text to the methods `logger.warn`, `logger.info`, `logger.error`, **and** `logger.fatal` **like this:** `logger.info("Hello, I'm a Rails application.")`. **The logged text goes into the application's log directory in** `development.log`, `test.log`, **or** `production.log`, **depending on the type of the application.**

Rendering Text Directly

You're used to the idea that actions are connected to view templates and layouts, but there's another way of rendering results back to the browser that's built into `ActionController::Base`: you can render text directly from an action back to the browser. The following Try It Out does just that.

Render Text Directly

To render text back to the browser, follow these steps:

1. Create a new application, `texter`, in the rubydev\ch09 directory:

```
C:\rubydev\ch09>rails texter
    .
    .
    .
```

2. Change directories to the texter directory:

```
C:\rubydev\ch09>cd texter
```

3. Create a controller named `Look` in the texter directory:

```
C:\rubydev\ch09\texter>ruby script/generate controller Look
    .
    .
    .
```

4. Edit rubydev\ch09\texter\app\controllers\look_controller.rb, adding this code in an action named `at`:

```
class LookController < ApplicationController

  def at
    render(:text => "<html><head><title>Welcome</title></head>" \
      + "<body><h1>Welcome to my Web page</h1>" \
      + "This page was created without a view template.</body></html>")
  end
end
```

5. Start the WEBrick server:

```
C:\rubydev\ch09\texter>ruby script/server
=> Booting WEBrick...
=> Rails application started on http://0.0.0.0:3000
=> Ctrl-C to shutdown server; call with --help for options
[2006-06-12 11:52:40] INFO  WEBrick 1.3.1
[2006-06-12 11:52:40] INFO  ruby 1.8.2 (2004-12-25) [i386-mswin32]
[2006-06-12 11:52:40] INFO  WEBrick::HTTPServer#start: pid=2304 port=3000
```

6. Navigate to `http://localhost:3000/look/at`. You should see the web page shown in Figure 9-11 — no view template necessary.

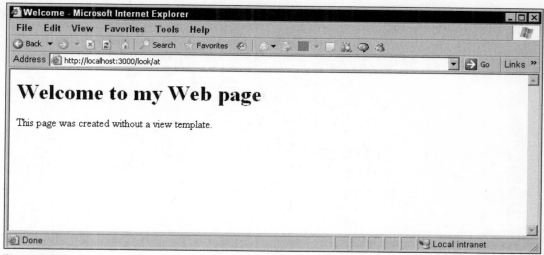

Figure 9-11

How It Works

The goal of this example is to write text to the browser without a view template, and it does that with the render method, assigning the text to be sent to the browser to :text:

```
class LookController < ApplicationController

  def at
    render(:text => "<html><head><title>Welcome</title></head>" \
      + "<body><h1>Welcome to my Web page</h1>" \
      + "This page was created without a view template.</body></html>")
  end
end
```

That's all it takes.

Want to send a file instead of text? No worries—just pass the ActionController::Streaming.send_file method the path to the file to send:

```
class LookController < ApplicationController

  def at
    send_file('c:\rubydev\ch09\texter\app\controllers\message.txt')
  end
end
```

The user will see a download dialog box like this one in Figure 9-12, allowing her to download the file.

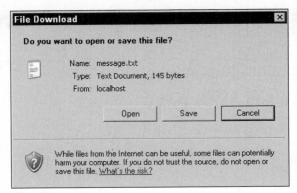

Figure 9-12

Caching

Sometimes it takes a lot of work to generate a page, including database lookup, and you don't want to have to re-create the page unless you have to. The solution is to cache the page, which means that the same page will be sent to the user over and over as he requests it (until you decide otherwise). You can cache a page in a controller file, using the `caches_page` directive:

```
class LookController < ApplicationController
  caches_page  :at

  def at
    render(:text => "<html><head><title>Welcome</title></head>" \
      + "<body><h1>Welcome to my Web page</h1>" \
      + "This page was created without a view template.</body></html>")
  end
end
```

You can also cache output on an action-by-action basis, using the `caches_action` directive:

```
class LookController < ApplicationController
  caches_action  :at

  def at
    render(:text => "<html><head><title>Welcome</title></head>" \
      + "<body><h1>Welcome to my Web page</h1>" \
      + "This page was created without a view template.</body></html>")
  end
end
```

In this case, the `at` action will only be executed once, and the results cached for later access.

When a page has changed, you can remove it from the cache with `expire_page` and `expire_action`, forcing Rails to deliver the new version next time the page is requested. Here's an example:

```
class LookController < ApplicationController
  caches_action  :at

  def at
    render(:text => "<html><head><title>Welcome</title></head>" \
      + "<body><h1>Welcome to my Web page</h1>" \
      + "This page was created without a view template.</body></html>")
  end

  def save
    if item.save
      expire_action :action => "at"
    end
  end
end
```

You can also specify the ID of the item to remove from the cache:

```
def save
  if item.save
    expire_action :action => "at", :id => item.id
  end
```

Caching is only enabled for production environments, by default. To enable it in other environments, execute this line of code:

```
ActionController::Base.perform_caching = true
```

Summary

In this chapter, you learned how to:

- ❏ Configure routing requests.
- ❏ Set and read cookies.
- ❏ Create a before filter.
- ❏ Control access to an action by time-of-day, and control access by asking the user to log in.
- ❏ Create an after filter that adds copyright information to web pages.
- ❏ Render text to the browser directly.
- ❏ Cache pages and the response from actions.

In the next chapter, you continue to get behind the scenes with Rails. Before proceeding, however, try the exercises that follow to test your understanding of the material covered in this chapter. The solutions to these exercises are in Appendix A.

Exercises

1. Set up a routing for an application named `timer` that lets the user specify hours/minutes/seconds in the URL like this: `http://localhost:3000/look/at/23/59/52`, and in the Look controller, recover the hours/minutes/seconds data.

2. Create a cookie that stores the text `"Not a good customer"` under the key `:customer` for 365 days.

3. Create a before filter that accepts only requests that were made with the `POST` method.

Getting the Big Picture
with Views

As you know, the view is responsible for interacting with the user — without the view, you wouldn't have much of an application in most cases. You might think you know all about views — they're those .rhtml templates that you use embedded Ruby with, right? Sometimes, yes. But there's more to views. For instance, you can create XML instead of HTML. How does that work?

Creating XML

Of course you can use .rhtml templates to generate HTML documents to send back to the browser. But you can also use .rxml templates to create XML to send back to the browser. You'll see how that works in the following example.

> *If you're not familiar with XML, it's a big topic. You can find the XML specification at* http://w3.org/TR/REC-xml, *but it's a hard-to-read document. If you're interested, take a look at some of the tutorials you can find on the Internet by searching for "XML tutorial."*

Try It Out   Create XML

To create XML, follow these steps:

1. Create a new application, xml, in the rubydev\ch10 directory:

```
C:\rubydev\ch10>rails xml
    .
    .
    .
```

2. Change directories to the xml directory:

```
C:\rubydev\ch10>cd xml
```

3. Create a controller named Look for the xml application:

```
C:\rubydev\ch10\xml>ruby script/generate controller Look
   .
   .
   .
```

4. Edit rubydev\ch10\xml\app\controllers\look_controller.rb, adding this code to create the at action:

```
class LookController < ApplicationController
  def at
  end
end
```

5. Create rubydev\ch10\xml\app\views\look\at.rhtml and place this code in it, tying a text field containing the user's name to the displayer action:

```
<html>
  <head>
    <title>Enter your name, please</title>
  </head>
  <body>
    <h1>Enter your name, please</h1>
    Please enter your name!
    <br>
    <%= start_form_tag({:action => "displayer"}, {:method => "post"}) %>
      <br>
      <%= text_field_tag("text1", "", {"size" => 30}) %>
      <br>
      <br>
      <input type="submit"/>
    <%= end_form_tag %>
  </body>
</html>
```

6. Edit rubydev\ch10\xml\app\controllers\look_controller.rb, adding this code to create the displayer action:

```
class LookController < ApplicationController
  def at
  end

  def displayer
    @name = params[:text1]
    @data = ["red", "blue", "green", "orange"]
  end
end
```

7. Create rubydev\ch10\xml\app\views\look\displayer.rxml and place this code in it:

```
xml.instruct! :xml, :version=>"1.0"
xml.comment! "This is an XML document."

xml.document do
```

```
  xml.author(@name)

  xml.time(Time.now)

  xml.colors do
    @data.each do |item|
      xml.color(item)
    end
  end
end
```

8.   Start the WEBrick server:

```
C:\rubydev\ch10\router>ruby script/server
```

9.   Navigate to `http://localhost:3000/look/at`, shown in Figure 10-1.

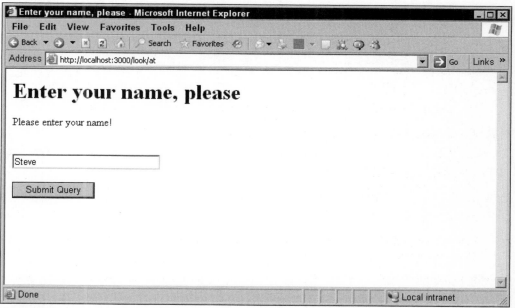

Figure 10-1

10.   Enter your name and click the Submit Query button. Your result should be similar to the XML document in Figure 10-2.

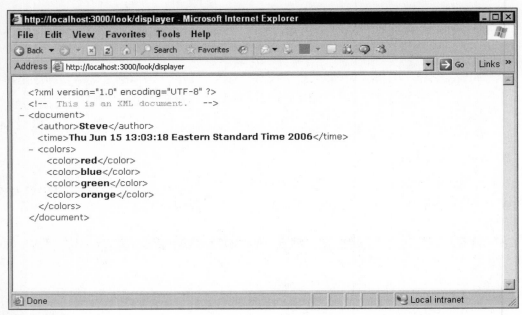

Figure 10-2

How It Works

This example creates an application that creates XML, including reading the user's name and installing him as the author of the XML document in an `<author>` element.

You first define an `at` action in the controller:

```
def at
end
```

Then you create a text field and a prompt asking for the user's name in the rubydev\ch10\xml\app\ views\look\at.rhtml view template. This page accepts the user's name and passes it to an action named `displayer`:

```
<html>
  <head>
    <title>Enter your name, please</title>
  </head>
  <body>
    <h1>Enter your name, please</h1>
    Please enter your name!
    <br>
    <%= start_form_tag({:action => "displayer"}, {:method => "post"}) %>
      <br>
      <%= text_field_tag("text1", "", {"size" => 30}) %>
      <br>
      <br>
```

```
        <input type="submit"/>
      <%= end_form_tag %>
    </body>
  </html>
```

Next, you create the `displayer` action in rubydev\ch10\xml\app\controllers\look_controller.rb
. `displayer` recovers the user's name and also creates an array of colors, `@data`, like this:

```
def displayer
  @name = params[:text1]
  @data = ["red", "blue", "green", "orange"]
end
```

Then you create the XML template, rubydev\ch10\xml\app\views\look\displayer.rxml, beginning
with an XML declaration, which must be at the start of any XML document:

```
xml.instruct! :xml, :version=>"1.0"
```

Next comes an XML comment:

```
xml.comment! "This is an XML document."
```

This line creates the following XML comment:

```
<!-- This is an XML document. -->
```

Next, you create the document element, which in XML must contain all the other elements in the XML
document. In this example, for simplicity, the document element is just named `<document>`, and here's
how you create it:

```
xml.document do
    .
    .
    .
end
```

In the template, the first contained element in the `<document>` element is the `<author>` element that
holds the user's name, gotten from the form he filled out. Here's how to create that `<author>` element:

```
xml.author(@name)
```

This code creates the `<author>` element like this:

```
<author>Steve</author>
```

So far, so good. Next, you create a `<time>` element holding the current time as its content:

```
xml.time(Time.now)
```

That creates the `<time>` element like this:

```
<time>Thu Jun 15 13:12:09 Eastern Standard Time 2006</time>
```

Now you can use the @data array that was filled with colors in the displayer action:

```
@data = ["red", "blue", "green", "orange"]
```

To display the colors, you start by creating a <colors> element:

```
xml.colors do
```

Then loop over all the colors in the @data array, creating <color> elements like this:

```
@data.each do |item|
  xml.color(item)
```

That creates the following output, with the <color> elements nested inside the <colors> element:

```
<colors>
  <color>red</color>
  <color>blue</color>
  <color>green</color>
  <color>orange</color>
</colors>
```

Very cool. Now take a look at adding attributes to your XML elements.

Creating XML Attributes

You can also add XML attributes to your output. The following exercise shows you how.

Try It Out   Create XML Attributes

To create XML attributes, follow these steps:

1.   Edit rubydev\ch10\xml\app\views\look\displayer.rxml, making this modification:

```
xml.instruct! :xml, :version=>"1.0"
xml.comment! "This is an XML document."

xml.document do
  xml.author(@name, :type => "primary")

  xml.time(Time.now)

  xml.colors do
    @data.each do |item|
      xml.color(item)
    end
  end
end
```

2. Edit rubydev\ch10\xml\app\controllers\look_controller.rb and place this code in it:

```ruby
class LookController < ApplicationController
  def at
  end

  def displayer
    @name = params[:text1]
    @data = ["red", "blue", "green", "orange"]
    @language = "English"
  end
end
```

3. Edit rubydev\ch10\xml\app\views\look\displayer.rxml and add this code in it:

```ruby
xml.instruct! :xml, :version=>"1.0"
xml.comment! "This is an XML document."

xml.document do
  xml.author(@name, :type => "primary")

  xml.time(Time.now)

  xml.colors do
    @data.each do |item|
      xml.color(item, :language => @language)
    end
  end
end
```

4. Start the WEBrick server:

```
C:\rubydev\ch10\router>ruby script/server
```

5. Navigate to `http://localhost:3000/look/at`.

6. Enter your name and click the Submit button. Figure 10-3 shows the resulting XML document, complete with XML attributes.

How It Works

This example adds XML attributes to XML elements. For example, instead of just the plain

```
<author>Steve</author>
```

you add an attribute named `type`, and assign it the value `"primary"`:

```
<author type="primary">Steve</author>
```

You can add attributes to XML elements in an `.rxml` template by adding a hash to the method call that creates the element. For instance, here's how to create the type attribute for the `<author>` element and assign it the value `"primary"`:

```ruby
xml.author(@name, :type => "primary")
```

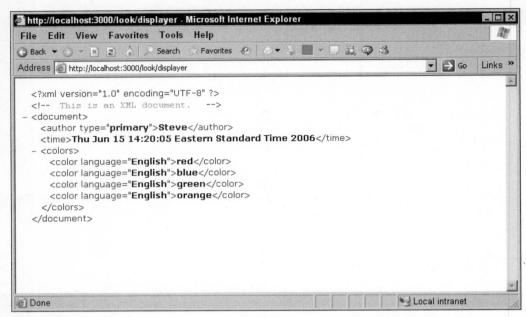

Figure 10-3

This creates the `<author>` element like this:

```
<author type="primary">Steve</author>
```

Similarly, you can create attributes from variables in the action; Adding the following line to the controller, rubydev\ch10\xml\app\controllers\look_controller.rb

```
@language = "English"
```

means you can use `@language` in rubydev\ch10\xml\app\views\look\displayer.rxml to create an attribute for each `<color>` element:

```
xml.color(item, :language => @language)
```

And that creates this kind of `<color>` element, complete with the `language` attribute:

```
<color language="English">red</color>
<color language="English">blue</color>
<color language="English">green</color>
<color language="English">orange</color>
```

You can also create XML declarations, as in the following example, which declares that the document is strict XHTML (Extensible Hypertext Markup Language) by referencing the XHTML 1.0 Strict DTD (Document Type Definition):

```
x.declare! :DOCTYPE, :html, :PUBLIC, "-//W3C//DTD XHTML 1.0 Strict//EN",
"http://www.w3.org/TR/xhtml1/DTD/xhtml1-strict.dtd"
```

And you can even create XML CDATA (character data) sections, using `xml.cdata!` this way:

```
xml.cdata! "Here is the character data."
```

to create this CDATA section:

```
<![CDATA[Here is the character data.]]>
```

As you can see, there's good support for integrating XML templates into your applications in Rails.

As time goes on, you may find yourself adding more and more code to your view templates. Don't do it. Use helpers instead.

Using View Helpers

It's a bad idea to pack too much code into `.rhtml` or `.rxml` templates — not only is the real place for code in controllers or models, but it mixes your code up with HTML and XML too much, making it prone to errors. Sometimes, you can't avoid using a fair amount of code in view templates, however, and Rails provides you an option: place that code in view helper files, not in the view template itself.

Try It Out   **Create a View Helper**

To create a view helper method, follow these steps:

1.   Create a new application, `helpers`, in the rubydev\ch10 directory:

```
C:\rubydev\ch10>rails helpers
    .
    .
    .
```

2.   Change directories to the helpers directory:

```
C:\rubydev\ch10>cd helpers
```

3.   Create a controller named `Look` for the `helpers` application:

```
C:\rubydev\ch10\helpers>ruby script/generate controller Look
    .
    .
    .
```

4.   Edit rubydev\ch10\helpers\app\controllers\look_controller.rb, adding this code to create the at action:

```
class LookController < ApplicationController
  def at
  end
end
```

5. Edit rubydev\ch10\helpers\app\helpers\look_helper.rb and add this code to it:

```
module LookHelper
  def content
    return "This content comes from the application's helper."
  end
end
```

6. Create rubydev\ch10\helpers\app\views\look\at.rhtml and place this code in it:

```
<html>
  <head>
    <title>Using helpers</title>
  </head>
  <body>
    <h1>Using helpers</h1>
    <br>
    <%= content %>
    <br>
  </body>
</html>
```

7. Start the WEBrick server:

```
C:\rubydev\ch10\router>ruby script/server
```

8. Navigate to `http://localhost:3000/look/at`, shown in Figure 10-4.

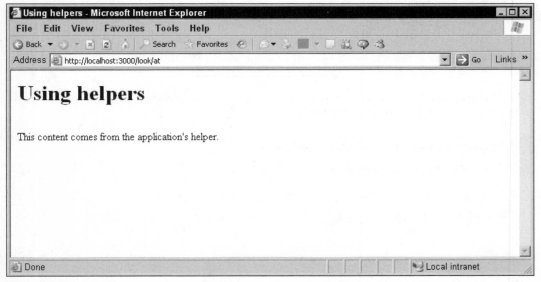

Figure 10-4

How It Works

This example demonstrates how to use helper methods, and it creates one that supplies the content of a web page. The controller supports a single action, at:

```
class LookController < ApplicationController
  def at
  end
end
```

You can add helper methods to rubydev\ch10\helpers\app\helpers\look_helper.rb to provide helper methods callable from the Look controller and its views. That's the way helpers are usually divided up — by controller. Here's how you create the content method:

```
def content
  return "This content comes from the application's helper."
end
```

Then, in the at action's view, rubydev\ch10\helpers\app\views\look\at.rhtml, you call the content method this way:

```
<html>
  <head>
    <title>Using helpers</title>
  </head>
  <body>
    <h1>Using helpers</h1>
    <br>
    <%= content %>
    <br>
  </body>
</html>
```

What if you've written a helper method that's so good you want to share it among all the controllers in an application? For that, you can create a shared helper.

Try It Out   Create a Shared View Helper

To create a shared view helper method, follow these steps:

1.   Create a new application, shared, in the rubydev\ch10 directory:

```
C:\rubydev\ch10>rails shared
   .
   .
   .
```

2.   Change directories to the shared directory:

```
C:\rubydev\ch10>cd shared
```

3. Create a controller named `Look` for the `shared` application:

```
C:\rubydev\ch10\shared>ruby script/generate controller Look
        .
        .
        .
```

4. Create another controller named `see` for the `shared` application:

```
C:\rubydev\ch10\shared>ruby script/generate controller See
        .
        .
        .
```

5. Edit rubydev\ch10\helpers\app\helpers\application_helper.rb, and add this code to it:

```
# Methods added to this helper will be available to all templates in the
application.
module ApplicationHelper
  def content
    return "This text comes from an application-wide shared helper!"
  end
end
```

6. Edit rubydev\ch10\helpers\app\controllers\look_controller.rb, adding this code to create the `at` action:

```
class LookController < ApplicationController

  def at
  end

end
```

7. Edit rubydev\ch10\helpers\app\controllers\see_controller.rb, adding this code to create the `me` action:

```
class SeeController < ApplicationController

  def me
  end

end
```

8. Create rubydev\ch10\helpers\app\views\look\at.rhtml, and place this code in it:

```
<html>
  <head>
    <title>Using shared helpers</title>
  </head>
  <body>
    <h1>Using shared helpers</h1>
    <br>
    <%= content %>
```

```
      <br>
    </body>
  </html>
```

9. Create rubydev\ch10\helpers\app\views\see\me.rhtml, and place this code in it:

```
<html>
  <head>
    <title>Also using shared helpers</title>
  </head>
  <body>
    <h1>Also using shared helpers</h1>
    <br>
    <%= content %>
    <br>
  </body>
</html>
```

10. Start the WEBrick server:

```
C:\rubydev\ch10\router>ruby script/server
```

11. Navigate to `http://localhost:3000/look/at`, shown in Figure 10-5. You see the text supplied by the helper method.

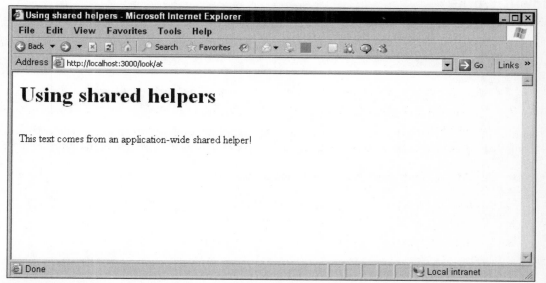

Figure 10-5

12. Navigate to `http://localhost:3000/see/me` as shown in Figure 10-6. You also see the text supplied by the helper method.

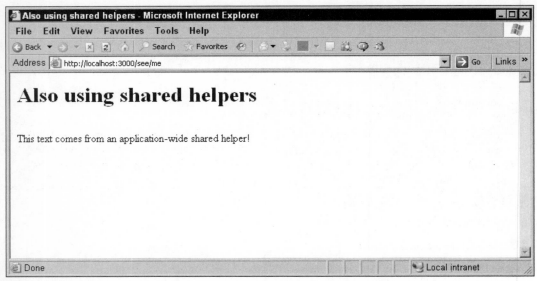

Figure 10-6

How It Works

This example shows how to create a shared, application-wide helper method. You start by creating the helper method named content in the file application_helper.rb (rubydev\ch10\helpers\app\helpers\application_helper.rb) like this:

```
def content
    return "This text comes from an application-wide shared helper!"
end
```

Putting the helper method in application_helper.rb rather than in a file connected with any particular controller—look_helper.rb or see_helper.rb—makes it available throughout the entire application.

Next, you add a controller named look with an action named at:

```
class LookController < ApplicationController
  def at
  end
end
```

And you added a controller named See, with an action named me:

```
class SeeController < ApplicationController
  def me
  end
end
```

Now you can access the shared helper method content in any view in the application.

As you can see, the helper method in this case is indeed application-wide: you can access it from any controller.

Using View Pagination

Sometimes you have more data to display in a view than you want to show on a single page. Rails *pagination* lets you choose how many records you want to show on a page. It can then determine how many pages you need and display page navigation links to previous and following pages in your view.

Try It Out **Create View Pagination**

To create view pagination, follow these steps:

1. Create a new application, `friends`, in the rubydev\ch10 directory:

```
C:\rubydev\ch10>rails friends
      .
      .
      .
```

2. Change directories to the friends directory:

```
C:\rubydev\ch10>cd friends
```

3. Create a controller named `Look` for the application:

```
C:\rubydev\ch10\friends>ruby script/generate controller Look
      .
      .
      .
```

4. Start the MySQL monitor:

```
C:\rubydev\ch10\friends>mysql -u root -p
```

5. Create the `friends` databases:

```
mysql> create database friends_development;
Query OK, 1 row affected (0.08 sec)

mysql> create database friends_test;
Query OK, 1 row affected (0.02 sec)

mysql> create database friends_production;
Query OK, 1 row affected (0.00 sec)

mysql>
```

6. Switch to the `friends_development` database:

```
mysql> use friends_development
Database changed
```

7. Create a table named `names`:

```
mysql> create table names (
    -> id    int    not null  auto_increment,
    -> name  varchar(80)     not null,
    -> primary key(id)
    -> );
Query OK, 0 rows affected (0.05 sec)

mysql>
```

8. Quit the MySQL monitor:

```
mysql> exit
```

9. Edit rubydev\ch10\friends\config\database.yml, adding username and password information as needed:

```
# MySQL (default setup).  Versions 4.1 and 5.0 are recommended.
#
# Install the MySQL driver:
#   gem install mysql
# On MacOS X:
#   gem install mysql -- --include=/usr/local/lib
# On Windows:
#   There is no gem for Windows.  Install mysql.so from RubyForApache.
#   http://rubyforge.org/projects/rubyforapache
#
# And be sure to use new-style password hashing:
#   http://dev.mysql.com/doc/refman/5.0/en/old-client.html
development:
  adapter: mysql
  database: friends_development
  username: root
  password: **********
  host: localhost

# Warning: The database defined as 'test' will be erased and
# re-generated from your development database when you run 'rake'.
# Do not set this db to the same as development or production.
test:
  adapter: mysql
  database: friends_test
  username: root
  password: **********
  host: localhost

production:
  adapter: mysql
  database: friends_production
```

```
username: root
password: *********
host: localhost
```

10. Create a model named `names` and a controller named `manage` for your application:

```
C:\rubydev\ch10\friends>ruby script/generate scaffold Name Manage
   .
   .
   .
```

11. Start the WEBrick server:

```
C:\rubydev\ch10\friends>ruby script/server
```

12. Navigate to `http://localhost:3000/manage`, shown in Figure 10-7, and add about 25 names to the database

Figure 10-7

13. Stop the WEBrick server with ^C.

14. Edit rubydev\ch10\friends\app\controllers\look_controller.rb, adding this code to create the `at` action:

```
class LookController < ApplicationController
  def at
    @name_pages, @names = paginate(:names)
  end
end
```

15. Create rubydev\ch10\friends\app\views\look\at.rhtml, adding this code to create the `at` action's view:

```
<html>
  <head>
    <title>Using pagination</title>
  </head>
  <body>
    <h1>Using pagination</h1>
    The names:
    <table>
      <% for friend_name in @names %>
        <tr><td><%= friend_name.name %>
      <% end %>
    </table>
    <%= pagination_links(@name_pages) %>
  </body>
</html>
```

16. Start the WEBrick server again:

```
C:\rubydev\ch10\friends>ruby script/server
```

17. Navigate to `http://localhost:3000/look/at`, shown in Figure 10-8. You see the first page of the names from the database.

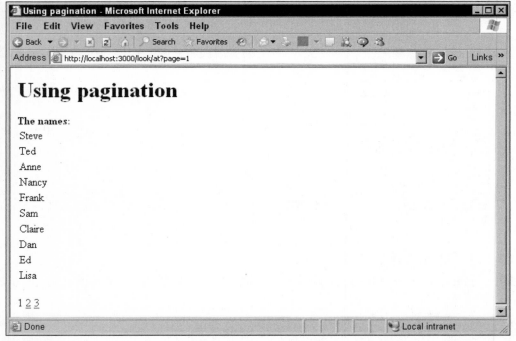

Figure 10-8

18. Click the 2 link at the bottom of the page to move to the second page of names. The second page of names appears (see Figure 10-9) — very cool. You can navigate to any of the three pages of names using links 1, 2, and 3 at the bottom of the page.

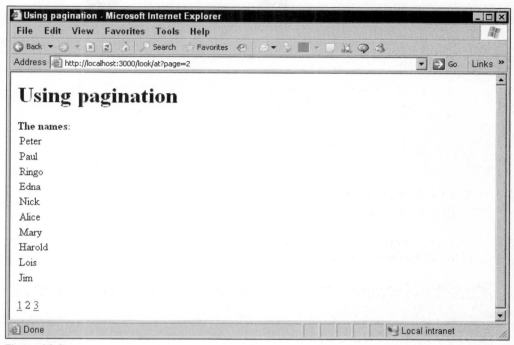

Figure 10-9

How It Works

This example fetches data from a database and displays it using pagination. It starts by creating a database named `friends_development`:

```
mysql> create database friends_development;
```

And then creating a table in that database named `names`:

```
mysql> create table names (
    -> id     int     not null   auto_increment,
    -> name   varchar(80)        not null,
    -> primary key(id)
    -> );
Query OK, 0 rows affected (0.05 sec)
```

After creating the application's `names` model, you navigate to `http://localhost:3000/manage` and add names to the database that will appear in the paginated pages.

The key is using the `names` model to provide the names to the view. To do that, you paginate those names in the `Look` controller:

```
class LookController < ApplicationController
  def at
    @name_pages, @names = paginate(:names)
  end
end
```

This returns a collection of name records, `@names`, and a paginator object, `@name_pages`. You can order the collection by using `:order` when calling `paginate`; here's how you can order the names returned, for example:

```
LookController < ApplicationController
  def at
    @name_pages, @names = paginate(:names, :order => name)
  end
end
```

The default number of items per page is 10, but you can change that by using `:per_page`:

```
class LookController < ApplicationController
  def at
    @name_pages, @names = paginate(:names, :per_page => 8)
  end
end
```

You can loop over the records in the collection, displaying them in the view:

```
<html>
  <head>
    <title>Using pagination</title>
  </head>
  <body>
    <h1>Using pagination</h1>
    The names:
    <table>
      <% for friend_name in @names %>
        <tr><td><%= friend_name.name %>
      <% end %>
    </table>
    <%= pagination_links(@name_pages) %>
  </body>
</html>
```

And you can also use the paginator object to display links to following and preceding pages by passing that object to the `pagination_links` method:

```
<html>
  <head>
    <title>Using pagination</title>
  </head>
  <body>
```

```
<h1>Using pagination</h1>
The names:
<table>
  <% for friend_name in @names %>
    <tr><td><%= friend_name.name %></td></tr>
  <% end %>
</table>
  <%= pagination_links(@name_pages) %>
</body>
</html>
```

That displays the links to other pages.

Using Partial Templates

Sometimes, you want to build up your view using layered templates; partial templates provide you a way of doing that. For example, if you have a set of links you always want to display at the bottom of web pages in a bar, partial templates would be a good solution.

Try It Out   **Create Partial Templates**

To create a partial template, follow these steps:

1.   Create a new application, `partial`, in the rubydev\ch10 directory:

```
C:\rubydev\ch10>rails partial
     .
     .
     .
```

2.   Change directories to the partial directory:

```
C:\rubydev\ch10>cd partial
```

3.   Create a controller named `Look` for the application:

```
C:\rubydev\ch10\partial>ruby script/generate controller Look
     .
     .
     .
```

4.   Edit rubydev\ch10\partial\app\controllers\look_controller.rb, adding this code to create the at action:

```
class LookController < ApplicationController
  def at
  end
end
```

5. Create rubydev\ch10\partial\app\views\look\at.rhtml, adding this code to create the at action's view:

```html
<html>
  <head>
    <title>Using partial templates</title>
  </head>
  <body>
    <h1>Using partial templates</h1>
    <br>
    This page uses partial templates to display this link bar:
    <br>
    <br>
    <br>
    <%= render :partial => 'links' %>
  </body>
</html>
```

6. Create rubydev\ch10\partial\app\views\look_links.rhtml, adding this code to create the link bar:

```
<center>
<%= link_to "Go to breakfast.", :action => "breakfast" %>
<%= link_to "Go to lunch.", :action => "lunch" %>
<%= link_to "Go to dinner.", :action => "dinner" %>
</center>
```

7. Start the WEBrick server:

```
C:\rubydev\ch10\friends>ruby script/server
```

8. Navigate to `http://localhost:3000/look/at` to see the results, shown in Figure 10-10. (Don't click the links — there's no corresponding action for them to link to!)

How It Works

This example uses a partial template to display a bar of links. That partial template is rendered with:

```
<%= render :partial => 'links' %>
```

To create a partial template, you preface the name of the file with an underscore, _, so it's not `links.rhtml`, but `_links.rhtml` (that is, rubydev\ch10\partial\app\views\look_links.rhtml). The links go in that file:

```
<center>
<%= link_to "Go to breakfast.", :action => "breakfast" %>
<%= link_to "Go to lunch.", :action => "lunch" %>
<%= link_to "Go to dinner.", :action => "dinner" %>
</center>
```

Using partial templates like this, you can build up your views piece by piece.

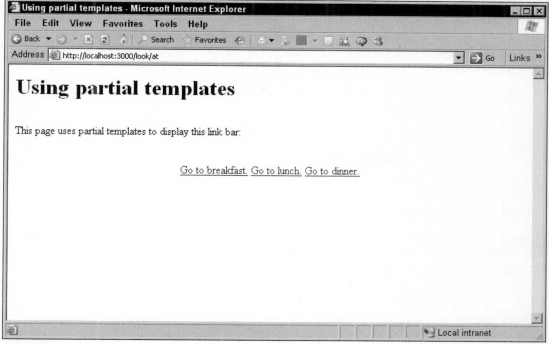

Figure 10-10

Passing Data to Partial Templates

You can pass data from controller code to a partial template, no problem. For example, you might create a variable, @title, in the controller's at action:

```
class LookController < ApplicationController
  def at
    @title = "The links"
  end
end
```

Then partial templates rendered from the at action's view template have access to @title:

```
<center>
@title
<%= link_to "Go to breakfast.", :action => "breakfast" %>
<%= link_to "Go to lunch.", :action => "lunch" %>
<%= link_to "Go to dinner.", :action => "dinner" %>
</center>
```

To pass data from a view template to a partial template takes a little work because the variables you declare in a view template are not accessible by default in a partial template:

```
<html>
  <head>
    <title>Passing data to partial templates</title>
  </head>
  <body>
    <h1>Passing data to partial templates</h1>
    <br>
    This page passes data to partial templates. Here's the passed data:
    <br>
    <br>
    <% @variable1 = "yes" %>
    <% @variable2 => "no" %>
    <%= render :partial => "data" %>
  </body>
</html>
```

You'll solve this problem in the following exercise.

Try It Out　　**Pass Data to Partial Templates**

To pass data to partial templates from a view template, follow these steps:

1.　Create a new application, `passdata`, in the rubydev\ch10 directory:

```
C:\rubydev\ch10>rails passdata
        .
        .
        .
```

2.　Change directories to the passdata directory:

```
C:\rubydev\ch10>cd passdata
```

3.　Create a controller named `Look` for the application:

```
C:\rubydev\ch10\passdata>ruby script/generate controller Look
        .
        .
        .
```

4.　Edit rubydev\ch10\passdata\app\controllers\look_controller.rb, adding this code to create the at action:

```
class LookController < ApplicationController
  def at
  end
end
```

5.　Create rubydev\ch10\passdata\app\views\look\at.rhtml, adding this code to create the at action's view:

```
<html>
  <head>
    <title>Passing data to partial templates</title>
  </head>
```

```
  <body>
    <h1>Passing data to partial templates</h1>
    <br>
    This page passes data to partial templates. Here's the passed data:
    <br>
    <br>
    <% @object = "Yes" %>
    <%= render :partial => 'data', :object => @object,
      :locals => { :variable1 => "indeed", :variable2 => "definitely" %>
  </body>
</html>
```

6. Create rubydev\ch10\passdata\app\views\look_data.rhtml, adding this code to create the link bar:

```
<%= data %>
<%= variable1 %>
<%= variable2 %>
```

7. Start the WEBrick server:

```
C:\rubydev\ch10\passdata>ruby script/server
```

8. Navigate to http://localhost:3000/look/at. The result, shown in Figure 10-11, should include the data passed to the partial template from the view template.

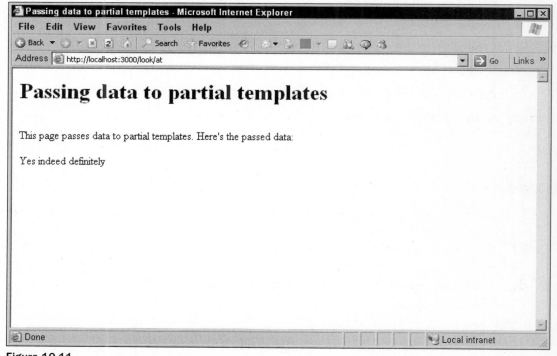

Figure 10-11

How It Works

This exercise starts by creating an object, `@object`, in the view template, and assigning that object to `:object` on the call to `render`. It also passes two local variables, `variable1` and `variable2`, after assigning values to them this way:

```
<% @object = "Yes" %>
<%= render :partial => 'data', :object => @object,
  :locals => { :variable1 => "indeed", :variable2 => "definitely"} %>
```

That data is accessible in the partial template. Note that you rename the object to match the name of the partial template without the underscore, making it just `data`:

```
<%= data %>
<%= variable1 %>
<%= variable2 %>
```

And that's all you need. You can pass data to a partial template in the call to the `render` method.

Summary

In this chapter, you did a lot of work with views, including learning how to:

❑   Display XML in the view.

❑   Display XML elements with attributes.

❑   Create and use view helpers and shared view helpers.

❑   Paginate a view.

❑   Use partial templates and pass data from a view template to a partial template.

Before proceeding to the next (and last) chapter, work through the following exercises to test your understanding of the material covered in this chapter. The solutions are in Appendix A.

Exercises

1.   Using an `.rxml` document, create an XML document that displays an `<author>` element, and a set of names from an array called `@names`.

2.   Create a view helper named `message` associated with a controller named `Look` that returns the text `This is the message`.

3.   What is the name of the partial template file referenced by this call to `render`?

```
render :partial => 'lookup'
```

Ajax and Rails

The future of the web is Ajax — Asynchronous JavaScript and XML. Ajax relies on the `XMLHttpRequest` object built into modern browsers to fetch data from the server behind the scenes asynchronously (which means it doesn't make the browser wait for a response from the server). The good thing about Ajax is the behind-the-scenes part, because you can fetch new data from the browser without waiting for a page refresh. In other words, data can just appear in part of a page in your browser, updated from the server, without needing to refresh the whole page.

Why is that a big deal? A major problem with web applications is that the display usually flickers and the display is reset — including the cursor position — when the browser needs to fetch new data. That's different from applications on the user's computer, where the display can be updated without refreshing the entire screen. For example, when you add an item to a table of data on a desktop application, the whole screen doesn't have to blink while that table is updated. Now the same can happen in your browser, using Ajax. And Rails has significant support for Ajax built in.

Using Ajax

To get started, take a look at an example that employs Ajax to connect to a Rails action behind the scenes. It uses Ajax to update the information in a `<div>` element in a web page by fetching data from the server — but without using a page refresh.

Try It Out   Use Ajax

You'll use Ajax in this exercise — just follow these steps:

1. Create a new application, `ajax`, in the rubydev\ch11 directory:

```
C:\rubydev\ch11>rails ajax
    .
    .
    .
```

2. Change directories to the ajax directory:

```
C:\rubydev\ch11>cd ajax
```

3. Create a controller named Look for the ajax application:

```
C:\rubydev\ch11\ajax>ruby script/generate controller Look
    .
    .
    .
```

4. Edit rubydev\ch11\ajax\app\controllers\look_controller.rb, adding this code to create the at action:

```
class LookController < ApplicationController
  def at
  end
end
```

5. Create rubydev\ch11\ajax\app\views\look\at.rhtml and place this code in it:

```html
<html>
  <head>
    <title>Using Ajax</title>
    <%= javascript_include_tag "prototype" %>
  </head>
  <body>
    <h1>Using Ajax</h1>
    <br>
    <%= link_to_remote("Click me to use Ajax", :update => "displayDiv",
      :url => {:action => :replacer }) %>
    <br>
    <div id = "displayDiv">The new text will appear here.</div>
  </body>
</html>
```

6. Edit rubydev\ch11\ajax\app\controllers\look_controller.rb, adding this code to create the replacer action:

```
class LookController < ApplicationController
  def at
  end

  def replacer
    render(:layout => false)
  end
end
```

7. Create rubydev\ch11\ajax\app\views\look\replacer.rhtml and place this code in it:

```
This text was downloaded using Ajax.
```

8. Start the WEBrick server:

```
C:\rubydev\ch11\ajax>ruby script/server
```

9.   Navigate to `http://localhost:3000/look/at`, shown in Figure 11-1.

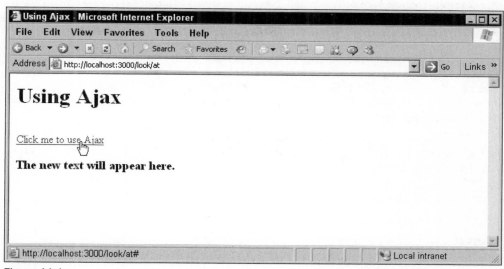

Figure 11-1

10. Click the link. The downloaded text appears, as shown in Figure 11-2. Congratulations, you're working with Ajax.

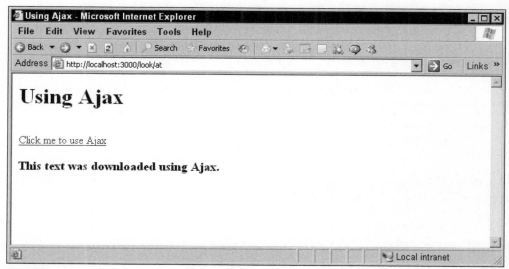

Figure 11-2

How It Works

In this example, you used Ajax to fetch data behind the scenes from the server, and to display that data in a `<div>` element. It all starts when you include the Rails `prototype.js` JavaScript library in any view template that wants to use Ajax, as you did in step 5:

```
<%= javascript_include_tag "prototype" %>
```

A call to `link_to_remote` (step 5) sets up a link that displays the text `Click me to use Ajax`, updates the `<div>` element named `displayDiv` with the fetched data, and fetches the text to display from the `replacer` action:

```
<%= link_to_remote("Click me to use Ajax", :update => "displayDiv",
  :url => {:action => :replacer }) %>
```

What does this call produce in HTML? It creates a call to the Rails `prototype.js` library function `Ajax.Updater` like this:

```
<html>
  <head>
    <title>Using Ajax</title>
    <script src="/javascripts/prototype.js?1151422045"
type="text/javascript"></script>
  </head>
  <body>
    <h1>Using Ajax</h1>
    <br>
    <a href="#" onclick="new Ajax.Updater('displayDiv', '/look/replacer',
{asynchronous:true, evalScripts:true}); return false;">Click me to use Ajax</a>
    <br>
    <br>
    <h3><div id = "displayDiv">The new text will appear here.</div></h3>
  </body>
</html>
```

The `replacer` action (step 6) simply renders its output — without including any layout:

```
def replacer
  render(:layout => false)
end
```

The actual text that the `replacer` action generates is in
rubydev\ch11\xml\app\views\look\replacer.rhtml:

```
This text was downloaded using Ajax.
```

Finally, this text is displayed in the `displayDiv` `<div>` element — without a screen refresh:

```
<html>
  <head>
    <title>Using Ajax</title>
    <%= javascript_include_tag "prototype" %>
```

```
    </head>
    <body>
      <h1>Using Ajax</h1>
      <br>
      <%= link_to_remote("Click me to use Ajax", :update => "displayDiv",
        :url => {:action => :replacer }) %>
      <br>
      <h3><div id = "displayDiv">The new text will appear here.</div></h3>
    </body>
  </html>
```

Downloading data into a `<div>` element gets you started with Ajax, but it's just a start. More often, you'll want to get your hands on the downloaded data yourself in JavaScript. For example, you may download a list of purchases the user has made and want to calculate the total price and display everything in an HTML table. Doing that kind of work takes some effort in JavaScript. So how do you get access to the downloaded data in your web page's JavaScript?

Getting Access to Ajax Data

You can configure `link_to_remote` to call a JavaScript function when your Ajax data is downloaded. Here are the possible parameters to pass to `link_to_remote` indicating when you want your JavaScript function called:

- ❏ `:loading`—Called when the remote data is being received by the browser.
- ❏ `:loaded`—Called when the browser has finished receiving the remote data.
- ❏ `:interactive`—Called when the user can interact with the remote data, even if it has not finished loading.
- ❏ `:success`—Called when the Ajax download is completed, and was successful.
- ❏ `:failure`—Called when the Ajax download failed.
- ❏ `:complete`—Called when the Ajax request is complete, whether it was successful of failed.

The following exercise uses the `:success` parameter to have a JavaScript function called with the downloaded data so you can handle that data in code.

Try It Out   Get Access to Ajax Data

To get access to Ajax data, follow these steps:

1. Create a new application, `ajaxdata`, in the rubydev\ch11 directory:

```
C:\rubydev\ch11>rails ajaxdata
     .
     .
     .
```

2. Change directories to the ajaxdata directory:

```
C:\rubydev\ch11>cd ajaxdata
```

3. Create a controller named Look for the ajaxdata application:

```
C:\rubydev\ch11\ajaxdata>ruby script/generate controller Look
      .
      .
      .
```

4. Edit rubydev\ch11\ajaxdata\app\controllers\look_controller.rb, adding this code to create the at action:

```
class LookController < ApplicationController
  def at
  end
end
```

5. Create rubydev\ch11\ajaxdata\app\views\look\at.rhtml and place this code in it, tying a text field containing the user's name to the getter action:

```
<html>
  <head>
    <title>Handling Ajax Data</title>
    <%= javascript_include_tag "prototype" %>

    <script language="JavaScript">
      function handleData(request)
      {
          var displayDiv = document.getElementById("displayDiv");
          displayDiv.innerHTML = request.responseText;
      }
    </script>

  </head>
  <body>
    <h1>Handling Ajax Data</h1>
    <br>
    <%= link_to_remote("Click me to handle Ajax data", :success =>
      "handleData(request)", :url => {:action => :getter }) %>
    <br>
    <br>
    <h3><div id = "displayDiv">The new text will appear here.</div></h3>
  </body>
</html>
```

6. Edit rubydev\ch11\ajaxdata\app\controllers\look_controller.rb, adding this code to create the getter action:

```
class LookController < ApplicationController
  def at
  end

  def getter
    render(:layout => false)
  end
end
```

7. Create rubydev\ch11\ajaxdata\app\views\look\getter.rhtml and place this code in it:

```
This text was downloaded using Ajax.
```

8. Start the WEBrick server:

```
C:\rubydev\ch11\ajaxdata>ruby script/server
```

9. Navigate to `http://localhost:3000/look/at`, shown in Figure 11-3.

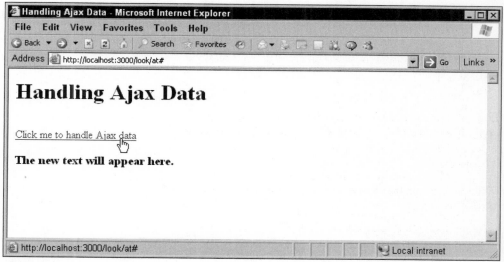

Figure 11-3

10. Click the link. The downloaded data appears, as shown in Figure 11-4.

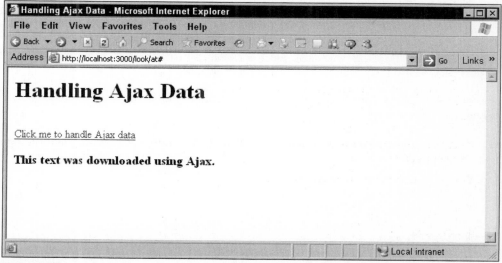

Figure 11-4

How It Works

This example gets its hands on the data that's downloaded using Ajax techniques. It starts by including the Rails `prototype.js` Ajax library in the view at `.rhtml` (step 5):

```
<%= javascript_include_tag "prototype" %>
```

Then it connects a successful download from an action named `getter` to a JavaScript function, `handleData`, which will be passed the data sent to the browser from the `getter` action (step 5):

```
<%= link_to_remote("Click me to handle Ajax data", :success =>
   "handleData(request)", :url => {:action => :getter }) %>
```

The `getter` action simply renders its view, without a layout:

```
def getter
  render(:layout => false)
end
```

And the `getter` view just passes this text data to the browser:

```
This text was downloaded using Ajax.
```

Back in the browser, that text is stored in the request object's `responseText` property, and the request object is passed to the JavaScript `handleData` function like this:

```
<script language="JavaScript">
  function handleData(request)
  {
       .
       .
       .
  }
</script>
```

In the `handleData` function, you recover the downloaded data using the `request.responseText` property:

```
var displayDiv = document.getElementById("displayDiv");
displayDiv.innerHTML = request.responseText;
```

This example just displays that text in a `<div>` element, but of course you can handle that downloaded data any way you want.

Here's what the `at` action's view looks like in HTML in the browser — note in particular the link, which sets up the callback to the `handleData` function:

```
<html>
  <head>
    <title>Handling Ajax Data</title>
    <script src="/javascripts/prototype.js?1151428997"
type="text/javascript"></script>
```

```
            <script language="JavaScript">
              function handleData(request)
              {
                  var displayDiv = document.getElementById("displayDiv");
                  displayDiv.innerHTML = request.responseText;
              }
            </script>

          </head>
          <body>
            <h1>Handling Ajax Data</h1>
            <br>
            <a href="#" onclick="new Ajax.Request('/look/getter', {asynchronous:true,
          evalScripts:true, onSuccess:function(request){handleData(request)}}); return
          false;">Click me to handle Ajax data</a>
            <br>
            <br>
            <h3><div id = "displayDiv">The new text will appear here.</div></h3>
          </body>
        </html>
```

So how about putting the XML into Ajax? After all, Ajax stands for Asynchronous JavaScript and XML. Working with XML is coming up next.

Using XML and Ajax

As you know, you can create XML documents using Rails and send them back to the browser. For example, you might send this document from the server to the browser using an `.rxml` view template:

```
<?xml version="1.0" encoding="UTF-8" ?>
<items>
  <item>Hello</item>
  <item>there</item>
  <item>today</item>
</items>
```

In fact, data is often sent from the server to the browser in XML format, because XML is the lingua franca of the Internet — it's the standard way to send data over the Web these days.

When you receive this XML document in the browser, you're going to need to extract the data held in it, and for that you can use JavaScript. The following Try It Out shows you how.

Try It Out   **Use XML and Ajax**

To use XML and Ajax, follow these steps:

1.   Create a new application, `ajaxxml`, in the rubydev\ch11 directory:

```
C:\rubydev\ch11>rails ajaxxml
          .
          .
          .
```

2. Change directories to the ajaxxml directory:

```
C:\rubydev\ch11>cd ajaxxml
```

3. Create a controller named Look for the ajaxxml application:

```
C:\rubydev\ch11\ajaxxml>ruby script/generate controller Look
    .
    .
    .
```

4. Edit rubydev\ch11\ajaxxml\app\controllers\look_controller.rb, adding this code to create the at action:

```
class LookController < ApplicationController
  def at
  end
end
```

5. Create rubydev\ch11\ajaxxml\app\views\look\at.rhtml and place this code in it:

```
<html>
  <head>
    <title>Handling XML with Ajax</title>
    <%= javascript_include_tag "prototype" %>

    <script language="JavaScript">
      function handleData(request)
      {
            var xmlDocument = request.responseXml;
            items = xmlDocument.getElementsByTagName("item");
            listItems(items);
      }

    function listItems (items)
    {
        var loopIndex, text;
        var displayDiv = document.getElementById('displayDiv');
        text = "";

        for (loopIndex = 0; loopIndex < items.length; loopIndex++ )
        {
            text += items[loopIndex].firstChild.data + " ";
        }

        displayDiv.innerHTML = text;
    }
    </script>

  </head>
  <body>
    <h1>Handling XML with Ajax</h1>
    <br>
    <%= link_to_remote("Click me to handle XML with Ajax",
      :success => "handleData(request)", :url => {:action => :getter }) %>
```

```
        <br>
        <br>
        <h3><div id = "displayDiv">The new text will appear here.</div></h3>
    </body>
</html>
```

6. Edit rubydev\ch11\ajaxxml\app\controllers\look_controller.rb, adding this code to create the getter action:

```
class LookController < ApplicationController
  def at
  end

  def getter
  end
end
```

7. Create rubydev\ch11\ajaxxml\app\views\look\getter.rxml and place this code in it:

```
xml.instruct! :xml, :version => "1.0"

xml.items do
  xml.item("Hello")
  xml.item("there")
  xml.item("today")
end
```

8. Start the WEBrick server:

```
C:\rubydev\ch11\ajaxxml>ruby script/server
```

9. Navigate to http://localhost:3000/look/at, shown in Figure 11-5.

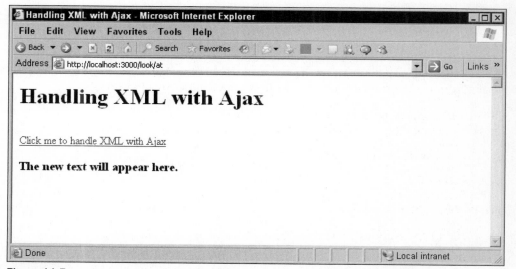

Figure 11-5

10. Click the link. The downloaded XML data appears, as shown in Figure 11-6.

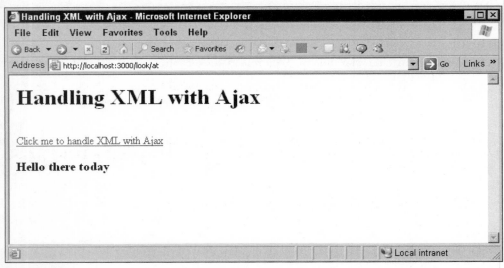

Figure 11-6

How It Works

The `getter` action's view, rubydev\ch11\ajaxxml\app\views\look\getter.rxml, looks like this:

```
xml.instruct! :xml, :version => "1.0"

xml.items do
  xml.item("Hello")
  xml.item("there")
  xml.item("today")
end
```

And here's the XML document it sends back to the browser; you start by passing the request object that holds the returned data from the server to the JavaScript `handleData` function:

```
<?xml version="1.0" encoding="UTF-8" ?>
<items>
  <item>Hello</item>
  <item>there</item>
  <item>today</item>
</items>
```

To handle that XML in your JavaScript, you use the `handleData` function:

```
<%= link_to_remote("Click me to handle XML with Ajax",
   :success => "handleData(request)", :url => {:action => :getter }) %>
```

In the `handleData` function, you use the request object's `responseXml` (not `responseText`) property to recover the XML data from the server. This XML is held in a JavaScript XML object, which means you have to use JavaScript techniques to extract data from it. For example, to extract an array containing <item> elements, you can use the XML document's getElementsByTagName method, and then you might pass that array to another JavaScript function, listItems, to actually extract the data in those elements and list them in the web page:

```
function handleData(request)
{
        var xmlDocument = request.responseXml;
        items = xmlDocument.getElementsByTagName("item");
        listItems(items);
}
```

In the listItems function, you can loop over the <item> elements in the items array, extract their text data, and concatenate that data into a variable named text, which you can then display in a <div> element in the web page:

```
<script language="JavaScript">
.
.
.
function listItems (items)
{
    var loopIndex, text;
    var displayDiv = document.getElementById('displayDiv');
    text = "";

    for (loopIndex = 0; loopIndex < items.length; loopIndex++ )
    {
        .
        .
        .
    }

    displayDiv.innerHTML = text;
}
</script>
```

How do you actually extract the text data from an <item> element? Here's what those items look like:

```
<item>Hello</item>
<item>there</item>
<item>today</item>
```

The text in each <item> element is stored in a text node. To access those nodes, you use the JavaScript property firstChild of each <item> element. Further, to access the actual text in each text node, you use that node's data property, which means you do the actual extracting of text data from the <item> elements like this in the listItems function:

```
text += items[loopIndex].firstChild.data + " ";
```

At the end of the listItems function, you assign the text of the <item> elements to the display <div> element.

Using HTML Controls and Ajax

The examples you've seen so far in this chapter rely on using a hyperlink to access Ajax data, but you may want to use controls like buttons instead. Tackle that now in an exercise that asks the user to log in.

Try It Out   **Use HTML Controls with Ajax**

To use HTML controls with Ajax, follow these steps:

1.   Create a new application, `ajaxcontrols`, in the rubydev\ch11 directory:

```
C:\rubydev\ch11>rails ajaxcontrols
        .
        .
        .
```

2.   Change directories to the ajaxcontrols directory:

```
C:\rubydev\ch11>cd ajaxcontrols
```

3.   Create a controller named `Look` for the `ajaxcontrols` application:

```
C:\rubydev\ch11\ajaxcontrols>ruby script/generate controller Look
        .
        .
        .
```

4.   Edit rubydev\ch11\ajaxcontrols\app\controllers\look_controller.rb, adding this code to create the `at` action:

```
class LookController < ApplicationController
  def at
  end
end
```

5.   Create rubydev\ch11\ajaxcontrols\app\views\look\at.rhtml, and place this code in it:

```
<html>
  <head>
    <title>Handling Ajax and HTML Controls</title>
    <%= javascript_include_tag "prototype" %>
  </head>
  <body>
    <h1>Handling Ajax and HTML Controls</h1>
    <br>
    <div id = "displayDiv">
      <%= render(:partial => 'form') %>
    </div>
  </body>
</html>
```

6.   Create rubydev\ch11\ajaxcontrols\app\views\look_form.rhtml, and place this code in it:

```
<% if (@username) %>
Sorry, <%= @username %> is not right.
<br>
```

```
<% end %>
<%= form_remote_tag(:update => 'displayDiv',
  :url => {:action => :login} ) %>
  Please log in:
  <%= text_field_tag :username %>
  <%= submit_tag "Submit" %>
<%= end_form_tag %>
```

7. Edit rubydev\ch11\ajaxcontrols\app\controllers\look_controller.rb, adding this code to create the `login` action:

```
class LookController < ApplicationController
  def at
  end
```

```
  def login
    @username = params[:username]
    if (@username == "Steve")
      render(:text => "You're in.")
    else
      render(:partial => 'form')
    end
  end
end
```

8. Start the WEBrick server:

```
C:\rubydev\ch11\ajaxcontrols>ruby script/server
```

9. Navigate to `http://localhost:3000/look/at`. Enter a name that is not Steve, as shown in Figure 11-7.

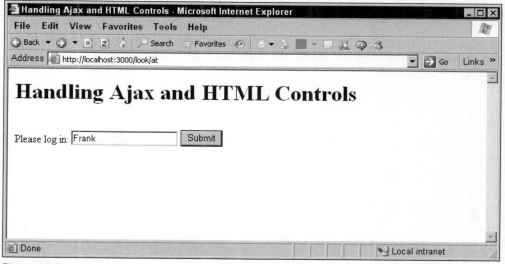

Figure 11-7

10. Click Submit. The result is shown in Figure 11-8.

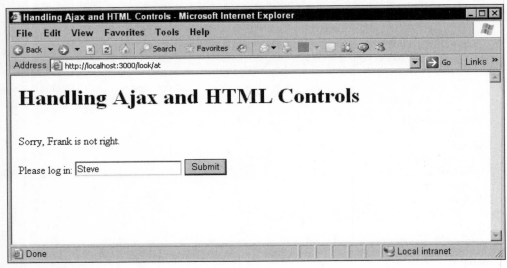

Figure 11-8

11. Now enter the username `Steve` and click Submit. You are accepted, as shown in Figure 11-9 — all without a page refresh.

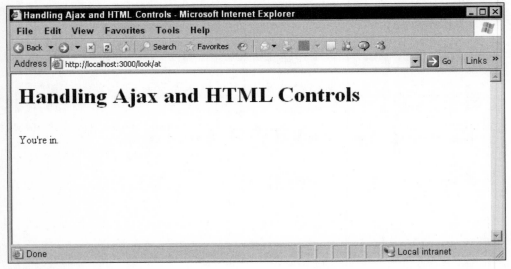

Figure 11-9

How It Works

This example starts by creating the `at` action:

```
def at
end
```

The `at.rhtml` template displays some basic information and then leaves the rest to a partial form, `_form.rhtml`:

```
<body>
  <h1>Handling Ajax and HTML Controls</h1>
  <br>
  <div id = "displayDiv">
    <%= render(:partial => 'form') %>
  </div>
</body>
```

In `_form.rhtml`, this example uses `form_remote_tag` to support Ajax:

```
<%= form_remote_tag(:update => 'displayDiv',
      .
      .
      .
<%= end_form_tag %>
```

Note the use of the `:update` parameter. It specifies the element that will display the updated data received from the server using Ajax techniques. In this case, that element is the `displayDiv` <div> element in `at.rhtml`:

```
<div id = "displayDiv">
  <%= render(:partial => 'form') %>
</div>
```

So when there's new data to display, the results will appear in the `displayDiv` <div> element — without refreshing the page.

The rest of the `_form.rhtml` partial template displays a text field named `username` that will allow the user to specify his name to log in, and a Submit button:

```
Please log in:
<%= text_field_tag :username %>
<%= submit_tag "Submit" %>
```

When the user enters his username in the text field and clicks the Submit button, the text in the text field is sent to an action named `login`:

```
:url => {:action => :login} ) %>
```

In the `login` action, you recover the text the user entered into the text field, and if it's `Steve`, you can send back the text `"You're in."`.

```
def login
  @username = params[:username]
  if (@username == "Steve")
    render(:text => "You're in.")
      .
      .
      .
end
```

Rendering the text "You're in." makes that text appear in the displayDiv <div> element—without a page refresh.

On the other hand, if the user enters an incorrect username, you render the form again asking him to enter his username:

```
else
  render(:partial => 'form')
end
```

In fact, you do better than that—you add code to _form.rhtml to display an error message if the user has entered an incorrect username, which you can test by checking on the presence of the variable @username:

```
<% if (@username) %>
Sorry, <%= @username %> is not right.
<br>
<% end %>
```

There you have it. You can support Ajax using HTML controls in HTML forms simply by using form_remote_tag and specifying the HTML element to update with the fetched Ajax data with the :update parameter. Not bad.

Performing Ajax Searches

One of the common Ajax techniques is to perform searches behind the scenes, as the user types in a search term. That's a perfect way to use Ajax—to grab data from the server as the user types a search term, displaying possible matches to that term—all without a page refresh.

Try It Out   **Perform Ajax Searches**

To perform Ajax searches, follow these steps:

1.   Create a new application, ajaxsearch, in the rubydev\ch11 directory:

```
C:\rubydev\ch11>rails ajaxsearch
    .
    .
    .
```

2. Change directories to the ajaxsearch directory:

```
C:\rubydev\ch11>cd ajaxsearch
```

3. Create a controller named Look for the ajaxsearch application:

```
C:\rubydev\ch11\ajaxsearch>ruby script/generate controller Look
        .
        .
        .
```

4. Edit rubydev\ch11\ajaxsearch\app\controllers\look_controller.rb, adding this code to create the at action:

```
class LookController < ApplicationController
  def at
  end
end
```

5. Create rubydev\ch11\ajaxsearch\app\views\look\at.rhtml and place this code in it:

```html
<html>
  <head>
    <title>Handling Ajax Searches</title>
    <%= javascript_include_tag "prototype" %>
  </head>
  <body>
    <h1>Handling Ajax Searches</h1>
    <br>
    <form>
      <%= text_field_tag :lookup %>
      <%= observe_field(:lookup,
        :update => :displayDiv,
        :frequency => 0.4,
        :url => {:action => :getter}) %>
    </form>
    <div id = "displayDiv">
  </body>
</html>
```

6. Edit rubydev\ch11\ajaxsearch\app\controllers\look_controller.rb, adding this code to create the getter action:

```
class LookController < ApplicationController
  def at
  end


  WORDS = ["This", "is", "a", "test", "here", "are", "the", "words"]

  def getter
    @term = request.raw_post
    regexp = Regexp.new(@term)
    @found = WORDS.find_all{ |term| term =~ regexp }
  end
end
```

7. Create rubydev\ch11\ajaxsearch\app\views\look\getter.rhtml and place this code in it:

```
<% if @found %>
Matches: <%= highlight(@found.join(', '), @term) %>
<% end %>
```

8. Start the WEBrick server:

```
C:\rubydev\ch11\ajaxsearch>ruby script/server
```

9. Navigate to `http://localhost:3000/look/at`. Enter a search term, such as `he`, and you'll see the matches to this term appear in the web page, without a page refresh, as shown in Figure 11-10.

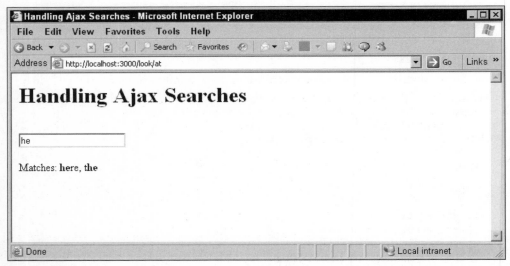

Figure 11-10

How It Works

This example uses a Rails observer to watch what the user types into a text field. As he types new terms, those terms are sent directly to the server, and any matches found in an array of strings is displayed back in the browser — as the user is typing.

It all starts with rubydev\ch11\ajaxsearch\app\views\look\at.rhtml, where you create a text field named `lookup` for the user to enter a search term into:

```
        <%= text_field_tag :lookup %>
          .
          .
          .
    </form>
```

You use the `observe_field` method to keep a watch on a field, notifying the server if any new data appears in the field. Here's what the call to `observe_field` looks like — it sets the frequency of checking the text field to every 0.4 seconds, and if there's new data there, it sends it on to an action named `getter`:

```
<%= observe_field(:lookup,
  :update => :displayDiv,
  :frequency => 0.4,
  :url => {:action => :getter}) %>
```

That raises the question, how do you read the text from the text field in the `getter` action? That text isn't submitted as it would normally be submitted from a form; instead, you access it using the request object's `raw_post` property:

```
def getter
  @term = request.raw_post
    .
    .
    .
end
```

Now you can use the support for regular expressions and the `find_all` method in Ruby to find any matches to the words "This is a test here are the words" like this:

```
class LookController < ApplicationController
  def at
  end

  WORDS = ["This", "is", "a", "test", "here", "are", "the", "words"]

  def getter
    @term = request.raw_post
    regexp = Regexp.new(@term)
    @found = WORDS.find_all{ |term| term =~ regexp }
  end
end
```

And in rubydev\ch11\ajaxsearch\app\views\look\getter.rhtml, you start by checking if any matches were found:

```
<% if @found %>
    .
    .
    .
<% end %>
```

And if a match or matches are found, you use the handy ActionView method named `highlight` to highlight (with a `<strong>` element) the matches like this:

```
<% if @found %>
Matches: <%= highlight(@found.join(', '), @term) %>
<% end %>
```

Cool—now you're able to watch on the server what the user is typing in the browser—no Submit button necessary at all.

Performing Visual Effects

One issue with Ajax is that changes made to a web page are sometimes so subtle that the user overlooks them—precisely because there is no page refresh. To make it evident that things are actually happening, Rails supports a number of JavaScript-based effects that you can use in Ajax-enabled web pages. The following table describes some of those effects.

Effect	Description
Effect.Appear	Makes an element appear.
Effect.Fade	Makes an element fade away.
Effect.Highlight	Makes an element's background fade from yellow to white, indicating that its data has been updated on the server.
Effect.Puff	Makes an element disappear in a "cloud" of smoke.
Effect.Squish	Squishes an element until it's gone.

You'll use the squish effect in the following exercise.

Try It Out   Perform Visual Effects

To perform Ajax-related visual effects, follow these steps:

1. Create a new application, ajaxeffects, in the rubydev\ch11 directory:

```
C:\rubydev\ch11>rails ajaxeffects
    .
    .
    .
```

2. Change directories to the ajaxeffects directory:

```
C:\rubydev\ch11>cd ajaxeffects
```

3. Create a controller named Look for the ajaxeffects application:

```
C:\rubydev\ch11\ajaxeffects>ruby script/generate controller Look
    .
    .
    .
```

4. Edit rubydev\ch11\ajaxeffects\app\controllers\look_controller.rb, adding this code to create the at action:

```
class LookController < ApplicationController
  def at
  end
end
```

5. Create rubydev\ch11\ajaxeffects\app\views\look\at.rhtml and place this code in it:

```html
<html>
  <head>
    <title>Handling Ajax and HTML Controls</title>
    <%= javascript_include_tag "prototype", "effects" %>
  </head>
  <body>
    <h1>Handling Ajax and HTML Controls</h1>
    <br>
    <div id = "displayDiv" style=
      "background: cyan; float: left; width: 100px; height: 20px">
      <%= link_to_remote("Delete me",
        :complete => "new Effect.Squish('displayDiv')",
        :url => {:action => :delete })
      %>
    </div>
  </body>
</html>
```

6. Edit rubydev\ch11\ajaxsearch\app\controllers\look_controller.rb, adding this code to create the `delete` action:

```ruby
class LookController < ApplicationController
  def at
  end

  def delete
  end
end
```

7. Start the WEBrick server:

```
C:\rubydev\ch11\ajaxeffects>ruby script/server
```

8. Navigate to `http://localhost:3000/look/at`, shown in Figure 11-11.

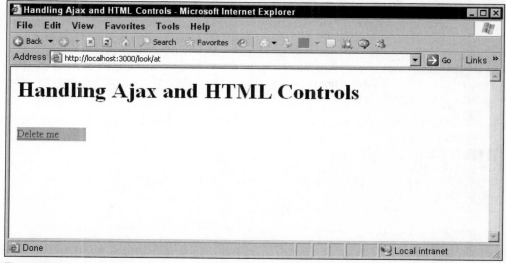

Figure 11-11

9.   Click the Delete me element and watch it squish down to nothing (see Figure 11-12).

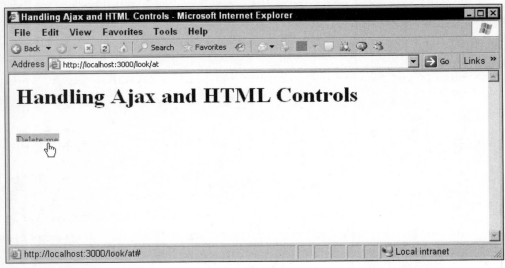

Figure 11-12

How It Works

This example squishes a Delete me element to nothing, providing visual feedback that a data item was deleted on the server. In this exercise, the good stuff takes place in the view, rubydev\ch11\ajaxsearch\app\views\look\at.rhtml. On completion of the delete action, the code uses the squish effect to make the <div> element containing the Delete me link disappear:

```
<div id = "displayDiv" style=
  "background: cyan; float: left; width: 100px; height: 20px">
  <%= link_to_remote("Delete me",
    :complete => "new Effect.Squish('displayDiv')",
    :url => {:action => :delete })
  %>
</div>
```

Using the Effects library like this, you can give your users instant visual feedback about what's going on in Ajax-enabled pages, and that's important because otherwise the user might not catch the action as the text content of his page changes.

Summary

In this chapter, you learned quite a bit about working with Ajax and Rails, including how to:

❑   Use the prototype.js library to support Ajax.

❑   Use link_to_remote to update elements with text fetched from the server as well as to fetch text data and XML data from the server that you can handle in JavaScript.

❑   Create Ajax-enabled pages that use HTML controls.

❑   Observe controls to see if the user has changed the data in them and, if so, to send that data to the server, as you may want to do with Ajax-enabled searches.

❑   Perform visual feedback in a web page, giving visual clues that Ajax has made changes on the server.

Try the exercises that follow to test your understanding of the material covered in this chapter. The solutions to these exercises are in Appendix A.

Exercises

1.   Use Ajax to download the text "Ajax rocks!" and display it in a web page, at.rhtml.

2.   Use JavaScript to display the Ajax-downloaded text "Ajax rules!"

3.   Make a <div> element containing a link that says "Smoke me" in a view connected to the at action appear to disappear in a cloud of smoke.

Answers to Exercises

Chapter 1 Answers

Exercise 1 Solution

```
array = [1, 2, 3, 4, 5, 6, 7, 8]
puts array[-6]
```

Exercise 2 Solution

```
array = {0 => 1, 1 => 2, 2 => 3, 3 => 4, 4 => 5,
  5 => 6, 5 => 7, 7 => 8, -1 =>8, -2 => 7, -3 => 6,
  -4 => 5, -5 => 4, -6 => 3, -7 => 2, -8 => 1}
```

Exercise 3 Solution

```
array = (1..8).to_a
```

Chapter 2 Answers

Exercise 1 Solution

```
def factorial(number)
  if(number == 1)
    return 1
  else
    return number * factorial(number - 1)
  end
end

puts factorial(6)
```

Exercise 2 Solution

```
def printer(text)
  yield text
end

printer("Hello") {|data| puts data}
```

Exercise 3 Solution

```
def array_converter(item_1, item_2, item_3, item_4)
  return item_1, item_2, item_3, item_4
end

array = array_converter(1, 2, 3, 4)

puts array
```

Chapter 3 Answers

Exercise 1 Solution

```
class Vehicle
  def initialize(color)
    @color = color
  end

  def get_color
    return @color
  end
end

vehicle = Vehicle.new("red")
puts "The new vehicle is " + vehicle.get_color
```

Exercise 2 Solution

```
class Vehicle
  def initialize(color)
    @color = color
  end

  def get_color
    return @color
  end
end

class Car < Vehicle
  def get_color
    return "blue"
  end
end

car = Car.new("red")
puts "The new car is " + car.get_color
```

Exercise 3 Solution

```
module A
  def get_color
    return @color
  end
end

module B
  def get_number_wheels
    return "four"
  end
end

class Car
  include A
  include B

  def initialize(color)
    @color = color
  end
end

car = Car.new("red")
puts "The new car is " + car.get_color
puts "The new car has " + car.get_number_wheels + " wheels."
```

Chapter 4 Answers

Exercise 1 Solution

1. Create the application:

```
C:\rubdev\ch04>rails test
C:\rubydev\ch04>cd test
C:\rubydev\ch04\test>ruby script/generate controller do
```

2. Edit C:\rubydev\ch04\test\app\controllers\do_controll.rb, adding this code:

```
class Do < ApplicationController
  def greeting
  end
end
```

3. Create C:\rubydev\ch04\test\app\views\do\greeting.rhtml and put this HTML in it:

```
<html>
  <head>
    <title>Hello</hello>
  </head>
  <body>
    <h1>Hello</h1>
  </body>
</html>
```

Exercise 2 Solution

1. Edit C:\rubydev\ch04\test\app\controllers\do_controll.rb, adding this code:

```
class Do < ApplicationController
  def greeting
    @hello = "Hello!"
  end
end
```

2. Change C:\rubydev\ch04\test\app\views\do\greeting.rhtml to this:

```
<html>
  <head>
    <title>Hello</hello>
  </head>
  <body>
    <h1><%= @hello %></h1>
  </body>
</html>
```

Exercise 3 Solution

1. Edit C:\rubydev\ch04\test\app\controllers\do_controll.rb, adding this code:

```
class Do < ApplicationController
  def greeting
    @hello = "Hello!"
  end

  def greeting2
  end
end
```

2. Create C:\rubydev\ch04\test\app\views\do\greeting2.rhtml and put this HTML in it:

```
<html>
  <head>
    <title>Hello Again</hello>
  </head>
  <body>
    <h1>Hello again</h1>
  </body>
</html>
```

3. Edit C:\rubydev\ch04\test\app\views\do\greeting.rhtml and put this code in it:

```
<html>
  <head>
    <title>Hello</hello>
  </head>
  <body>
    <h1>Hello</h1>
    <%= link_to "Greeting2", :action => "greeting2" %>
  </body>
</html>
```

Chapter 5 Answers

Exercise 1 Solution

1. `public\input.html:`

```html
<html>
  <head>
    <title>Using Text Fields</title>
  </head>
  <body>
    <h1>Working With Text Fields</h1>
    This Ruby on Rails application lets you read data from text fields.
    <br>
    <form action = "\look\at" >
      Please enter your name.
      <br>
      <input type="text" name="text1">
      <br>
      Please enter your age.
      <br>
      <input type="text" name="text2">
      <br>
      <br>
      <input type="submit"/>
    </form>
  </body>
</html>
```

2. `app/controllers/look_controller.rb:`

```ruby
class LookController < ApplicationController
  def at
    @data = params[:text1]
    @age = params[:text2]
  end
end
```

3. `app/views/look/at.rhtml:`

```html
<html>
  <head>
    <title>Reading data from text fields</title>
  </head>
  <body>
    <h1>Reading data from text fields</h1>
    This Ruby on Rails application reads data from text fields.
    <br>
    <br>
    Your name is <%= @data %>.
    <br>
    Your age is <%= @age %>.
    <br>
    <br>
  </body>
</html>
```

Exercise 2 Solution

1. `app/views/look/input.rhtml`:

```
<html>
  <head>
    <title>Using Text Fields</title>
  </head>
  <body>
    <h1>Working With Text Fields</h1>
    This Ruby on Rails application lets you read data from text fields.
    <br>
    <%= start_form_tag ({:action => "at"}, {:method => "post"}) %>
      Please enter your name.
      <br>
      <%= text_field_tag ("text1", "", {"size" => 30}) %>
      <br>
      Please enter your age.
      <br>
      <%= text_field_tag ("text2", "", {"size" => 30}) %>
      <br>
      <br>
      <input type="submit"/>
    <%= end_form_tag %>
  </body>
</html>
```

2. `app/controllers/look_controller.rb`:

```
class LookController < ApplicationController
  def at
    @data = params[:text1]
    @age = params[:text2]
  end

  def input
  end
end
```

3. `app/views/look/at.rhtml`:

```
<html>
  <head>
    <title>Reading data from text fields</title>
  </head>
  <body>
    <h1>Reading data from text fields</h1>
    This Ruby on Rails application reads data from text fields.
    <br>
    <br>
    Your name is <%= @data %>.
    <br>
    Your age is <%= @age %>.
    <br>
    <br>
  </body>
</html>
```

Exercise 3 Solution

1. `app/views/look/input.rhtml`:

```
<html>
  <head>
    <title>Using Text Fields</title>
  </head>
  <body>
    <h1>Working With Text Fields</h1>
    This Ruby on Rails application lets you read data from text fields.
    <br>
    <%= start_form_tag ({:action => "at"}, {:method => "post"}) %>
      Please enter your name.
      <br>
      <%= text_field ("cruncher", "crunch", {"size" => 30}) %>
      <br>
      Please enter your age.
      <br>
      <%= text_field ("cruncher", "crunch2", {"size" => 30}) %>
      <br>
      <br>
      <input type="submit"/>
    <%= end_form_tag %>
  </body>
</html>
```

2. `app/models/cruncher.rb`:

```
class Cruncher
  attr_reader :crunch
  attr_writer :crunch
  attr_reader :crunch2
  attr_writer :crunch2

  def initialize(data, age)
    @crunch = data
    @crunch2 = age
  end

end
```

3. `app/controllers/look_controller.rb`:

```
class LookController < ApplicationController
  def at
    @data_hash = params[:cruncher]
    @cruncher = Cruncher.new(@data_hash[:crunch], @data_hash[:crunch2])

    @data = @cruncher.crunch
    @age = @cruncher.crunch2
  end

  def input
  end
end
```

4. `app/views/look/at.rhtml`:

```html
<html>
  <head>
    <title>Reading data from text fields</title>
  </head>
  <body>
    <h1>Reading data from text fields</h1>
    This Ruby on Rails application reads data from text fields.
    <br>
    <br>
    Your name is <%= @data %>.
    <br>
    Your age is <%= @age %>.
    <br>
    <br>
  </body>
</html>
```

Chapter 6 Answers

Exercise 1 Solution

`config\database.yml`:

```yaml
# MySQL (default setup).  Versions 4.1 and 5.0 are recommended.
#
# Install the MySQL driver:
#   gem install mysql
# On MacOS X:
#   gem install mysql -- --include=/usr/local/lib
# On Windows:
#   There is no gem for Windows.  Install mysql.so from RubyForApache.
#   http://rubyforge.org/projects/rubyforapache
#
# And be sure to use new-style password hashing:
#   http://dev.mysql.com/doc/refman/5.0/en/old-client.html
development:
  adapter: mysql
  database: store_development
  username: orson_welles
  password: rosebud
  host: localhost

# Warning: The database defined as 'test' will be erased and
# re-generated from your development database when you run 'rake'.
# Do not set this db to the same as development or production.
test:
  adapter: mysql
  database: store_test
  username: orson_welles
  password: rosebud
  host: localhost
```

```
production:
  adapter: mysql
  database: store_production
  username: orson_welles
  password: rosebud
  host: localhost
```

Exercise 2 Solution

Enter this command on the command line:

```
ruby script/generate scaffold  Item Merchandise
```

Exercise 3 Solution

scaffold.css:

```
body { background-color: #fff; color: #333; }

body, p, ol, ul, td {
  font-family: verdana, arial, helvetica, sans-serif;
  font-size:   16px;
  line-height: 18px;
}
      .
      .
      .
```

Chapter 7 Answers

Exercise 1 Solution

rubydev\ch07\app\views\buy\display_cart.rhtml:

```
<html>
  <head>
    <title>Your Cart</title>
  </head>

  <body>
    <h1>Your Shopping Cart</h1>
    <% if (@purchases == []) %>
      <b>There are no items in your cart:</b>
      <br>
      <br>
      <%= link_to 'Shop some more!', :action => 'index' %>
    <% else %>
      <b>Here are the items in your cart:</b>
      <br>
      <br>
      <table cellpadding="6">
        <tr>
```

```
              <% for column in Item.content_columns %>
                <th><%= column.human_name %></th>
              <% end %>
              <th>Quantity</th>
            </tr>
            <% for purchase in @purchases
                  item = purchase.item
            %>
              <tr>
              <td><b><%=h item.name %></b></td>
              <td><%=h item.description %></td>
              <td><%=h item.price %></td>
              <td><%=h purchase.quantity %></td>
            </tr>
            <% end %>
        </table>
        <br>
        <b>Total: $<%=h @total %></b>
        <br>
        <br>
        <%= link_to 'Clear cart', :action => 'clear_cart' %>
        <br>
        <%= link_to 'Shop some more!', :action => 'index' %>

        <form action = "\buy\checkout" >
          Please enter your name to check out:
          <br>
          <input type="text" name="text1">
          <br>
          <br>
          <input type="submit"/>
        </form>
      <% end %>
    </body>
  </html>
```

Exercise 2 Solution

rubydev\ch07\app\controllers\buy_controller.rb:

```
class BuyController < ApplicationController

  def index
    @items = Item.return_items
  end

  def add
    item = Item.find(params[:id])
    @cart = get_cart
    @cart.add_purchase(item)
    session[:shopping_cart] = @cart
    redirect_to(:action => 'display_cart')
  end

  def display_cart
```

```
      @cart = get_cart
      @purchases = @cart.purchases
      @total = @cart.total
    end

    def clear_cart
      @cart = get_cart
      @cart.initialize
    end

    def checkout
      @name = params[:text1]
      @cart = get_cart
      @total = @cart.total
    end

  private
    def get_cart
      if session[:shopping_cart]
        return session[:shopping_cart]
      else
        return Cart.new
      end
    end
end
```

Exercise 3 Solution

rubydev\ch07\app\views\buy\checkout.rhtml:

```
<html>
  <head>
    <title>The Store</title>
  </head>

  <body>
    <h1>Checkout</h1>
    <br>
    <%= @name %>, you owe $<%= @total %>.
  </body>
</html>
```

Chapter 8 Answers

Exercise 1 Solution

rubydev\ch08\app\models\item.rb:

```
class Item < ActiveRecord::Base
  validates_presence_of :name, :subtitle, :description, :price

  def self.return_items
    find(:all)
  end
end
```

Exercise 2 Solution

rubydev\ch08\app\models\item.rb:

```
class Item < ActiveRecord::Base
  validates_presence_of :name, :subtitle, :description, :price
  validates_uniqueness_of :subname

  def self.return_items
    find(:all)
  end
end
```

Exercise 3 Solution

rubydev\ch08\app\models\item.rb:

```
class Item < ActiveRecord::Base
  validates_presence_of :name, :subtitle, :description, :price, :number
  validates_uniqueness_of :subname
  validates_numericality_of :number

  def self.return_items
    find(:all)
  end
end
```

Chapter 9 Answers

Exercise 1 Solution

1. rubydev\ch09\timer\config\routes.rb:

```
ActionController::Routing::Routes.draw do |map|
  # The priority is based upon order of creation: first created -> highest
priority.

  # Sample of regular route:
  # map.connect 'products/:id', :controller => 'catalog', :action => 'view'
  # Keep in mind you can assign values other than :controller and :action

  # Sample of named route:
  # map.purchase 'products/:id/purchase', :controller => 'catalog', :action =>
'purchase'
  # This route can be invoked with purchase_url(:id => product.id)

  # You can have the root of your site routed by hooking up ''
  # -- just remember to delete public/index.html.
  # map.connect '', :controller => "welcome"

  # Allow downloading Web Service WSDL as a file with an extension
  # instead of a file named 'wsdl'
  map.connect ':controller/service.wsdl', :action => 'wsdl'

  # Install the default route as the lowest priority.
```

```
    map.connect ':controller/:action/:id'

    map.connect "look/at/:hours/:minutes/:seconds",
      :controller => "look",
      :action     => "at",
  end
```

2. rubydev\ch09\timer\app\controllers\look_controller.rb:

```
class LookController < ApplicationController
  def at
    @hours = @params[:hours]
    @minutes = @params[:minutes]
    @seconds = @params[:seconds]
  end
end
```

Exercise 2 Solution

rubydev\ch09\cookies\app\controllers\look_controller.rb:

```
class LookController < ApplicationController
  def set
    cookies[:customer] = {:value => "Not a good customer",
                          :expires => 365.days.from_now}
  end
end
```

Exercise 3 Solution

rubydev\ch09\post\app\controllers\look_controller.rb:

```
class PlayController < ApplicationController
  before_filter :check_method

private
  def check_method
    unless (request.method == :post)
      redirect_to(:action => "nogo")
    end
  end
end
```

Chapter 10 Answers

Exercise 1 Solution

rubydev\ch10\timer\config\routes.rb:

```
xml.instruct! :xml, :version=>"1.0"

xml.document do
  xml.author(@author)
```

```
xml.names do
  @names.each do |name|
    xml.name(name)
  end
end
```

Exercise 2 Solution

helpers\look_helper.rb:

```
module LookHelper
  def message
    return "This is the message."
  end
end
```

Exercise 3 Solution

_lookup.rhtml.

Chapter 11 Answers

Exercise 1 Solution

1. at.rhtml:

```
<html>
  <head>
    <title>Using Ajax</title>
    <%= javascript_include_tag "prototype" %>
  </head>
  <body>
    <h1>Using Ajax</h1>
    <br>
    <%= link_to_remote("Click me to use Ajax", :update => "displayDiv",
      :url => {:action => :replacer }) %>
    <br>
    <div id = "displayDiv">The new text will appear here.</div>
  </body>
</html>
```

2. look_controller.rb:

```
class LookController < ApplicationController
  def at
  end

  def replacer
    render(:layout => false)
  end
end
```

3. replacer.rhtml:

```
Ajax rocks!
```

Exercise 2 Solution

1. at.rhtml:

```
<html>
  <head>
    <title>Handling Ajax Data</title>
    <%= javascript_include_tag "prototype" %>

    <script language="JavaScript">
      function handleData(request)
      {
          var displayDiv = document.getElementById("displayDiv");
          displayDiv.innerHTML = request.responseText;
      }
    </script>

  </head>
  <body>
    <h1>Handling Ajax Data</h1>
    <br>
    <%= link_to_remote("Click me to handle Ajax data", :success =>
      "handleData(request)", :url => {:action => :getter }) %>
    <br>
    <br>
    <h3><div id = "displayDiv">The new text will appear here.</div></h3>
  </body>
</html>
```

2. look_controller.rb:

```
class LookController < ApplicationController
  def at
  end

  def getter
  end
end
```

3. getter.rhtml:

```
Ajax rules!
```

Exercise 3 Solution

at.rhtml:

```
    <div id = "displayDiv" style=
      "background: cyan; float: left; width: 100px; height: 20px">
      <%= link_to_remote("Smoke me",
        :complete => "new Effect.Puff('displayDiv')",
        :url => {:action => :delete })
      %>
```

Index

Index

L

M

Get more Wrox
at Wrox.com!

Special Deals

Take advantage of special offers every month

Unlimited Access. . .

. . . to over 70 of our books in the Wrox Reference Library. (see more details on-line)

Meet Wrox Authors!

Read running commentaries from authors on their programming experiences and whatever else they want to talk about

Free Chapter Excerpts

Be the first to preview chapters from the latest Wrox publications

Forums, Forums, Forums

Take an active role in online discussions with fellow programmers

Browse Books

.NET	XML
SQL Server	Visual Basic
Java	C# / C++

Join the community!

Sign-up for our free monthly newsletter at
newsletter.wrox.com